Royal
Roots

Royal Roots

Reimagining a Life through Humor, a Castle, and the US Navy

Patricia Wynn Brown

Variations of "Butter Knives" and the Patti LaBelle
tale appear in Regina Barreca's anthologies *Fast Fierce
Women* and *Fast Funny Women,* Woodhall Press.

Excerpts from the *Virginian-Pilot* (Kimberlin 2012)
reprinted with permission.

Cover photograph by Richard L. Wynn, 1955.
Frontispiece photograph of Gwydir Castle and its
courtyard Knot Garden by Judy Corbett.

Published 2024
Printed in the United States of America by
Biblio Publishing, Columbus, Ohio, 43212

ISBN: 978-1-62249-699-0

—For Steve, the knight in shining armor

Contents

PART IV
Jolted Forward and Conquering New Lands

PART V
Let the Truth Be Known

PART VI
The Revolution of Resolution

It's never too late in fiction or in life to revise.

—BONNIE FRIEDMAN

A textbook case of the eldest child, a leader, a doer, a convincing veneer of personality and confidence atop a bottomless pit of insecurity and need.

—ANNA QUINDLEN

If you make them cry then you make them laugh, then you've done your job.

—JACKIE GLEASON

"King" Richard Wynn, also, my dad, Richard Leo Wynn,
with his rifle and two squirrels he bagged.

Prologue

WHEN I saw Gregory Peck standing there with Sophia Loren, as other people milled around in front of the stage in the auditorium at the Oscar rehearsal in 1991, I did this; I walked up slowly and just stood with them as if I were part of their conversation. They continued chatting. I was drawn to them like a magnetic force. I stood beside them directly in front of the massive stage, on the floor with the poster-sized picture placards of the stars to attend, sitting on the chairs like paper dolls. I smiled and nodded, me, the add-on. They did something extraordinary. They let me stand there with them. I existed in their orbit.

I had my moment with that wonderful movie dad, Atticus Finch, and the most gorgeous woman I had ever seen in real life, Sophia Loren. I stood with greatness. They could not know my mission to, for a moment in time, exist in this celestial galaxy. Or do stars have extra sensory mission-of-need detectors? Particularly those stars with actual talents?

Seeing Peck as Atticus Finch in *To Kill a Mockingbird* revealed the unattainable father I always wanted, and here he was in the flesh. Fantasy stood close to reality. At that moment, in my mind, they were one.

I attended the Oscars at the invitation of my cousin Debbie, who worked on the show. Sophia Loren, Peck's dear friend, was being given a special award. I stood with Hollywood royalty. Destiny had been decreed by association, I decided. Dreams could bestow treasures. My dad was not at all like Atticus, and it seemed, as I look back, that Dad may have been the one most disappointed by this fact. He was well aware of falling short of greatness in character and deeds. He displayed his Big Fish bravado as a shield. I always thought Dad could have been an Atticus, with his humor, talents, and people skills, and something went wrong even before I was born in 1951, but what? Answering that question has plagued me my entire life.

Where Atticus was predictable, Dad was volatile. Where Atticus took time to explain things to his children, my dad would blow a gasket. Where Atticus attended children's events, my dad would be with

At that Academy Awards® rehearsal in 1991 on the stage with Cousin Debbie Williams (right). Debbie comes from my mother's side of the family and worked on specials and live shows as a stage manager. We decided to give ourselves the Oscar for Best Cousins.

his drinking buddies. Where Atticus would reason, Dad would yell, threaten, and, on several occasions, spank and belt me. Movie Atticus was present and ruled benevolently. Dad was often absent either at the Veteran's Hospital or on his getaways at "the union hall" or beer joint. Dad's reign rivaled Henry VIII: heads rolled.

The one thing Dad and Atticus had in common was compassion for people suffering through rough spots in life, which in Dad's case did not necessarily include his own family. Dad was more of an outside-the-home-base empath.

Some people realize very early in life that essential choices need to be made, or else the furies of hell will burst through their personal protective portcullis castle gate. I am one of those people. In my childhood, I found solace and hope in my imagination and show business. Throughout my life, I've built the capacity to fly away and soar above it all on the magic carpet ride of stories. Humor is my jet fuel. Dance is my engine. Performing is my jet stream.

Stories double as my salvation. They sustain me, and I employ them to nourish and entertain others as a performer and writer. Rather than simply living through the random and uncontrollable events in the dizzying spin of the wheel of fate, I frame my life experiences in stories because they help me see meaning and purpose in my existence. Stories pull all the fragments of my life together into a stained-glass window of colors and light instead of scattered slivers of piercing pain. They build a moat around my daily life castle, allowing me to dwell unharmed and free. With storytelling, I garner renewal, redemption, and restitution.

Stories have been part of my life since babyhood: my mother read *Wynken, Blynken, and Nod* to me at bedtime and sang that sad song of departure, "Danny Boy." When Mom sang the other song in her two-song repertoire, Doris Day's hit, "Que Sera, Sera," and the musical question lyric "What will I be?" would arise, I gave this much thought. I must have been three years old.

While growing up in our house, where chaos reigned between all too brief bouts of calm (and those peaceful times would remain suspect, held out at a distance like a not-quite-dead mouse in a trap that required vigilance and possible murderous action), a girl needed to stay on her toes and develop some protective battle armor. Images of Joan of Arc were helpful in times of distress. Safety and security were a foreign land of desire for us Wynns.

In our house, our lives swirled around the eye of the storm, Dad. He did not go to work like the other dads. We could be peacefully sleeping one minute, then abruptly awakened by the six-foot-long brass medieval buisine trumpet blast of his nightmares. Mom would attempt to

This is the Wynns of Wales's coat of arms. My imagination also has me claiming royal roots, as the Wynns were the kings and princes of Wales in the 1500s and 1600s. I learned of this not so many years ago.

calm him down with, "Rich, Rich, you're having a nightmare. Wake up, Rich!" as Dad flailed and yelled about explosions.

One family dinner ended abruptly with a plate of steak thrown at my head as Dad became upset by something I said, and by that time, in my teen years of the 1960s, I was expressing a lot of my frustration and anger. My mom called me "Miss Smart Mouth." She labeled my blond and agreeable younger sister "The Pretty One." There was a permanent dent in the wall above Miss Smart Mouth's head, just behind my place at the table, caused by that very dish. I had had it with Dad by then, fighting with our mom and with us kids, physically and emotionally. I mouthed off.

Dad's depression and psychosis set the scene for our days and nights. If I walked into the living room and he was grunting his dissatisfaction at the world at large and settled glumly in His Chair, or I saw him pacing and looking out the windows, unable to still himself, or heard Mom and Dad quarreling and coming to shoves, I eventually learned in my teens to find the safest place in our house, my room, a.k.a. "the keep" of my castle. Marauders dared not enter. I do not know why it was a respected, safe, demilitarized zone. Could the lingering smog of Aqua Net hairspray for my bouffant teenage hair have been my protective Kryptonite?

Dad had been honorably medically discharged after seven years in the Navy in 1944. What I was told was that when he returned from the war, he worked for a while at General Motors as an inspector of layouts but frequently broke down mentally and eventually went on total disability before I was even born. I never saw Dad go to work. I was never told what had happened to Dad in the war other than this from Mom, "there was some explosion on his Navy base at Norfolk." That's all any of our nuclear family knew until very recently.

I researched and discovered what happened while writing this. Grandma Aggie, an excellent storyteller, knew the truth, but it was the darkest story she had never told.

When I saw *To Kill a Mockingbird* on television for the first time, so many revelations came to me. There! That Man! Atticus! That's who I wished Dad to be. It pressed on me that Dad was incapable of Atticus' qualities. Why? I wondered. Why can't Dad make his and our

Dad in the Navy.

Two of my three siblings. I have Scout hair, center. Grandma Aggie made my bikini from cottage curtain fabric.

lives easier by being like Atticus? And there was Scout, a tomboy like me. She loved her father. I did, too, when I was very little. Scout rode inside a big black tractor tire down the street. I wanted to do that. I could use a friend like Scout, and when I went to her house, her dad would be there.

Boo Radley's character, though, made me feel uneasy. He had a mental illness like my dad did. The kids made fun of Boo as some kids made fun of my dad, and that part of the story makes my stomach churn even now. Boo had his kind side but could not act like other people. As I watched the movie, I realized my dad could not be Atticus because his problems were more in Boo's camp. Of the town's people, it was Atticus who understood Boo and showed him kindness and compassion. The scene at the end, when Boo has protected Scout and Atticus speaks of Boo's heroics, affording Boo the dignity he deserves, dissolves me into tears every time I see it.

Standing beside Gregory Peck for that brief time at the Oscars had me silenced in radiant, healing awe. Had we had a conversation, and I explained my adoration for Atticus, he would have said that many people have shared those exact feelings with him about the Atticus character.

I invite you to sail off with me "into a sea of dew," like in the fairy tale poem Mom read me when I was just a little thing, "Wynken, Blynken, and Nod." Allow me to tell you my stories of getting through. By our journey's end, the mystery of what initially and what finally happened to Dad is revealed, at long last. Like a Maypole dance, my days and nights weave in and out of the stories, with Dad always at their core. He held reign. Many decades later, I reclaimed *my* throne of identity.

It's all in how you look at it.

But first, what about my mom?

There is a country song called "Mama Tried" about how the singer's father left her a heavy load. My mom carried that load and more.

Royal
Roots

PART I

Shining a Light in the Darkness

Candle glowing at Gwydir Castle, Wales, the Wynn ancient
ancestral home. Photo: Judy Corbett of Gwydir Castle, Wales.

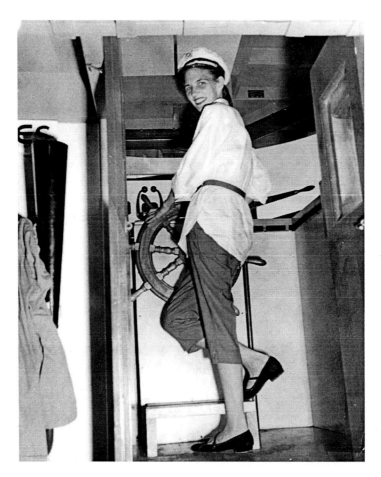

My mom, Dorothy Mary Cavanaugh Wynn.
Before kids. A time of smoother sailing.

Chapter 1

The Unsinkable Dorothy Wynn

MY MOM, Dorothy Mary Cavanaugh Wynn, waged a daily battle of survival on the high seas of marriage to a mentally ill World War II vet with her children close aboard. But that hadn't been the lookout from the beginning. It wasn't until a couple of years into their marriage that the tide turned.

Mom and Dad spoke of alleged halcyon days in the peaceful waters of dating. Not long after their marriage, it seems, things fell apart. The nasty riptides of Dad's mental illness rolled in. My mother's previously stable life changed. *Did Mom know this from the start? Was Dad in an exceptional mental health period when they courted and married?* All I know is that when I was about three or four years old, as far back as I can remember, their physical shoving fights and the yelling already had me taking cover.

Money issues were Mom's never-ending advancing war front. Survival does not mean constant victories; it means not being conquered.

Mom performed the duties of daily survival like a nimble grenadier guard by shielding each dollar in our meager treasury, paying what she could on bills in a near shell game, handling Dad's ins and outs of our home for extended stays for his psychiatric treatments, keeping up appearances (a major task employing smoke, mirrors, and a sublime sense of humor), getting us four kids schooled, and echoing strict warnings to us about right and wrong.

Her number one ideology: the worst thing her two daughters could become were tramps. (The two boys were considered princes above the law and denunciations of any nature.)

But our mom-directed battle plan/credo also included respecting and caring for our family elders, adoring the Blessed Virgin, and attending weekly Mass. Obey the nuns whether they are right or wrong. Protect our siblings from others (but they were free game at home because

Mom only had two hands), and never ever speak of the troubles in or outside our home about Dad. Belly aching and whining were exempt from family protocol. If anyone broke ranks and wept from exhaustion from the winds of in-family-country war, a quick retort from Mom of "If you wanna' cry, I will give you something to cry about" blew our boohoos out to sea.

Some adults to whom she was beholden for assistance in *Dad Gone Wild Days* were saints on earth and helped keep us afloat: The neighbors who stepped in when the roof blew off from the screaming, bringing calm and humor. Our aunt Cornie, my mother's sister, would not let us sink into the depths of poverty. A few family friends gave our strife an air of normalcy and laughter. The Blessed Virgin Mary seemed to be Mom's chief of staff and her comfort. Allies are essential for victory over life's struggles.

There was the good Doctor Forrester, our family doctor, who would have been paid in chickens if we had any chickens (excluding the dyed pastel-colored chicks we found one year frolicking and chirping all over our candy in our Easter baskets). Instead, Dr. Forrester gave our family excellent care without consideration of our frequently delinquent account. He made house calls. He always treated us with dignity and never condescended to our situation. I distinctly remember his mint gum breath, a cover-up for his smoking, which he did at his desk during office visits.

Many decades after his death, I ran into his wife, who managed his office in the 1950s, when she was in the same nursing home as my Uncle Tom. I told her of her husband's help for our family, and it touched her, but it was no surprise. She did his books.

Food budgeting prevailed. Soda pop at home was a luxury, only for special occasions, like the second coming of Christ. Mom hid some chocolate for herself in her bedroom, but sleuth *Swamp Fox* that I am, I could find it for a stolen nibble. Mom's budgeting employed alchemical skills. With all this abracadabra Wizard Merlin allocating and earmarking, and the ongoing mental health crises with Dad's dips into depression, risings into mania, and swoops into rages ignited by the slighted spark, Mom grimly sailed the waves like a seasoned sea captain, though always with carefully painted fingernails.

Her orders about falling into line were *sui generis*: "If you think you're going to wear that, you have another think a-comin." Misbehavior was met with this proclamation, "You are flirtin' with the undertaker." And who can forget the time check when the hammer would come down on us with, "Get in here faster than Billy be gone," which we would learn meant that when mystery boy Billy flees, he flees fast.

Thespian Mom would often fake call the "orphanage" and ask them to come and get us. Other times, at the end of her rope, she said she would send us away to the "island of Pago Pago," wherever that was (Mom had her own language and geography). Dr. Spock's child-rearing practices were not part of her navigation of a troubled life. She leaned more towards General Patton's side of discipline. "Because I said so" would do the trick.

A scene facsimile from an *I Love Lucy* episode would be Mom trying to reprimand me by chasing me, pushing her Hoover vacuum cleaner (to suck me up?). She would inevitably be defeated as I would run to the bathroom, close the door, and pull out the top drawer to barricade me in until she cooled off. I could tell the coast was clear when the Hoover became silent.

We three older kids attended Catholic school, which involved tuition payments that I would carry to the office in a small, sealed white envelope. My sister was the first to drop out of parochial school early on because she required the availability of a special reading teacher in public school. She went on to become a voracious reader. My brother made it to high school, but when Sister Clarette demanded he play five-year-old Winthrop in *The Music Man* school musical, which he did with great skill, that kind of nun-tyranny was too much for him. He went over to the Protestants, a.k.a. public school.

My other brother, the youngest, never began Catholic school. I, the eldest child, continued in Catholic school through high school graduation, working two jobs during my junior and senior years to help with costs. This education became another arrow in my quiver of success.

While growing up, new clothes were few and far between, so wearing a uniform to school shielded me from potential mean-girl social rebuke.

Our Christmas and Easter holidays and various gatherings were spent with Mom's side of the family, the Cavanaughs. My abundance of aunts, uncles, and cousins buoyed me up. We were a tribe.

When it came to Easter in the 1950s and 1960s, Mom managed (a deal with the Bunny?) to pull out all the stops with bonnets, purses, white gloves, and crinolines for the girls, accompanied by new and stiff shiny black patent leather shoes with straps. The boys had little suits that made them look like midget undertakers for some years, while in other years, they wore jaunty caps and looked like they were going to the track to bet the ponies.

Crying scenes of distress at the kitchen table mark my memories, a table that now resides in my kitchen. It should be able to float from Mom's sodden, desperate hours when hope seemed as far away as your fondest dream dashed. Even women warriors of true grit sometimes must take a knee.

Dad, in a manic state, during which times he becomes bravado-laden Richard the Lionhearted, bought our second house, which he could ill afford, on a whim. Mom was pregnant with the last sibling, Robert, a "surprise baby." The house was on a big hill in the new Holiday Hills development. Dad christened our "estate" Wynndy Knoll and commissioned a white wooden sign declaring such, which he hung from a big hickory tree in the front yard, as though we were neighbors of Downton Abbey or around the corner from Scarlett O'Hara's Tara.

We joined a new working-class neighborhood with enough kids on the street for two baseball or football teams. We spent much of our time down at the creek catching tadpoles or swinging on tree vines like Tarzan. Our summers included the area swimming pool, where I also worked, and I did swim team and the synchronized swimming shows. We Wynn kids now had lives outside of our house, and we gravitated to them most of the day.

The riches and treats would flow if Mom won at Bingo that week. Bingo was to Mom what candy is to a toddler. She needed the R and R thrill of gambling. The treasures of that heavily Catholic-supported game where erupting white balls did a path to riches lead, once did spill

Some of the Cavanaugh clan, my mother's side of the family. Eventually, there would be eighteen cousins. Mom and Dad are center, back row. I am in the second row, second from the right.

Left: My pre-patent leather shoe Easter rebellion circa 1954. My cowboy-boots-on-Easter era arrived a couple of years later.

Right: Dad was having a bad day that Easter; you can see it on his face. Circa 1963.

My niece Michelle Wynn now has the Wynndy Knoll sign perfectly set in her pretty garden.

bountifully when Mom won a thousand dollars at the St. Agnes Church Bingo in the mid-1950s. She bought each of us a bicycle. Like many of her fellow Bingo participants, she spread out about four hundred cards in front of her and mastered them all with the efficiency of an ace air traffic controller.

Dad's disability checks disappeared into the tides as quickly as they arrived. He had a penchant for throwing money into the wind with careless spending and a taste for fashion, including derbies, a deer skin coat, motorcycle boots, and, during one style era, neckerchiefs. There was also that fanciful-fronted white shirt that would have suited a Mexican warlord.

I remember a "Sure Fire Lobster Deal" that immediately fell through. His bar buddies always seemed to see an easy mark in Dad with their bogus schemes. Dad budgeted in guns and rifles, of which he had many. And, at the Keg Room, drinks were on him!

Mom struggled to continue a "loaves and fishes" approach to home finances. Eventually, it necessitated her return to work at the phone company, in the billing department where she had worked before marriage. That return to her job required daycare for us since Dad was unreliable as a parent and, at that time, once again hospitalized at the Veteran's Hospital in Chillicothe, Ohio, about an hour or so from our house.

Into our house came Shirley, our new babysitter. Though recruited into our troubled crew, she proved unseaworthy. This was in the 1950s; we kids were about seven, five, and three years old. A fourth child, brother Rob, was yet to be born. We Wynn kids were sometimes as undomesticated as feral alley cats despite Mom's commands from on high. Our reputations preceded us.

(Later, in high school, I met my classmate's mother, Mrs. Marsili. She recalled that once, when I was a tiny child, I had run up to a casket in the church at a funeral and knocked over the big burning candles on golden stands surrounding it. Mrs. Marsili told this story, shaking her head and tsking. It was clear she had never recovered from the Requiem Mass incident.)

The new babysitter, Shirley, was the quiet type. She was a large-boned country girl with long, straggly hair. She dressed as though she were in *The Grapes of Wrath and* had a Southern accent, just like in the film. I do not know where my parents found her or why they thought this reserved and introverted young woman could be a match for their often airborne-from-dressers "Flying Wallenda" children. When Shirley arrived, I immediately knew the fit was just like too-tight Easter patent leather shoes.

For starters, Shirley was not enamored of our playful aerodynamics or our to-the-death wrestling matches. Add to that mix the chivalrous jousts with the clothesline wooden props in the backyard. Forget about my acting out scenes, with volume up, from the Mickey Mouse Club shows as if I were Annette Funicello, pretend tap dancing on any hard surface, ground level or elevated.

These activities did not peacefully co-exist with Shirley's day-long Bible reading from a living room chair, her fixed perch. Yet, interestingly, our behavior probably matched many of the Bible stories, such as those in Revelations about the apocalypse or the vicious murder of John the Baptist.

Babysitter/Theologian Shirley lasted a very short time and quit after her punitive hell term with us. We kids celebrated. But who would care for us? Who would dare?

I have thought about this one terrible day so often over the decades, but there are gaps in my memory. *Does childhood trauma play a role in forgetting essential facts?* It seemed we three little kids were home alone, *but how could that be?* We were about the same age as I described: seven, five, and three. *Was this post-Shirley? Did Mom leave us there unattended to go to work out of dire need?* I remember Mom coming home just as the horrific drama unfolded, and she was in a dark, floral work dress with makeup, including her red lipstick, which we were not to kiss directly.

What happened was this: My brother, Rick, and I were in the living room by the front door with our neighbors, the two Gordon boys, who were about our ages. They were on the other side of the storm door window, outside on the front porch. We were playing and pushing on the glass at each other. *We were not allowed out, and they were not allowed in.* I do not recall any adults in our house.

Suddenly, the plate glass window broke, and sharp and deadly sheets of it came sailing down on us, a dangerous feature of that type of glass. The shattering sound rings in my ears even now. Shards cut my brother on his wrists and head, so severely slicing him that he started bleeding like a rolling river. The Gordon boys had rivulets of blood running from lacerations on their lips and faces. I had jumped back from the waterfall of glass and was not injured. I had not one clue what to do.

We all started screaming. Blood was everywhere. Then I saw my mother running toward our house, and my bloody brother was running down the street the other way . . . *to escape?* It appeared to me he did not want to get in trouble for breaking our glass door. *Was Mom coming from the bus stop where she would ride to and from work? I do not know.*

Now, Mom was screaming, too. Our neighbor George, who worked from home for a Las Vegas business, flew out of his house next door. He was the father of my best friend, Stevie. George started treating my brother by pressing cloth on his wounds, and he, Mom, and my brother all dashed away in George's car to the hospital. *Or was there an ambulance?* The Gordon kids, slightly injured, went home to seek help.

I do not recall where my little sister was during all of this. I was sent next door to the Hatfield's house alone. Whether the Hatfields made me sit there or I chose to sit there, I stayed seated on their front porch steps, waiting while they ate dinner. I sat there until my mother came home from the hospital and fetched me. My brother was alive but had many stitches, she told me, and he was bandaged on his head and wrist. His scars remain to this day.

As for our life and limbs, which Dad's out-of-control tirades of foul words, bodily threats, and physical aggressions attacked just like shards of slicing plate glass, we were at the mercy of the gods. I failed to save my brother from the accident caused by us kids horsing around with the glass door. Very early on, though, I saw it as my honor-bound duty, as eldest, to keep our family alive, as aspirational and delusional as that seems now.

The constant family worry about money pushed me to build my coffers through summer and after-school jobs. Money would buy me safe passage to new lands. My vivid imagination would create charts to follow and scaffolds to cross the abyss that had no obvious bridge to the other side. I became a conquering conjurer with my trusted banner of hope unfurled.

My Davy Crockett-era.

Chapter 2

Living in My Imagination

FOR RELIEF FROM the battlefront of real life, I spent a lot of time as a little child imagining myself to be someone else, to be somewhere else. When things in our home grew dicey from Dad's angry flare-ups, at times near-spontaneous combustion at the slightest provocation, say, for instance, the sun came up that day, I saddled up the mighty steed of my imagination and rode off into the fantasy sunset. Davy Crockett and I sported raccoon skin caps. Dale Evans was my fellow cowgirl with our hat and boots, complete with holster and gun.

I secretly tunneled out of real life to escape into TV Land when Dad started swinging and threatening Mom while she cringed and cried. Once the coast was clear—and we never knew how long the tirade would blaze on—I would laugh at Lucille Ball and Desi Arnaz as the Ricardos, along with the Mertzes, on the *I Love Lucy* show.

Jackie Gleason in *The Honeymooners* reminded me of Dad with his outbursts. He threatened his TV wife, Alice, by yelling and drawing back his fist to say he was going to send her to the moon, just like my dad would do with Mom. Ralph Kramden had a funny neighbor named Norton. We had funny neighbors. The show made me feel at home, a place where domestic violence masqueraded as standard comedy fare.

I craved the comedian acts on *The Ed Sullivan Show* on Sunday nights. *Stiller and Meara* were favorites of mine because she was Irish. The morning *Ten O'Clock Theater* on my local TV station showed old movies, many of them about show business, revealing the backstage happenings, star romances, and crazy mishaps.

The stuff of my daydreams sprang from the television, which I had thought came from inside the TV set. To discover the wonders of how it all worked, one day, I crawled into the narrow floor space between the wall and the hippo-sized TV and looked inside. All I saw were giant glass tubes, gray in color, with thin wires of light inside them. No singing man from the kids' show within, warbling, "Yoo hoo, it's me, my name is Pinky Lee," and no dancing teenagers doing the stroll from Dick Clark's *American Bandstand* to be found.

In contrast to my daytime TV viewing, the nighttime plots of my frequent childhood nightmares were heavily influenced by the neighborhood dads, home from WWII. Those who told their stories took me to the battlefields of wars, into the bunkers of WWII, on flights on foot from Nazi soldiers, or to the decks of the exploding ships of Pearl Harbor.

The war ended in 1945. I was born in 1951. The dust was still settling in the United States for most of the families in the US. Our house was a continuous dust storm of what we now know as post-traumatic stress syndrome (PTSD). For this, we were not alone, but we thought we were.

An additional night terror of mine involved tornadoes, which I attribute to repeated viewings of *The Wizard of Oz*. I also have an abnormal distaste for Flying Monkeys. I liked that Dorothy sought help from various sources other than her family. I did, too.

The ultimate of my "presto change-o" I-am-not-really-here acts to avoid the friction of the home front lines was my sincere wish to enlist in a fun TV brigade as a Mouseketeer. Annette Funicello, *Prima Mouseketeera*, set the bar high for the life I would seek. It seemed I would need to become Italian.

One afternoon, when I was about four years old, I became a Mouseketeer. I napped on my parent's bed, and a warm breeze billowed through the sheer white curtains. To this day, wisps of fresh air swirling through a window transport me to that embracing chenille bedspread of my parents. Their bed was directly against the window facing the backyard, where my mother would hang the wash on the clothesline, especially the sheets. She would shout howdy-dos over the fences to the other mothers at their laundry tasks. The scents of Tide and Clorox informed our families we were cared for and clean.

The aroma of summer's possibilities and honeysuckle filled the bedroom that soft and quiet afternoon of my Mickey Mouse Club initiation nap. In my dream (which I now know was of the lucid variety termed *hypnagogic)*, the Mouseketeers climbed in that very window in their sparkling white sweaters with their respective names across their chests and sporting their "mouse ears." They invited me to be part of their troupe. There she was, my favorite, Annette! I dream-climbed back out the window to be on the show with them. Then I woke up, not wanting the moment to pass.

Turning seven, I desired to run away and join my cousin Debbie (who later became that TV stage manager) and her family act in *Holiday on Ice*. My aunt, uncle, Debbie, and her brother, Robbie, were professional ice skaters. We would visit them at Grandma Cavanaugh's and see them perform in Columbus or Cleveland.

My aunt wore bright, sequined costumes and make-up and looked strikingly different from the moms in my neighborhood. They were always in some stage of pregnancy, ironing for centuries in their living rooms in front of the soap operas and bribing our good behavior with red Kool-Aid containing one full cup of sugar. The fact that I did not know how to ice skate never compromised this wishful thinking, nor did my abject terror of being away from home. My dream world kept me planted and secure in my insecurity.

Severe stage fright thwarted my show business goals for many years. Due to my family circumstances, I felt inferior and diminished. I tried to be a strong cowgirl, but inside, I was as squishy with anxiety as a shaky cherry Jell-O mold. There came a time when I slayed this dragon. He was not an easy kill.

Another escape route never pursued (as it was problematic for a child to obtain a train ticket in those days without raising suspicion) was taken by my dad's cousin on the Wynn side, actor Mitchell Ryan. He was in theater in New York, on TV in westerns and soaps like *Dark Shadows* and *All My Children*, and later movies including *Liar Liar*, *Lethal Weapon, Gross Pointe Blank*, and hit TV series like *Dharma and Greg*.

While we Wynn kiddies only knew of Mitch's career and did not know him personally while we were growing up, he and I connected

Cousin Debbie and Uncle Johnny in the Williams family skating act. What's not to like there?

My mom's younger sister, Patricia Ann, and Uncle Johnny Williams are from Columbus, Ohio. As teens, they won nationwide skating competitions and then became professional ice skaters.

Mitchell Ryan, actor.
My dad's cousin.

years after my dad died in 1980. We then regularly talked and visited until his death at eighty-eight. He was among the few family members who affirmed my later-in-life work in performing and writing.

These peripheral, genetically linked family members continued to succor me. It is not uncommon to want to be your TV and movie heroes or follow your relatives living lives you admire. In the second case, you hope some of that DNA seeped into your system, too.

Then came a touchstone moment, a turning point made possible by my now well-honed ability to step into another life and imagine the maybe not-so-crazy possibilities. I learned about a castle in Wales named Gwydir, the ancient home of the Wynn dynasty, the kings and princes of Wales. My imagination catapulted me back to the 1500s.

Could they be my own Wynn ancestors? Wynn was an uncommon US surname when I was growing up. Reading and learning about the powerful ruling Wynns of Wales caused me to see alternative genetic programming potential. Mental illness and infamy appeared to be our family's central claim. But. Maybe we also have royal roots, and my visions of the best we could be were more than figments of my elaborate and persistent Walter Mitty reveries. *Can we decide to cherry-pick our DNA selections or how we view them?*

All this blossomed like a June red rose when I discovered the memoir *Castles in the Air* (2005), about a young couple who purchased the dilapidated Gwydir Castle in 1994 and brought it back to life. Judy Corbett, the book's author, and her husband, visual artist Peter Welford, continue to renovate the castle. My dream life expanded like a blue and white striped circus tent as I devoured their journey and learned more

Gwydir Castle in Wales is the ancient ancestral seat of the powerful Wynn family. It was built around 1500. Photo: Judy Corbett

about the Wynns who inhabited the castle. I began to mentally clear the stigma that had been laid on my family name, resulting from my dad's hellzapoppin' living days and his brutal death when he was sixty.

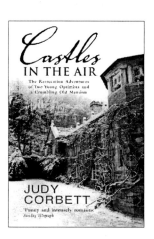

The book that turned my thinking around.

My new thinking had me stirring something constantly in the back of my mind: *Do we have an alternative life script we could have followed if not for some strange twist of fate?*

After over half a century of being labeled "the Wynn family with the crazy dad," I now had another point of view: the phrase in the book *Castles* that author Judy chose, "the illustrious Wynns." Those three words affected me to my core because we had born so much emotional pain, shame, and guilt as the *family of Wynn*. I had seen unrealized glimmers of "illustrious" in Dad, who could sing like Bing Crosby, dance like Astaire, draw, tell stories, create photography, do one-handed push-ups, hunt, fish, and use his humor on sacred rare occasions.

My husband and I made plans to visit Gwydir in Wales, our own royal pilgrimage. Judy and Peter had made Gwydir into a two-bedroom Bed and Breakfast with their living quarters in another wing of the stone manse so they could have guests stay in the castle. The trip did not disappoint; it fired up my hopes that we Wynns were once of this clan.

After all, the Wynns in the old castle paintings and drawings prominently displayed are Richard Wynn (my dad and brother's name), Robert Wynn (my brother, uncle, and grandfather's name, and my son's middle name), and John Wynn, (my uncle and cousin's name). We named our only son Wynn Robert in 1979, unaware of Gwydir Castle. This enhanced my thinking that if you are a Wynn, you might have the *Dieu et mon droit* license in your composition to reject the hand you were dealt.

Through the "wicket gate" of the main gate to the large castle door of Gwydir.

The gracious and charming Gwydir Castle proprietors, Judy and Peter, have taken on the formidable task of restoring the castle's ruined condition to its majestic glory, with ongoing constant repairs and colossal calamities. They are beating the odds, gallantly battling the initial vermin, water leaks, cold, hours-long workdays, "chainsaw gardening," financial scrapes, continuing prodigious flooding, and total discomfort. Their noble quest is to save the castle.

By the time of our stay in 2011, the castle was more than fit for guests. It was enchanting from the start, with peacocks strolling the grounds. Judy told us guests with the name of Wynn often visit. She jokes about the Wynn royal wannabes in her book. Judy and Peter were extraordinarily gracious and tolerant toward my wishful claim for royal Wynn-ness.

I settled into the "Illustrious Wynn" world of the castle; these 1500s and 1600s Wynns added to my pride: they were patrons of the arts and education, as am I. A high school classmate once said, "I heard your dad is crazy. Is that true?" The centuries between mattered not. Gwydir lopped that memory off.

When I spoke to Judy and Peter about that cognitive shift during our stay, they mentioned that Gwydir possesses some powerful energies. The castle's energy, maybe even more than the possibility of royal connections, began scraping away my mossy veneer of shame. I had pulled the Excalibur of positive perception out of the stone of my false narrative.

We were on this visit with our friends Anita and Lindsay Jenkins. We took a nearby day trip to my teen mecca of Liverpool. Our Magical Mystery Tour of Beatleland added an extra dose of fairy dust to the adventure since I am a Paul McCartney devotee. It all became a psychic make-over: music in The Cavern Club, visiting the childhood homes of each Beatle, driving down Penny Lane, and gazing in the gate of Strawberry Fields.

This just added to the treasure chest of the visit to the castle with its restored rooms, gorgeous gardens, colorfully proud peacocks, exqui-

Judy Corbett (standing), author and castle owner, also served the delicious breakfasts. Friend Anita Jenkins, left; husband Steve, center; friend Lindsay Jenkins, right.

sitely painted chapel, morning scones, and other nourishing breakfast goodies, with a pot of delicious tea. It was a turning point and set me in a new direction. It righted my ship. I felt my shame slip away as smoothly as Judy removed the marmalade from the table. I was a brand-new royal me. Those included in this stay, and Judy and Peter, humored me as I frequently voiced exclamations and grateful revelations.

Judy's present-day Gwydir Facebook posts of photographs and glorious descriptions of the grounds, the building, and nature are like a priest's daily readings of a Divine Office or a Magnificat for me. They lift me. They nourish my soul. My spirit, indeed, rejoices.

I started reading up on "royal blood" ancestry. I ran across some studies that have bolstered my sense that I could tap into alternate strains of DNA for my identity, "reclaim my throne" of self-worth, and free myself of the shroud of household trauma and embarrassment that had settled on my soul, like the dying embers and morning soot I had seen in the colossal hearth of Gwydir.

In one 1999 Yale study, researcher Joseph Chang concluded everyone

Gwydir peacocks. The medieval knights took the "Vow of the Peacock" during Christmas week. They would place their hands on a peacock and vow to keep to their code of chivalry for the year. Photo: Judy Corbett

alive today shares a common ancestor. We are all intertwined: royals, court jesters, horse thieves, murderers, mule skinners, and cooks. Our life scripts are not prescribed or limited by our circumstances. Another study in 2013 by Peter Ralph and Graham Coop determined all Europeans come from the same people. Everyone in Europe is descended from royalty back to Charlemagne, so all Europeans who came to America are descended from royalty. Ergo, any American with a drop of European blood comes from royalty. I'm buying it.

In my family of birth, we gave not an inch to considering our ancient forbearers since our very existence in the here and now was constantly at risk. I was extremely attentive to and observant of my immediate and (living) extended family, taking a loyalty pledge in my self-styled "Vow of the Peacock." In so doing, I remained quiet about our hidden pain while guarding it inside our tainted fortress. I kept to our mandated family script of secrecy about our troubles. Carl Jung said secrets are "psychic poison." I had a massive swig of that evil potion to spit out.

We misjudged, however. Despite our heroic efforts to put up a good front in our "Wynn Abbey" on the hill, this assumed privacy protection we disciplined ourselves to project was as impervious as a sieve. Everyone knew. But no one talked. But it was not all doom and gloom at our house. Some days, the sun peaked through the clouds, and we caught rare glimpses of that fleeting apparition, "Good Dad."

Dad circa 1948.

Chapter 3

Good Dad

"GOOD DAD" WAS Dad on his best days. Dad's lifetime loves were guns, fishing poles, beer (though he did not drink at home), the Catholic Mass, St. Patrick's Day, steak and potatoes, Neapolitan ice cream, Peter Sellers, the Army–Navy game, his mother, my mom's mother, my sister Kathleen, leather boots, and the Keg Room bar.

In his days of yore, Dad was a good singer and knew the words to many songs. He was born on February 12, 1920 and his voice sounded like a Bing Crosby/Elvis Presley blend. One minute, he might be crooning a 1940s hit like "I'll Be Seeing You," and the next, Roger Miller's 1965 hit, "King of the Road." He was a smooth and skilled dancer. Dad had a good hand with a pencil and may have been a bit of an artist at heart. Dad loved riding a motorcycle. For a brief while, he had been a part-time professional photographer, and we had a dark room in the basement of our first house where he developed photos from weddings he shot. Most of the family pictures of me in this memoir are by him. The for-hire photography went by the wayside when he entered the No Job Permanently zone right before I was born. In 1963, he bought a Polaroid camera and loved snapping pictures with that magical device that spit out photos.

When he went into a depressive state, Dad didn't like anything, mainly himself and us. Those days, brooding became his pastime.

Compromised people with sad lives can have days of Ohio Eastern Bluebirds on their shoulders. The about-face emotions are enough to give the peripheral people whiplash and a reason to wear a neck brace as a fashion accessory. When Dad had a flash-in-time "well period," his charms, humor, and talents shone through. He warbled with his beautiful voice. He would show me how to draw. He taught me to dance to singers like Patti Page or Rosemary Clooney while standing on his feet, just like in commercials showing children at weddings.

The Good Times. Mom and Dad on the left.

He demonstrated to us kids how to eat sardines on saltines with mustard and encouraged us to try this snack that was in direct opposition to a peanut butter and jelly sandwich. The sardine can was a little culinary treasure chest with its unique key to peel back the lid, revealing its bounty in a briny oil. The teeny, salty, greasy fish and the tart mustard offered a new taste sensation. We looked like hungry baby birds around Dad as he fed us the concoction while standing around the kitchen counter.

On rare occasions when I was very little, and before my three siblings were born, Mom would dress up, and Mom and Dad would go out with friends. I have the white milk glass brooch with rhinestones my mother would wear on those night-out-on-the-town occasions.

As the family grew, the laughs dwindled. With four children and an increasingly depressed husband who had adverse feelings about socializing the white brooch went into hiding in Mom's jewelry box. I exhumed it from this box, which I inherited in 2011 upon Mom's death.

Glass brooch coiffure.

Our son Wynn was very close to my mom. I wore the brooch in my hair for his 2019 wedding day.

Mom always accompanied Dad from Columbus to the VA hospital in Chillicothe, Ohio, during his attacks of mania or depression or both. He required supervision during the trip. However, Mom did not receive her driver's license until later in life. One rendition of the driving story is she flunked her test nine times. Mom was a terrible driver.

It was typical Good Dad that on one of his many trips to the VA, he rescued a stray piglet waddling down the side of the road. Dad had the designated helpful driver stop the car for the piglet and made my mom promise she would see to the squealing pink orphan. Good Dad often created additional tasks for others, so again, Dad's folly became Mom's cross to bear in the form of a piglet to ferry.

My mother hated animals. We were permitted no pets beyond a little turtle that somehow got lost for a year, only to be discovered hunkered under our living room sofa, having survived on escaped Rice Krispies and falling cookie crumbs. When Mom grew elderly and entered assisted living, she rued the days they brought the emotional support dog to her room. She told me she would act like she liked it, not to insult the dog's human.

On the other hand, Dad loved wildlife and brought home an assortment of frogs, rabbits, turtles, and once an entire snake's skin. One day, he drove up the driveway only to emerge from the car with a live chicken for dinner, which he chased around the yard. He then cut off its head, and the chicken continued running headless. The Good Dad horror show mesmerized us.

Back to the story of poor Mom and her new porcine charge. She wrangled the piglet while wearing her going-to-the-hospital proper dress-up clothes and stored it where? In a bag? In her purse? In the trunk? She incredibly got the pig to a farm. She added this task to her 5,000 additional to-dos as the primary parent of our litter.

Once, when I was a little girl, I went into the kitchen to find a teenage girl who was dripping wet, shivering, and weeping seated at our table. My mom and dad were talking to her in consoling tones. Seeing them working as a team in a stressful situation was strange. I was missing a script page, so I stayed in the background of the small yellow kitchen nestled under the wall phone twirling its spiral black cord. This scene was for responsible adults as primary players, with me as a riveted audience.

Earlier, Dad had exited his home-away-from-home, the beer joint, only to happen upon the forlorn girl, rain-soaked and trembling on the street sidewalk. She was a runaway, and he took her home with him. My mom fed her, and my dad dialed her number. Again, he spoke to the people on the other end in reassuring and well-adjusted parental tones. Then he and the teen left, and he returned her to her parents.

It was as though Mom and Dad were trained and official Red Cross volunteers at the disaster scene. Hot cocoa in a mug warmed the girl's hands. A sandwich sat on a plate before her. Mom wrapped her in a terry cloth towel. My parents played off each other with their language and mannerisms like they had rehearsed it and relied on each other's responses for the next word or action. This was a one-time-only performance.

Mom and Dad, in personal crisis, were usually at loggerheads resembling *Who's Afraid of Virginia Wolf*-level volleying. Perhaps those battles contributed to their skill set when challenged to work together.

Later, I realized they were doing something I learned from them:

calming a situation of emotions gone wild. When the tables were turned in the revolving staircase of our family scenes, and I felt lost, I learned to calm myself. I am also good at comforting others—all four Wynn kids are. If we were firemen, we would run into the fire to help another person and then counsel them when they were safe. Compassion comes from our firehose.

During some of the infrequent rainbows and unicorn days, Dad taught me to fish, frog gig—where you use a little pitchfork pole to stab and catch the frogs—hunt, box, fly a kite, swing on a swing set, and ride a bike.

Dad, his beloved motorcycle boots, and his guns. The gun case was in the room where my little brothers slept. Do notice the dead pheasant hanging in it.

After my dad's frog gigging trip. Our neighbor kids, my brother,
my little sister, and Mom.

When I recall the funny family stories, I always question what might
have been: Why couldn't many more of our own life stories have been
I Love Lucy episodes, too, like this one?

Dad would go frog gigging. One day, in the 1950s, he brought a tin
bucket of frisky frogs home to our first house, and the neighbors came
over. Frog legs on the backyard grill were on the menu. These frogs had
been alive in their container in the house but got loose, and as Dad told
the story, all he saw were the neighbor women "ass up" trying to catch
the frogs with pots and pans all over the living room.

Those early-on happy gatherings in the kitchen to celebrate a birth
or for the neighbor men to come for a beer and watch the Friday night
fights tickle my memories. Dad and the men would laugh and tell stories
and jokes. I loved seeing Happy Dad.

The neighbors made over me when I was little and played with me,
tossing me about. I loved being airborne. My teenaged neighbor Carol,
whom I adored, and thought was even more beautiful than the dancers
on the Dick Clark American Bandstand show, would play a game with

I can imagine my dad and his buddies watching the fights and, for laughs, setting up this picture of me with a potty on my head, slugging down a 7-Up.

me where she would sing, "Tra la la Boom Dee Ay," and I would run across the yard and leap into her arms. I also have a home movie of our game taken by her dad.

I was my dad's buddy as a toddler and in preschool. We took joy rides on his bicycle. He would put me in the basket with the little multi-colored wool quilt blanket lining it, and we would fly around the neighborhood. Mom tasked Dad with taking me to the beer joint when my younger brother was born so she could have some quiet. Dad would prop me up there on the bar with a 7-Up and a cute, blue, sparkly plastic straw, and I would listen to the other veterans of WWII tell their war stories. We were lost in a fog of cigarette smoke, their remembrances, and the smell of spilled beer.

When I saw the movie *Paper Moon,* Tatum O'Neal's adult/child character riding shotgun with her charlatan dad reminded me of my dad and me. My favorite part was that Tatum was his match.

For too short a while, my dad was my best ally. In my first neighborhood, all the kids my age were boys. Boys who did not want to play with a girl. My dad had a solution. He worked in naval aviation during the war and, later, out of the service, became a pilot (and by "became a pilot," I guess he did this by just going and flying planes without certification). One day, he rallied all the neighbor boys in the garage and told them, "Gentlemen, if you let Trish play with you, I will let you swing in this parachute seat."

He had hung up this elaborate kid magnet in the garage in all its alluring glory. The boys were sold, and each took a turn in the honest-to-God parachute seat swing. I was in!

Some of these gender experiences were useful later in my life. For instance, with my college summer job as one of the first female mail carriers in Columbus in 1971, I needed to remember how to *get in with the boys*. Most of the men in the station were angry that a "girl" "stole" a "man's job" from a "family man." It wasn't long before I suffered their reprisals in various forms.

I mouthed off to the haranguing guys when they taunted me about depriving a man of this job. Because I played rough house and sports with neighbor boys, including tackle football, until high school, I was not intimidated by the mailmen who shoved open the bathroom door on me or placed pornographic literature on my car seat. My dad taught me to box, so I understood aggression, and I used it with my words, posture, and walk with the few revengeful men.

Once they simmered down and knew I would not be cowed, I became one of the guys, and we joked around together. I was nineteen.

My dad had a great sense of humor during his *Just Being Funny Dad* times. One day, he took the parachute out onto the street and pretended he had just landed from jumping out of an airplane. There was only one snag to his comedy act: it was a windy day, and the parachute filled with air and dragged him down the road. As he was about to go airborne, good neighbor George† saw what was happening, ran out from next door, tackled, and saved Dad as they pulled in the parachute. (I have a home movie of this scene filmed by a neighbor.) This is the same George who helped save my brother when play at our plate glass door turned deadly.

† George made illegal weighted dice for Las Vegas in his basement, and my mother sewed the blue velvet bags that contained them. I don't dare to guess their employer as I understand a healthy omertà (the Italian code of silence).

Dad standing on a car because, well, just because.

Dad took me to Westgate Park and taught me to pump my legs to go higher on the swings. He would swing me up to the skies, it seemed. I felt like Peter Pan flying, and I adored Peter Pan. He would take us to the river where people would picnic, and we would skip rocks and buy peanuts from the Peanut Man with his little glass cart on the side of the road above the river. Dad took us to the cowboy movies, and I could buy a root beer.

At some traffic lights, Dad had a particular game. It was called Hit the Deck. No other kids in the neighborhood played this game. Dad would pretend that enemy fire rained down on our car, and we had to *hit the deck* to avoid certain annihilation. We would scramble off our seat positions, unencumbered by seat belt laws in the 1950s, and dive onto the floor of the red Nash model car until Dad gave the all-clear. We never knew when an attack would occur, so we remained on high alert.

But as we got older and Dad found handling us kiddies a D–Day-sized task, fun times diminished to those of our own making, and Dad

Dad in the Navy "admiring art."
A joke photo.

continued slipping further and further away from us into the troubled fugue of his existence.

Good Dad reappeared at the odd time and place, just when needed. When I became a teenager, Dad was especially protective of me with boys. He didn't trust them. He had been one on the prowl as a young man. Dad would give me what he called "mad money" in case I needed to make a clean escape from a bad boy. And most boys were bad at heart, my dad counseled.

When I was in college, I received only one letter from Dad. I was stressed out with finals and had called home in tears. My anxiety monster was getting the better of me, as it too often did. In the short letter with his jagged and pointed left-handed script, he advised me to have some fun and stop worrying so much.

My mother never spoke with me about boys or sex, but she had an ironclad rule about the girls shaving their legs. We were not to shave our legs until we were older (perhaps retirement age?), as shaving legs too young was some kind of sign that we were loose women.

When I was about thirteen, I decided to shave my legs, fallen woman or not. So, I secretly went into my parents' bathroom, took out my dad's razor from his drawer, and began to shave the hair away. Not having had any lesson in the proper procedure, I also scraped all the skin in a long strip up my entire shin. It's interesting what happens next from a medical point of view; the blood does not seep out all at once. It bubbles to the top of the flesh in dots, like the candy in little circle puddles on register paper, and then it gushes *everywhere!*

I dashed out of the bathroom screaming and ran into the living room, leaving a trail of blood. My dad hit the wooden ejector lever on the side of his chair. *POP!* That swung his relaxing recline to "Ten Hut" upright attention from his easy chair cockpit, catapulting him to a standing position, wearing his usual leisure wear of boxer shorts.

"What in the hell happened!"

I moaned, tears streaming down my face and blood streaming down my leg onto the carpet, "I shaved my legs, and I cu- cu- cut myself!!!!!"

"Did you use *my razor*?"

What? This stifled me. I am bleeding all over holy hell and his concern was for his razor? (I later learned from my husband after I used his that this was a primary offense and affront.)

Dad ran from the room (Dad running, not pacing!), grabbed some towels, and started pressing them on my leg like a medic called to the scene. He staunched the blood. He also cleaned up the "murder scene" in their bathroom and the blood on the carpet.

When my mom returned and heard the tale, she probably assumed God already had punished me for turning into a street walker, with only one good leg left to practice my newfound oldest profession. No remonstrations from her to me. Perhaps she had also unsuspectingly crossed the proprietary razor restriction line.

Dad took this picture of me on the day of my eighth-grade graduation. My leg had healed. Before the shot, Dad showed me how a model stands.

My dad staged and took this picture. I remember this day. He had
me draw my arm up as if I was about to shoot. That is his real pistol
and holster. I still take direction well. It has served me.

Chapter 4

Operation Kill Daddy

I SUPPOSE BEING a potential murderer at the age of five might give you a new and jaded impression of me. But here it is. Bad Dad emerged much more than Good Dad. Even as a young tyke, I needed the brutality and abuse to stop. By now, my first brother was born, and then my little sister. Something had to be done. The potential casualty list was expanding.

Sure, our family had laughs and fun times early on, between the skirmishes with weeping Mom and roaring Dad. But there were also times of supreme angst, yelling, and violence. When I was very little, these fights were much more physical, with Dad pushing and punching Mom. I could not bear it.

Even as a little child, I would enter the fray. Dad would fight with Mom, and I would rush to interrupt with a Shirley Temple-style stomp and a shouted protest. On a couple of occasions, my efforts were misplaced. Apparently, on one attempted rescue mission of mine, when they were in their bedroom behind a closed door, my mom's moans were what they both assured me was "Daddy tickling Mommy."

Even so, Dad's suddenly erupting volcanoes of anger and violence presented a clear and present danger to my vulnerable child self and the rest of my family. I knew it from the start. One day, I decided to act after a night of fighting had me unsettled and on edge. Mom had been sobbing and pleading with Dad to stop screaming at her and shoving her. I spied this fracas from my floor seat before the television, casting my eyes into their bedroom. Dad had pinned Mom up against the dresser, where she begged him to stop. The fighting lasted a long time.

Had my parents ever realized my crusade to right this wrong the following morning, foster care could have been my fate. I steeled myself to joust.

Little brother Rick and me.

The very next morning, before my parents emerged from the bedroom, I enlisted the assistance of my little brother. I was five, and my little brother was three. I knew I had to do something. I was a determined child. (When I was around two, they told me I bit my Grandma Aggie on the butt at the grocery store when she refused my toy request.)

I strategized. I went into the kitchen of our small tract house on the West Side of Columbus, Ohio. Out of the flatware drawer, I chose two butter knives. I gave one to my little brother, Ricky, as he was known then, and I held one in position to stab Dad, mimicking what I had seen on the TV cowboy show, *The Adventures of Jim Bowie*.

I positioned Ricky and me behind Dad's Eakin Road throne, the green leather easy chair in the living room. I told Ricky to crouch down with me and hide, and we would wait for Dad to come out of the bedroom with butter knife daggers at the ready. We were in our footed jammies with the rubber-dotted bottoms, preventing a running child from crashing into a wall or flying aloft and barreling down the basement stairs.

I told Ricky, "We gotta kill Daddy." Ricky just looked at me. He was accustomed to following my orders, but this seemed a bridge too far.

My quest was to save Mom, us, and a baby sister. Kathleen was not enlisted to murder as she was too young to walk, talk, or understand directives. Her knife skills were nil, but she did have an abnormal affection for sharp objects. (Example: Mom could not locate the "good scissors" one day and did not discover them until she changed Kathleen's diaper, where the toddler had stashed them. There were no injuries.)

Back to the scene of the potential crime.

I encountered a snag in "Operation Kill Daddy." As we hid, ready to pounce, Ricky refused to go along with me, being three and all and not having developed the fierce skill set that I had. He handed me his weapon. Also, the climate in our house had demonstratively changed. My mood detector abilities (no trendy ring necessary) served.

Dad came out of the bedroom to our battle position. I can still see him looming over us. He appeared smiling and cheerful. An atmospheric recalibration snapped into place. I could not figure out how to start killing him because it was a "Good Dad" morning. It would be like a standing high jump with the bar twenty feet off the ground.

Dad smiled his broad Celtic smile and said, just like TV Dad Ozzie Nelson, "What are you two kids doing back there?"

Eakin Road, present day. Those trees did not exist when I lived there.

Ricky, dumbstruck, just looked at Dad.

Searching for cues, Dad locked eyes on me, the general, who had charted the maneuvers to take this hill. I offered the universal child subterfuge surrendering answer, "Nuh . . . thing."

Dad took the butter knives, shaking his head like, *you crazy kiddies,* and walked my weaponry back into the kitchen, not knowing he was just seconds from being whacked.

Dad's deteriorating mental health continued, as did battles, heartache, grossly tragic incidences, physical fights, and misery, with Good Dad Days diminishing with the years. Mercifully, our family was spared. Many years later, others were not.

I still have those exact butter knives.

PART II

The Royal Court: Who's Who

Hieronymus Janssen (Belgian, 1624–1693), *Charles II Dancing at a Ball at Court*, c. 1660, oil on canvas, Royal Collection Trust, UK

If you cannot get rid of the family skeleton,

you may as well make it dance.

—GEORGE BERNARD SHAW

The advantage of growing up with siblings

is that you get very good at fractions.

—ROBERT BRAULT

About 1961. Kathleen, me holding Robbie, and Richard.

Chapter 5

The Line-Up

THERE WERE eventually four of us, the first three siblings born two years apart, then a baby ten years my junior. The second child, named Richard after Dad, is my first brother. Dad had boxed in the Navy, and when he taught his kid to box, Dad acted as if his young, elementary-school-aged son were an equal opponent and beat the crap out of him. The novel *The Great Santini* comes to mind. Mr. Tough Guy-Dad whipping his seven-year-old opponent in the ring, now *that's* significant to our saga.

This brother became a lifelong protector of our mom. Mom was his champion, too.

The third child, Kathleen, was born when I was four. Mom and Dad brought her home, and many neighbors came over to celebrate. While they were gathered in the kitchen, the new baby girl was in her bassinet in the living room. I had no idea we were going to receive a baby, as this, too, was never addressed. Had it been discussed with me, I might have suggested we get a kitten instead. But here she was, a tiny human.

I pulled myself up on the side of the crib and peered in. There was this pink, chunky baby with a round face and wisps of blonde hair. She looked like a perfect baby doll you would buy at the store. She turned her attention to me hovering over her. She had big blue eyes and started to cry. Dad came roaring out of the kitchen and gave me a spanking. He told me never to touch my sister. I protested that I hadn't touched her, but he didn't listen. At this young age, I understood that no appeals court would help. Dad's edicts in our house were final.

Kathleen was a favorite of Dad's. She was overtly affectionate, while I was guarded and defiant. For instance, one day, on the city bus going downtown to shop with Mom, when she was about three or four, Kathy sashayed down the central bus aisle and kissed passengers down the row. Kathleen's baby doll appearance made her a welcome bus greeter, whereas my six-year-old tomboy look likely threatened them. Any affectionate overtures from toughie me might have been met with a clutched purse, a rolled-up newspaper whack, or a poke with an umbrella.

In 1961, we were in for a family surprise. We were all in the car when Mom entered Dr. Forrester's office for her OB/GYN test and exam. I was nine at the time. Dad initiated the Hit the Deck game, but we quickly tired of being on the car floor. All during her appointment, we three kids were roughhousing in the backseat with Dad irritated, doing his raging bull nose breathing, and shouting orders to cease and desist. All that was ignored. We would settle and then ignite all over again with wrestling, tickling, and crossing all personal boundaries to annoy each other. We found it great fun and ignored Dad's irritated mood. The three of us teamed to outnumber him.

Mom came out of the doctor's door, which had a round leaded cut glass window on the top. Their conversation was brief: Dad said, "Yeah?" and Mom answered, "Yes." It was a tone more in line with a verdict. Finances most likely proved the happiness damper for my parents. Money management was Mom's mandate. Dad's penchant rested in ignoring accounting.

That was how we learned Mom was going to have a baby, and the three of us Wynn kids, with no checking account nor bills to stew about, could not have been happier. Robbie was and is much loved.

During Mom's pregnancy with Robbie, I would sidle up to my teacher's desk some mornings before class began and give Sister Agnes Clare updates on how many days until the baby's arrival. I assumed she would be as delighted as I was about the new baby. No matter that, she, childless, had a teaching career amid the post-war baby boom in a Catholic school where birth control's rhythm method proved more suitable to tap dancing.

The long-awaited blessed event of the birth of our baby brother finally went into motion. Neighbor Margaret, a German War Bride, walked Mom up and down the street. Margaret said Mom needed to walk to give birth. This, I now assumed, was how a woman had a baby; you walk it out of your body.

Then, Dad took Mom to the hospital. After she had the baby, Dad brought us to visit. Standing on the sidewalk outside the hospital, the three of us waved to Mom, who stood at her window many floors up. My guess is her stay at the hospital, much longer than nowadays, felt like a week at the Canyon Ranch Spa compared to life in our house. She had room service! No screaming kids! No wrathful husband! They probably had to evict her forcefully.

Dad went to the hospital to bring Mom and the new baby home. They drove up the long driveway hill of our second house by now. We were thrilled and bounced around the living room in anticipation. Mom came up the basement steps from the garage in her fancy New Year's Eve two-piece maternity outfit (even though it was June). It was white, made of a satin floral brocade. As was the custom then for maternity clothes, the top was pup tent-sized and flared, billowing over a skirt with a vast, expandable half-moon piece of elastic fabric that could grow with you. She wanted to look her best in her finest outfit.

The minute Mom walked in the door, with Dad carrying the baby, they began screaming about whatever they had quarreled about in the car. Having lost the debate, Mom cried and stowed baby Robbie safely away into his white woven wooden bassinet in their bedroom as Dad shifted topics in some indecipherable pattern.

When Dad squawked about whatever, you name it, we learned to stay out of the way and continue our lives (unless we were targets). It was like remaining distracted or even oblivious as a cobra eats a live chicken: unconditional indifference. Some people label this defense tactic disassociation. I call it either that or escalating the danger. (The character Alice Kramden on *The Honeymooners* was a fine example for me: in the face of Ralph's tirades, she remained impassive and unmoving. Ralph would eventually sputter and downshift.)

Dad kept harping at Mom, then he denounced her and touted his injustice of that hour. He stomped back down the basement steps to the garage, got in his car, ripped down the steep driveway backward, and sped to the bar. Mom went to lie on her bed in her pretty dress-up clothes. At times like these, Mom would take her rosary and pray for help from another mother, the Blessed Virgin Mary, who also suffered.

We kids turned to our distractions: television and sibling mortal combat, without the aid of the video games to come much later. This was living room trench warfare.

We had been instructed sternly not to hold the baby, so naturally, I would sneak into their bedroom, hoist baby Robbie out of the white wicker bassinet, and rock him in my arms when no one was looking. Mom was forty years old, tired, and probably suffering post-natal depression, so when Robbie cried at night at some length, I would sometimes get up and change his diaper and give him his bottle.

Baby Robbie became an excellent sideshow diversion for everyone, including Dad. When Dad left for the VA hospital during spells, focusing on Robbie's antics became a way for me not to cry. Despite Dad's offenses, I always teared up when he left for the psychiatric stays, but I would hide it from him.

We marveled at Robbie's developmental stages, all of us taking part in his learning and growing and inadvertently nearly killing him. We called him "Circus Baby" because I would grab him when he was about two and put him on my feet as I lay on the ground with my legs stretched up into the air. There, he would extend his arms and legs and "fly." He was a breath of fresh air in our house. Yet, even a very amusing little boy could not lift Dad's morose state of mind for long, and once it built to the crisis phase, he would be back in the hospital.

Recently, when I thought of asking my siblings, I learned I was the only one who received corporal punishment. Other than brother Rick's battering boxing match with Dad, which turned out to be an isolated incident, I was the only child in the family who ever got hit numerous times.

Here is one of the times I got whacked: Remember that pretty, little curly blond-haired baby? She is now about six or seven in the story.

When we arrived home from church, I jumped out of the car and slammed the door shut, not realizing Kathleen was climbing out the same door. She got her finger caught in the door. That resulted in a belting from Dad; one Mom tried to stop. Other times, I just faced the music alone.

Dad whipped his belt out of the loops when we came home from skating at the pond near our house. My siblings skedaddled home when they heard the cowbell ring, which is how we were summoned when scattered hither and yon. I had to gather up sleds, hockey sticks, and pucks, so I was later than they were, trudging home in the heavy snow. Dad met me at the garage door. My attempts at an explanation were ignored. I was belted across my rump.

No one came to my defense that time.

Corporal punishment was not on my regular schedule. Some of my infractions resulted in a tongue-lashing from Dad. Other times, they might erupt in corporal punishment, especially if I defied Dad verbally. Emotional jujutsu was the air I breathed.

The Koreans have a name for being able to "read the room." It is *nunchi*. I practiced *nunchi*, but knowing the attack was coming did not necessarily mean I could avoid it. Often, pending trouble filled the air like thunderclouds and then rained down only on me. No escape route was available.

A time when I thought we would be seeing the face of Sweet Baby Jesus was when Dad began a tirade with such ferocity that I was not sure we could contain him. He paired the ranting about his gripe du jour with his legendary accusation thrust at my mom repeatedly: "If you had half a brain, you'd be dangerous," accompanied by physical jostling. Mom cried and shouted back.

All this happened that day in our home's narrow hallway, too small of a ring for fights, where all six of us were corralled. I was maybe twelve years old. The friction heating the thermostat-o'-craziness raised the temperature in the house. On this occasion, Mom chose a new strategy and brought divine reinforcements.

Mom shepherded all of us into the room where my two brothers slept and had us kneel in a circle with her in the shadow of the arsenal in the gun case. She armed herself with a Rosary, and, as if we were the children of Fatima, Portugal, to whom the Blessed Virgin appeared, she had us recite the Rosary prayers as we would with a priest: Mom offering the beginning of the Hail Marys and Our Fathers and us responding with the final portions of the prayers in chant. It was a blessed call-and-response General Eisenhower-level battlefront tactic.

I can still envision my father stalking and huffing in the hallway, like a furious lion in a cage whose blood-red steak had been maliciously devoured by his tiger neighbor. Dad's puffed-out-to-bursting capillaries gave off incensed gasses, furious that Mom would pull the Virgin Mary card that guarded us and prevented him from entering the room. It was like a panel from Marvel Comics with the villain foiled.

By the time Mom finished the last Hail Mary with the final line, "pray for us sinners / now / and at the hour of our death. Amen." That day of the incensed Leo the Lion King of Beasts, which **could have been** the hour of our death, Dad had cooled down and surrendered by fleeing to his sanctuary, the Keg Room. After these upheavals in our house, everyone would disperse and rejoin the everyday world as if nothing had happened.

In theater parlance, it would be *End of Scene.*

When Mom was dying at age eighty-nine, extremely incapacitated, and deliberately hanging on to life by a slim optic fiber filament, the palliative care people asked her why she was fighting so hard to stay alive. Mom said, "I can't leave these kids alone."

We were in our fifties.

Dad's anger would build like the green haze of hail on the horizon. His depression would descend like a hot, humid, cloudy summer and smother all of us. Then he would leave. We knew if Dad was gone for an extended time, he would be at a place Mom called the "VA." It stood for Veterans Administration and also, in our house, the "Vanishing Act." Poof! Dad was gone.

Once we were old enough to drive, we would be dispatched to the VA to pick up Dad. (Transporting him to the VA amid his mental crises required experienced adult supervision.) The VA institution was a Georgian Revival building in Chillicothe, Ohio, but it was a foreboding-looking monster of a fortress to my eyes. I did not like going there. It looked haunted by the past and the present.

In 1997, Ken Kesey, the author of *One Flew Over the Cuckoo's Nest,* and his wild band of Merry Pranksters came to Ohio with their new hippie bus, Further II, to deposit it at the Rock and Roll Hall of Fame in Cleveland. I was writing my humor column then and interviewed Kesey.

I told him that his character McMurphy, played by Jack Nicholson in the movie, reminded me so much of my dad during his psychiatric hospital times.

Kesey looked at me intently and asked, "Is that a good thing?"

I answered, "Oh yes, a very good thing. I saw my dad's strength and skills in Nicholson and the humor."

With Country Joe McDonald and the Fish singing the "Fixin' to Die Rag" in the background on Rock Hall Plaza during the bus's investiture ceremony, Cosmic Kesey said, "Well then, you'd better get up on top of the bus with the Pranksters and dance!"

Up the bus ladder, I climbed. I danced.

By age twelve, I had my exit strategy within our home and could go into hiding. At about this time in my life, I became aware of Anne Frank and her secret annex, where she would journal, dream, and ponder life. Far from her attic in Amsterdam, that place of exile for me was my bedroom, which I shared with my sister Kathy. I do not recall my dad *ever* entering our bedroom for any reason.

I received a desk for one birthday. Now, my command center materialized, and I could begin master plans for my real life to come. I reasoned that a desk is where a person can create a different reality. Other than occasional letters to my cousin, doing homework, or doodling and drawing something, it acted more as a vessel I commanded with the potential to steer me toward future writings. I knew stories; I did not know how to put them onto paper yet, but I wanted to create them.

I reasoned that an architect sits at a desk, and poof! A new building begins to exist. A novelist can travel anywhere she wants and write at her desk. A besotted girl of twelve can connect to her heartthrob Beatle Paul at her desk, and she did.

The day I received it, I was so thrilled I feigned some vague illness and asked to stay home from school. Mom let me. I sat at my desk, my ship of dreams, and I, her captain.

I learned of the aristocratic women's hideaway. Judy Corbett writes of the lady of the castle's "still room" in Gwydir Castle, and she conjures what would have been contained within it before the eighteenth century. As the mistress of the manor places her key in the lock and enters, according to Judy, she sees:

> Herbs hang in bunches from iron hooks in the ceiling and the walls are lined with shelves that hold tall, narrow-necked phials and alembics filled with scented elixirs and vermilion-coloured liquids . . . There the sun falls across the floorboard, large earthenware crocks contain a concoction of root of angelica and white wine vinegar. . . . It is a paradise for the senses, with that dark edge of mystery that you often find in a room exclusively used by a woman.

In my "still room" bedroom in the new second house where we moved when I was nine, with the levered roll-out windows that overlooked our steep driveway on one side and our neighbors, the Bolin's, house on the other, I had a record player, records that included my very first 45, *Let's Get Together* (Hayley Mills, from the movie *The Parent Trap*), the *Meet the Beatles* LP, a transistor radio in a brown leather case, pens and paper and books, my brushes and combs for my hairdo experiments (pitiful failures), one school uniform, my beloved blond wood desk, and, for holding my bouffant hairdo together, Aqua Net. I could remain there for years, which I mostly did. My room did not smell of orris root or myrrh, as Judy describes, as much as it did of Ambush perfume in a pink bottle by Dana. Heavy is the hand of a teenage girl and her cologne.

It was at this desk with a suspended shelf on the left side for storing essentials of paper, pencils, crayons, tape, a ruler, a metal compass for the sole purpose of drawing circles, the Anne Frank paperback book, and a magazine about the Beatles that I found I could teleport myself into a newly imagined future. I went to work.

Branches of the Family Tree

Another tactic I had long used was to look back on the family and see our history from the perspective of "best practices" and traits. Dad had talents. Mom remained burdened but steadfast. My siblings and relatives had great senses of humor and were storytellers all. A few were in show business. We were all loyal to each other in our ways.

These are the Mitchells, my paternal Grandma Aggie's family, c. 1929. My great-grandmother, Anna Timany Mitchell, is front and center. My dad is the boy on the bottom row far right . . . with the rifle.

I became convinced that we could take our DNA and genetics, pump up the good parts, and deflate the bad parts with learned behaviors by studying outside sources, like movies, biographies, song lyrics, TV shows, and famous people. I theorized we had control, not over the incidents themselves but how we framed them in our life stories via attitude and perspective adjustments. It all depends on how the story is told in our heads.

Cowboy Dad—1920s. With a pistol.

Chapter 6

Contrary to All Propriety

We have always found the Irish a bit odd. They refuse to be English.
—WINSTON CHURCHILL

CAST OF CHARACTERS

My dad—Richard Wynn

Dad's parents—Agnes and Robert Wynn, a.k.a. Grandma Aggie
and Grandpa Wynn

My dad's maternal grandparents—Anna Timany Mitchell and
Charlie Mitchell

Dad's maternal uncle—Freddie Mitchell

Dad's maternal cousin and actor (their mothers were sisters)
—Mitchell Ryan

Our Story Continues . . . Whence does Dad's belligerence and shoulder chip come? As I pore over the family history, I find clues, and the torrential tide is awash in potatoes.

The stubborn streak of my great-grandfather Charlie Mitchell, my dad's maternal grandfather, almost sacrificed the lives of his future descendants in America. The pig-headedness remains ingrained in our lineage. Ask anyone. It can either bolster determination to squelch adversity or, if employed injudiciously, cause a cloudburst of personal misfortune.

As I follow the present Facebook news about the repeated flooding of the Gwydir castle and its grounds, I am struck with the hellbent resolve of owners Judy and Peter not to allow the work, expense, frustration, and extensive damage to drown their dreams for their life's work prize. They dig in their heels, rally volunteers, set to work with sandbags, and act in sheer defiance of the natural disaster, with waters rising, sometimes up to their hips and beyond.

A few weeks later, we see a picture of a beautiful sunrise over the Welsh fairy tale scene on the Gwydir Facebook site. Disaster receded.

Gwydir Castle. "It's the loveliest of lovely Easter mornings here at Gwydir, and the fountains are throwing diamonds in the air," writes Judy Corbett.

That same resilience can be seen in the needy and lonely refugees packing up what they could carry and coming to America from Ireland because of the potato famine (1845–1852). A few of my great and great-great-grandparents, from both sides, came to America then so they wouldn't starve, thereby escaping the barbarity and its soul-crushing deluge of aftereffects.

Most blame the English for this atrocity. I will leave that to the historians, but I theorize that the resentment for this cruelty stows away internally to the next generations. Trauma is a traveling tramp in the boxcar of our body. Science proves it so.

When the Irish people were forced to eat nothing but grass, staining their lips green, while nutritious foodstuffs were being exported to England, genetic codes took roll call. The Welsh possess equal abilities to hold grudges for centuries regarding British rule, abilities barreling down our family line via my grandfather Wynn's family and my dad's dad, who are of Welsh stock.

I heard more elaborate versions of the well-known Mitchell (my paternal grandmother) obstinance from Cousin Mitch Ryan and how his grandfather, my great-grandfather, committed his obdurate childhood action to foul up his exit from Ireland to his emigrating family's horror.

The way Mitch told it, according to family lore, is that as a boy of about nine or ten, my great-grandfather, Charles Mitchell, and his family got on a ship in Ireland to come to America. Charlie Mitchell did not want to go to America, so he handed a prized possession of those times, his shoes, to his mother and, to the shock of his family and all on board, jumped overboard while the ship was still docked. They assumed he drowned and mourned his passing, as the story goes.

But no, headstrong unrepentant Charlie, Mitch Ryan recounts, walked nine miles in his bare feet to his uncle's home only to be put on the next ship, alone, to come to the USA. How they kept him on board is a mystery. So, too, is whether he ever got his good shoes back.

Young Charlie Mitchell was reunited with his astounded family, who had given him up as drowned. Then, underaged Charlie, enticed by the "brimming river" of combat (thank you, Tennyson), decided to join the Civil War. His angry father retrieved him from the Northern army. Charlie returned home, only to run away again and reenlist with his older brother. The army kept the rebellious Mitchell boys.

As a teen Union Army soldier, my great-grandpa Charlie Mitchell was in McLaughlin's Squadron Ohio Volunteer Cavalry. He fought in the Siege of Knoxville and the Siege of Atlanta. He was enlisted for three years. After the war, he returned to Georgetown, Ohio, and married my great-grandmother, Anna Timmany, whose parents came from Ireland. Charlie made bricks and farmed. He died many years later when his mule, who had a cantankerous history of his own and lived up to the gossip about mules being stubborn, kicked Charlie to death.

Guns and war play an on-going role in our family saga on this paternal side, and they feature in my civilian analyses of my dad's life. The shadow of WWII clouded baby boomers'—our generation's—days. I was a city girl, but Dad taught me to shoot and hunt. We Wynn kids respected guns and knew their potential harm, so we *never* played with the guns that were plentiful and frighteningly accessible to us by any era's standards. We only needed to go as far as my brothers' bedroom and open the unsecured gun case, the door fastened by a mere hook and eye.

We never did.

This was not the restraint exhibited by my paternal great-uncle Freddie Mitchell (Charlie and Anna's son), one of Grandma Aggie's brothers, on the Mitchell farm in Georgetown when he was a boy. One day, when he was fooling around with his gun, he accidentally shot his brother Leo dead in 1918. My father's middle name is Leo in his memory.

My dad's family were gun owners and hunters. Cousin Mitch told me the Charlie Mitchell tales, including one with Mitch in the starring role.

Young boy Mitch Ryan visited the Mitchell farm with his mother, my Grandma Aggie's sister, and my dad's aunt. All the men had been hunting that day and returned for dinner. Mitch was eight years old and went over to their guns and began playing with a rifle that fired, wounding his leg. It was a flesh wound, and he was ministered to and declared just fine. *Pass the potato salad.*

Mitch recounted that story to me about three weeks before his death. His incredulity at their casual handling of guns as though they were toys still had him chuckling drily at the absurdity of it all. In contrast, my dad offered repeated warnings and instructions regarding gun safety and security.

My great-grandparents Charlie and Anna Mitchell's eighth of nine children, my grandma Agnes, and her future husband, Grandpa Wynn, first met as teachers at the Boys Industrial School (BIS) in Lancaster, Ohio (a school for "wayward boys"). The boys received military training along with vocational studies. They were also used as forced farm labor. Grandpa Wynn was the "military commandant," and Grandma Aggie taught classes. She received teaching certification from Ohio University, Athens, Ohio.

The BIS was established in 1857 to house and educate male juvenile offenders. Grandpa did a nine-year stint in the army, then took a job at the BIS. The boys arrived at the school with several demerits commensurate with their crimes. Good behavior reduced the demerits, and they

Agnes Mitchell Wynn, my
paternal grandmother.

Boys Industrial School, Lancaster, Ohio.

were released when their ledger reached zero. Comedian and actor Bob Hope was one of these boys for a time and later donated large amounts of money to the institution. In 1980, the school became an adult prison.

I have the *billet-doux* my grandmother wrote to my grandfather at the BIS when they first became enamored with each other circa 1915. Grandma Aggie's face had all the Irish traits, from her thick black hair, apple cheeks, slightly wide and upturned nose, and full top lip, the same features often disparagingly illustrated in demeaning cartoons about the Irish. She was also leprechaun short and had a spirited spark of humor in her peppy personality.

Grandpa Wynn was tall, strong, and handsome. Unlike Aggie's Irish Catholic recently immigrant clan, Grandpa Wynn's family was Welsh protestant and had been in America since the 1700s. Grandpa often spoke of his "great, great . . ." fighting in the Revolutionary War with close military ties to George Washington. He repeatedly mentioned the term "aide-de-camp."

The note Grandma Aggie wrote to her new protestant boyfriend (which was *a thing* then) at their school is addressed on the envelope this way:

Mr. Wynn
Local

It reads as follows:

Sunday Night, March 26
I, too, shall adopt this means of communication to thank you for your very kind thoughts of me and shall be equally frank in telling you that the desire for further acquaintance is mutual. There it is—contrary to all propriety for me to have said that? Can't help it. I was always contrary—even went against the laws of nature and grew down instead of up. Do we swing the clubs Monday night? And incidentally—no I shan't say it but that old soldier I was telling you about 'Major Orion' is a wonderful chaperone and I am very truly yours,

Agnes Mitchell

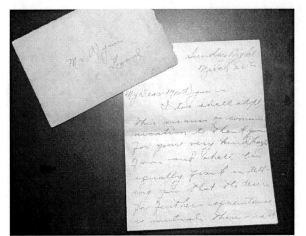

Billet-doux.

Indian Clubs.

The clubs are "Indian Clubs" used for exercise and, in Grandpa's estimation, chick bait. Grandpa Wynn was a talented aficionado of the clubs. *Major Orion* was code for the constellation under which they would court.

They married. Early on, they had to move home to the Mitchell farm where Grandma was born, probably for financial reasons. By 1909, Aggie's father, Charlie, had died.

When my grandparents moved to the Mitchell farm, my Grandpa Wynn's well-known temper was an issue (and remained so until his old age when he mellowed into a warm puppy with huge Lyndon B. Johnson ears). My great-grandmother, Anna Timany Mitchell, was not one to toy with on her Mitchell acres, as slender and delicate as she was, with her upswept, whitening, coifed hair. When my grandpa Wynn, her son-in-law, became mean and abusive to that cranky mule, great-grandma Anna came out with a pistol and threatened to kill my grandfather Wynn if he did not let up, according to Cousin Mitch. She made delicious pies, I am told, but apparently, everyone gave way to Anna Timany Mitchell.

Grandpa Wynn's family was Protestant and well-established before the influx of immigrants, so they were readily accepted in America. It was a different story for the Irish Catholics and the Mitchell clan.

Grandma and Grandpa Wynn, with Uncle Bob (who would later be on the USS West Virginia at Pearl Harbor) and Baby Dad, Richard Wynn, right. Two more sons to come.

Aggie was smitten despite Grandpa Wynn's religion and Welsh family tree, which must have irked Aggie's staunchly Irish Catholic parents. This prejudice about non-Catholics also came down the family line.

It was assumed I would marry a Catholic, which I did in 1973. A few years later, my brother married an Italian American Catholic woman. My mother had to get her head around having a mini-Sophia Loren in the family, which she accomplished after some handwringing. After the Irish migration, the Italians came to America. They were also met with unwarranted bias in my mother's generation.

My sister married a Protestant. He was, and still is, such a good man that everyone overlooked this religious "flaw." My other brother married a Catholic of German descent. My mother's mother was also of German ancestry, so the scales could balance. (We are talking about the 1970s and 1980s when ethnicity could break a relationship.)

I would beg Grandma Aggie to tell me the stories about her father coming from Ireland and the potato famine, but she was a "water over the dam" girl with eyes focused forward. However, she did possess a steel trap memory for injustices and slights.

The Irish prejudice was slowly being diluted in the 1940s and 1950s with the warbling of Bing Crosby as Father O'Malley, the quaint humor and pub singing/fisticuffs in the movie *The Quiet Man*, and the ultimate

Aggie (b. 1892) must have seen the newspaper cartoons
depicting the Irish in the 1900s as drunks, simian-like
with ape features, and raggedy lazy souls.

vindication: the charms and good looks of President John F. Kennedy.
Grace Kelly and Gene Kelly helped, too. I will throw in James Cagney.

Still, Grandma Aggie told me I should not claim Irish heritage:
"You are American," she would reprimand, "Do not tell people in job
interviews about being of Irish people."

The "Irish Need Not Apply" signage in shop windows she had witnessed and statements in newspaper classified ads from the past, she
assumed, would compromise my chances at a successful life decades
later. The floodwaters of hurt ran deep and wide. A line from James
Joyce's poem, *Flood*, comes to mind, "vast wings above the lambent
waters brood."

After centuries of British Rule and the potato famine, a particular
impermeable island of bitterness could be found in Irish souls, passing through generations like a cold raging stream. The famine here is
described in a History Channel publication: "Beneath the auld sod,
festering potatoes bled a putrid red-brown mucus as a virulent patho-
gen scorched Ireland's staple crop and rendered it inedible." †

The Irish people ate seven million tons of potatoes yearly until the

---

† History Channel program, March 16, 2017, program title: "When America Despised the
Irish: The 19th Century's Refugee Crisis."

famine. The starvation and poverty resulted in the deaths of a million people and the emigration of two million more. Ireland lost a quarter of its population. As the Irish poured into America, they were labeled as disease-ridden criminals, a burden on society, and job stealers. They were poor, unskilled, hungry, and, worst of all, according to the Anglo nation of states, Catholic.

Secret societies such as the Star-Spangled Banner group formed to bring "Protestantism" back to America and punish the "ignorant bogtrotters" who they maintained were loyal only to the Pope and a threatening scummy mold on society.

The Irish started at the bottom of the employment ladder, creating canals, digging ditches, laying rails or sewer pipes, and becoming maids for the rich. They assumed power in the US only when they began to organize politically, but they always remembered their past. Those struggles lived in their bones and ran in their veins: our family's veins. Our bones. Former US senator Daniel Patrick Moynihan once said, "To be Irish is to know that, in the end, the world will break your heart."

One specific Irish strength is part of our upbringing: "slog through the bog." Grandma Aggie certainly possessed that. In my dad, I saw similar courage, but it was more of a desire, a veneer that also seemed to disguise a debilitating sense of weakness within him. It was like two sides cohabitating in a lava lamp of bubbling and fluctuating liquid colors of courage, one overtaking the other in the undulating rhythms of the moon and tides. I frequently experience this, too, but I can work with it most of the time. Dad could not handle the crashing and colliding surges of anger and fear by the end of his life at the age of sixty.

Near where I grew up in Columbus and even nearer where Dad grew up with my grandpa Wynn and grandma Aggie, a historic flood occurred decades before I was born in 1951 and before Dad was born in 1920. It was called *The Great Flood of 1913*. Hundreds were killed, and thousands became homeless. It destroyed five hundred buildings in the working-class neighborhood.

This tragedy became an opera performed by Opera Columbus and the Pro Musica Orchestra in 2019. (Composed by Korine Fujiwara

The Franklinton area of the West Side of Columbus, Ohio, 1913.

with a libretto by Stephen Wadsworth.) The opera tells of the traumatic effects, not only to the people who experienced the flood but to subsequent generations, even when many years later, the descendants were not even conscious that the flood had occurred. The tragedy deposited into and floated indiscriminately within their psyches.

Trauma remains embedded in our bodily systems. Researchers say it can click on and off specific genes when triggered. Some learn to tame the deluge of gene ignitions. When faced with extraordinary circumstances, a particular history, personality make-up, emotional fault lines, and specific disposition, some cannot.

A careful review of Dad's time on earth that I did know about as I got older reveals exposure and susceptibility to trauma: He had a golden boy older brother and struggled to measure up to him, especially during WWII. Dad's dad, a cop and later chief of police was tough on all four boys, using corporal punishment freely. Dad was slightly built and had a young-looking face, necessitating a quick-trigger tough guy façade in his mind. Dad did not do well in school and always struggled with authority figures. Dad loved guns and looking "badass" while holding one.

Grandpa Robert E. Wynn

Chapter 7

King of the Clan

I THOUGHT Grandpa Robert Elmer Wynn, Dad's dad, had to be the strongest man in the world. He chopped and sledgehammered big things in his yard. He whacked tall brush with a scythe. He had a workbench in his garage that smelled of the oil he rubbed on the wood, and heavy tools hung efficiently on the walls. He plowed his garden with a push tiller. He had a big pile of sticks, grass, and leaves in the backyard and created a funeral pyre to rid himself of the detritus. He wore a workman's uniform of khaki shirt and trousers. No one could be stronger.

I knew this: Grandpa Wynn had run away from his boyhood home in Canton around fifteen and then held a job involving horses. (I recall seeing him astride a horse playing polo when I was little.) The story was that Grandpa's attorney-dad was an alcoholic and cruel to him, and after his mother died young, his stepmother was no fan of Grandpa's. So, Grandpa boot-scooted out of town.

After his stint at the Boys Industrial School, Grandpa Wynn began his career as a cop walking the beat, where he saved a young girl's life. She was stabbed in the neck and left for dead on the sidewalk. Grandpa had finished his duty that day but felt the urge to return to his beat, and there she was. He held the wound closed on the way to the hospital and was proclaimed a hero, not for the first time.

Grandpa Wynn became a cop in the 1920s, in the days of gangsters like Al Capone. He must have been a good one because he was made a lieutenant and then Captain of the Vice Squad. He ended up as Chief of Police.He relentlessly pursued and busted syndicates and mobsters for vice. He employed a red ax to destroy gambling machines.

Grandpa's club-swinging exercise regimen was the subject of a newspaper cartoon by famed cartoonist and watercolorist Leland E. McClelland. We once saw him perform with his clubs at an outdoor

Grandpa Wynn, on the left rear, during the city's first marijuana bust.

Wielding his ax to destroy gambling machines.

A MASTER OF THE INDIAN CLUBS IN HIS SPARE TIME IS POLICE LIEUTENANT ROBERT WYNN.

LSM.

Cartoon of Grandpa Wynn by Leland S. McClelland, whose work can be found in the Billy Ireland Collection at The Ohio State University.

arena. He opened with an elaborate removal and folding of his shirt. I was about eleven years old and thought this part of the act deserved a sarcastic eye-roll.

Grandpa was a strong swimmer. When he retired after twenty-two years on the police force (1922–1944), he moved from Columbus to Millersport, Ohio, out in the country where corn fields lined the roads like an Ohio honor guard. There, his oasis was Buckeye Lake. Summers had him heading to the lake for his floating time, a restorative antidote after years of people's nasty, carnal habits. The lake was just minutes away from his home.

We Wynn kids heard the tragic story, breathless and riveted, of what happened to Grandpa one floating day in 1947 at Buckeye Lake. Grandpa would tell it in a cadence rivaling a fireside opening for a thrilling PBS episode of Masterpiece Theater. It was a story of horror, gore, and mob retaliation. Who wouldn't be fascinated? After hearing it 16,000 times, it lost a little of its power. Still, there were usually refreshments.

Here is the true story.

Grandpa was taking his float when the motorboat with his mobster enemies' henchmen (as he always titled them) zoomed up to him and ran over him. The boat's outboard motor shredded his leg. He was

Attempted murder.

bleeding profusely. The attempted murderers sped off and left him for dead. Two men in the distance fishing from their boat heard him yelling. A newspaper article about the "Hit-Skip Speedboat" attack said Grandpa's "right leg was shattered, and he was reported in fair condition . . . [and] surgeons were fighting to save his injured leg."

The surgeons saved the leg, but it had a steel rod the entire length, which kept it stiff and permanently extended. He could balance about four grandkids on it and did.

A crime family involved in an assortment of vice had hired the hit men to run over Grandpa in the lake. The men in the boat that attacked him were identified, and the family who contracted the attack settled a monetary amount of $5,000 with my grandfather to not prosecute them. I have the legal contract agreement. That family eventually went legit in business.

Bob and Rich as children and then in the service.
Dad is on the right in both pictures.

Grandpa saw the world unquestionably divided between good and evil and had a particularly zealous fanboy admiration for Joseph McCarthy's fight against "communism." He frequently spoke to us of McCarthy's "list of communists" in the 1950s and 1960s despite demagogue McCarthy's lies being debunked.

When Grandpa's sons served in WWII, their enlistment doings made the papers, too. Uncle Bob was the oldest of the four Wynn boys. Dad's downfall begins in the shadow of Bob's rise to glory as a war hero.

Grandpa was still recovering from the attempted murder-by-boat when my parents married in August of 1947. Maybe there was a lull in my dad's mental illness during their courtship for my mom to willingly leap into that bubbling emotional cauldron in a white satin wedding gown. A lot appeared to be riding on the efficacy and drenching of the wedding Mass holy water.

Everyone looks happy in the family picture outside of Holy Rosary

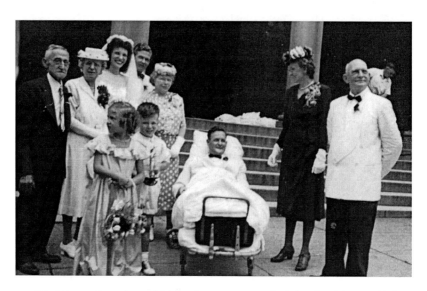

My parents, Dorothy and Richard Wynn, are on the left side of the rear. Grandpa Wynn is on the stretcher. The couple on the left are my mother's grandparents. Aggie is in front of Dad in the rear. My mom's parents are to the left of Grandpa Wynn, HRH.

Church, posed on the steps as if the future were bright and cheery, filled with apple blossoms, woodland fairies, and lilacs. Despite the mounting evidence, it is just in the human spirit to hope for the best.

Grandpa Wynn is in the photo, his post-op leg from the motorboat ambush evident, and he is still recovering. His star power shines through, taking center stage, sporting a white tuxedo while supine on a stretcher. He is the focus of attention, with the bride and groom barely visible on the left. Grandpa Wynn remained King of the Clan until his death at age ninety-three.

When I was born in 1951 (the first of my parents' four children), fathers were stationed in the waiting room, smoking and pacing until the baby's arrival. My dad and Grandpa Wynn were together in the waiting room the night of my birth, November 7, 1951. I have heard the story.

The nurse came to the waiting room and announced, "Mr. Wynn, you can go up now."

My grandpa Wynn then stood, followed the nurse, and went up as the first, the primary Mr. Wynn to, as he said, "inspect the baby." Grandpa declared me "the prettiest baby he had ever seen." Then, he allowed his successor, my dad, to meet his first child. I was told that Dad was confident I would be a boy named Michael Patrick Wynn. Mom said it took him some time that day to accept a firstborn baby girl named Patricia Ann.

Grandpa Wynn was stern and direct with his grandchildren, but he never laid a hand on us. I learned later that this was far from the case with his four sons. Corporal punishment came frequently and swiftly when Grandpa's orders were not followed at home.

Uncle Bob and Dad shared one thing: both men felt resentment toward their father, and we kiddies could sense it. Our family lived about an hour away and visited Grandma and Grandpa Wynn frequently despite the tension in the room. Uncle Bob, who married and remained childless, only returned to Ohio from his home in San Diego once after the war. We little nieces and nephews could not get enough of this handsome, funny, and charming man on that visit.

Grandpa cast a shadow as big as the Hindenburg over the family, which seemed to have shaded his sons. We kids navigated the aphotic chasm of feelings between Grandpa and his sons on that monumental day of Uncle Bob's triumphant return, like highly trained Navy SEALs, avoiding possible booby traps and angry seas. Ours was not to make waves but to act as court jesters, distracting all from family tensions.

L-R Brother Rick, Me, Cousin Janice, Uncle Bob Wynn, and Cousin Bonnie.

Easter. My grandparents and me. Grandma's homemade dresses always resembled this style, with the little bolero jacket in a variety of prints.

Grandpa's interactions with the grandkids were more regimental; we were "in his charge." We followed orders. We did not converse with Grandpa as much as we received instructions here or there regarding what was happening next on our visit.

I don't think he knew much about our lives in Columbus, our schooling, or our interests. I had more respect for him than a feeling of love, but only because he didn't seem to offer love—if he had those feelings, he shut them away. He did not need to reprimand us; none of us would dare disobey him. This was an established protocol, and we knew our roles as well as we knew the sun would rise in the morning.

Though retired, my other impression of Grandpa was that he was wildly popular and respected by all the police officers at police picnics, which we attended with him. So many people addressed him with salutes and hellos that I half-expected someone in the crowd around his procession, which emanated an aura of admiration, to bow to him.

Robert E. Wynn was not a playful grandpa as much as dutiful; he built a wooden teeter-totter and a sandbox in their backyard for us. In the summer, we would accompany him to the sound of cooing mourning doves and bees buzzing into his luscious garden to pick and shuck the corn, pluck some juicy red tomatoes off the oil-scented vines, and tote a big round Irish baby head-sized cabbage back to Grandma in the kitchen for her coleslaw.

Aggie said cutting parts of the core and eating them for vitamins after grating the cabbage was healthy. I do this to this day and think of her.

We were not accustomed to Grandma and Grandpa Wynn's deliberate and austere ways at home; theirs was reminiscent of the 1850s rather than the 1950s and their time as staff at the Boys Industrial School. Grandma and Grandpa regarded our usual monkeyshine hijinks as discipline problems, household crimes of vice, which would not wash in their house.

Grandpa spared us the red ax he used to bust the gambling machines. Still, he never shied from letting us know he witnessed executions at the Ohio Penitentiary (which once housed writer O. Henry) and that the electric chair's name was "Old Sparky," known for its inefficiency in its task. That got our attention.

Yet, we were wily and lively children with short memory spans, so my little sister and I got away with the ransack of Grandma's clothes from her closet (where she kept a small homemade still to make her sugary sweet wine from the grapes in her arbor). After examining all the items on top of her dresser, including a small delicate china dish with

a matching cover and a hole where she stuffed hair from her brush, we rifled through her drawers.

This photo, shot through their living room window, identified us as the brazen perpetrators. Exhibit A, Your Honor, shows the ringleader (me) boldly sticking it to the man, sporting Grandma's girdle, garters, and hose.

Grandma was tiny compared to big, strong Grandpa, but she seemed to hold her own with him. She had a touch of that Mitchell headstrong attitude about her, and when Grandpa said something she

Shenanigans ensued. My sister, Kathleen Agnes (left).

did not like, she would fold her arms under her bosom, look at him, and utter his name, "Bob!" Worked every time.

I believe Grandma was the only person on earth Grandpa would heed.

Grandpa watched baseball on TV. He played cribbage by himself. I never saw Grandpa read a book. No one snacked between meals in their house. It was an honor to ring the three little rope-connected bells hanging outside the kitchen in the cottage hallway to announce supper was ready. "Bless us, oh Lord, and these thy gifts . . ." we'd intone together with heads bowed around the table.

Grandma and Grandpa Wynn would take us kids to Buckeye Lake, the scene of the mobster hit, in the afternoons after a peanut butter and marshmallow sandwich lunch. The water in the lake was dark, and the mud bottom would squish between our toes. The motorboats on the lake cast gentle waves our way that rushed at our legs and elicited screams of laughter. We could not swim yet, so we splashed, made sandcastles, and ran from shore into the water, kicking sprays onto each other.

At Buckeye Lake, we were carefully supervised by Grandma Aggie. Grandpa would leave us behind on the brown sand shore of Fairfield Beach, swim far out into the lake, turn over onto his back, and crest the water like a one-man armada inching along the horizon the entire time of our beach visit. I guess he just spat in peril's eye, returning to the scene of his near death. Since he was not afraid of another attack, we weren't either.

We knew it was time to return to the cottage when we saw Grandpa swimming up to shore, emerging from the lake, walking against the weight of the water in long steps like Neptune rising from the sea. We would all dry off and head to the car. Grandpa would look refreshed and happy.

As I write this memoir, I am connecting with other Wynns. A fellow choir member said I resembled her Wynn friend in Canton, Ohio. We discovered Pam Wynn's great-grandfather and my great-grandfather were brothers. Pam's family even had some of the same newspaper clippings about Grandpa Wynn.

Imagine my surprise when I encountered Becky Thill, a Wynne of the Wynne Society, during my research for this memoir (spelling of names in Wales is not an exact art form). She did a little preliminary research as I sought clues connecting me to my rightful Gwydir throne, the Welsh ancestral home of the Wynns, dating back to the Middle Ages.

Becky did some internet digging and, in a shocking turn of events, informed me with documentation, not about Gwydir, but that my grandpa Wynn had been an army deserter. He was dishonorably discharged in 1913. He went AWOL, it seems. He was apprehended in Mansfield, Ohio, and returned to military control, tried, and found guilty. I was incredulous and, simultaneously, curious about the lack of vetting for his subsequent jobs, a much different story in these times. This story was also never told. I even wonder if Grandpa's children knew of this.

My grandpa was a convert to Catholicism since my grandma Aggie and her family, the Mitchells, were staunch Irish Catholics. Grandpa was baptized the same day as my newborn dad in 1920 and remained devout his whole life.

Grandpa Wynn died three days after my dad passed in 1980. My dad was living with his parents in the Millersport cottage then. The family story of the entanglements and tragedy of that week makes the angels weep. There was no hiding what happened that awful day. The family became another news story.

PART III

How to Grow Up by Really Trying

A happy childhood is the worst possible preparation for life.

—KINKY FRIEDMAN, American singer

Children surviving childhood is my obsessive theme and my life's concern.

—MAURICE SENDAK

When I look back on my childhood, I wonder how I survived at all. It was, of course, a miserable childhood: the happy childhood is hardly worth your while. Worse than the ordinary miserable childhood is the miserable Irish childhood, and worse yet is the miserable Irish Catholic childhood.

—FRANK MCCOURT, in *Angela's Ashes*

The author aged one. Happy hands in the icing.

Chapter 8

Say Kids, What Time Is It?

Life goes on if you are one of the lucky ones.
—JUDY BLUME

TV BECAME a primary stabilizer early in my life, and I not only gazed at it, I studied it. The shows I watched fascinated me not just for the escapist entertainment, which nourished me like a Fred Flintstone multivitamin. They satisfied my microscopic mental queries into how shows were made and what the talented people did to jolly us up. It intrigued me how they learned such things as singing, dancing, and acting.

Were they knighted explicitly by the powers that be?

It may seem odd for a little child to be interested in production and talent casting, but I watched TV like I was in my tower, wrapped in ermine-edged ceremonial robes, poring over sacred scrolls. When I was one with the TV, any disruption in our home was a battle in a war well beneath my royal notice.

My presentation to the Court of Television came at a surprisingly young age. My mom must have sent the request to the local TV station, and I can imagine my begging her to do so. During my R and R free time from sentry duty at home when I was five or six, I was thrilled to be one of the two chosen birthday guests, a regular feature, on a popular local 1950s kid TV show in Columbus. It was not my ultimate wish list shooting star TV show debut, being a featured player on the Mickey Mouse Club, but it would do for starters.

To "begin my show business career" on our local show, my mom bought me a lovely new dress with a crinoline underlay to spread it out like a dainty Japanese umbrella. As was her custom for any critical event, the day before the show, she had me choking on the fumes of a Toni Home Permanent to turn my blunt hair into wild Medusa-like mini snakes.

My dad drove me to the TV station. We arrived a little early, so we waited on a bench outside. We were relaxing before the big show on a summer day so bright that it seemed to light my path to the constellations.

Is this how Annette Funicello started?

To pass the time while waiting in various places, Dad would have me name the purpose of each key on his populated key ring. The keys were many. The purpose of the exercise was to silence my chatter.

It was here, in our alfresco green room, that the tables were suddenly turned on my dad. Shifting winds. New storm saga twist. Switched leading role. New script pages.

As the time was nigh to go inside, the host of the kiddie show (I will call him Sam) came up the walkway from the parking lot to the studio, escorted . . . nay, carried and dragged, by a couple of men in suits. Sam was blubbering something incomprehensible, and the men patiently tried to talk sense into him. This yin-yang interaction of wild-one-to-calm-one was familiar, with Dad commonly in the loose cannon role.

Then and there, Dad was overthrown from my world's Emperor of Creating Big Noise and Commotion position. Kid show host Sam now held the crown. In these situations, and those of much more severe consequences, my dad would "presto change-o" into his alter persona: Sir Galahad, to the rescue, just like Superman into the phone booth. Later, I realized that it had always seemed like he cherished these moments and spent his time pacing, waiting to be called to action.

I could feel their roles repositioning like a ship changing course. Dad was now emerging as my protector in the face of a TV personality gone blotto. Blasts of caution blared in my head. *What would Dad do? What would Sam do? How do I handle this? Can't we ever let me live a dream?*

I asked my dad what was wrong with the show host while the men in suits, who seemed part of the TV team, manhandled Sam into the station, with Dad and me following as instructed.

My dad told me Sam was sick. As I continued to scan the host's shocking behavior, even I could see he was drunk. The men in suits gave Sam some coffee and a pep talk. Years later, we learned they had harvested him from some beer joint to get him to the studio in time for the live afternoon show.

The first birthday party I attended, about 1954. I was a keen observer and always felt like an outsider looking in on the lives around me. I took mental notes.

We entered the studio, and the headset-wearing assistant promptly put an oversized gray sweatshirt on me. It featured the show name and covered up my brand-new dress, crinoline and all. A little boy was my co-guest. We were both the show's "birthday children." The assistant also put a sweatshirt on him, a meek child, in my opinion.

For this boy-child character joining my première, think of the role of "Dill" in the movie *To Kill a Mockingbird* only without the verbosity. My slight six-year-old costar faded like a flower tucking into itself at bedtime. He did what he was told without responses and seemed to settle into the background like an extra.

Unlike Dad, whom I could see through the whole show in the shadows beyond the studio's own Northern Lights, the boy's parents dutifully allowed themselves to be swallowed into the room's darkness. The space was filled with big metal hooded lights in the ceiling, bulging black cords on the floor that looked like garden hoses, a massive camera on wheels with a man peering into the binocular-looking part in the back of it, and a couple of helper men with clipboards. None of these things were part of my TV viewing at home. I was not privy to the sorcery until now, and the imprint was indelible—I had the keys to the castle.

Helpful hint! You know that scene in *The Wild Ones* starring Marlon Brando where the woman asks, "Johnny, what are you rebelling against?"

And Johnny answers: "Whadda ya got?"

That one scene clarified my dad's attitude in so many situations. Like this one: My dad, who defied any authority or others' rules, sometimes just for the hell of it, objected vocally about the oversized sweatshirt on me and wanted my unobstructed pretty dress to be on camera. He and the assistant had words, and I thought: *What if Dad and Sam BOTH go nuts?*

Dad had been a part-time photographer of wedding shoots before he went on disability, and he had an artistic eye and an artful hand for drawing. He always staged the photos he took of me. He did not like the optics of this TV ensemble on me that day.

Dad's sartorially influenced command directed at the crew member caused my emotional litmus paper to fire red hot colors into my psyche

One of Dad's set-up shots shows my most beloved teen queen babysitter, Carol, and me as we "plant a tree." I am in my onesie PJs in the dirt.

strategic map, as I could feel the acidity of conflict rise. Up welled the *nunchi*. Then, Sam stepped into the fray.

Would Dad and Sam joust? Dad was always expecting injustice and punitive measures from those in charge. He played defense as offense. He would not abide by custom or protocol if he deemed them antithetical to his sketchy game plan and skewed worldview.

Dad lost the sweatshirt battle; he had met his match with booze-soaked Sam, the "TV star" who put the ultimate kibosh on any costume adaptations. There could not be two kings in this tale.

However, Sam and his delicate condition would not be given a break with his regalia dictum. Sam should have been warned: *you have seen my father as a foe; now watch little me, his well-trained mouthy apprentice. She is on a sacred campaign to figure out how to run this Show Business business. She has questions and is demanding answers.* At this age, I already possessed verve and nerve.

As the show started, there we were on the set, the birthday boy and girl on the very show I watched on my home TV. Sam, now standing upright on his own, held a long microphone with a cord, and he talked directly to the man at the other end of the big black camera. Sam was sweaty and corpulent. He looked overheated, and I got the feeling he did not want to be there, and he might need to throw up into a bucket. That would have to wait.

I needed to address a few issues as soon as the live show started. From the top of the half-hour to the closing moments, I relayed these directly to Sam, to Sam's on-air annoyance. I was explicitly vocal about those issues relating to the differences between what was happening during the broadcast there at the studio and what I had observed on the screen at home. I needed to understand them if I were ever to become a Mouseketeer.

For instance, when we entered the TV kid show "elevator" to go down into the "mine shaft," a somewhat bizarre setting for a kid's show, the elevator did not move like on TV! We went into a big box with 2x4s on the insides, looking like an unfinished house closet, and closed the door. In post-war America, many homes were being built in my neighborhood, and I would explore their progress. Someone needed to complete this TV elevator.

We stood stock still as the familiar music played *doo doo doo doo . . . doo doo doo doo*, but we were not going anywhere, let alone down into a mine. Sam signaled me with a finger to his lips to be quiet. The camera with the man behind it could not see us inside the closet.

This did not compute: There were supposed to be shapes that appeared on the TV at home to show the *movement* of the elevator. The shapes that I saw on TV looked like carrots to me. They were MIA on my show day.

"Where are those carrots that fall when the elevator goes down?" I asked Sam.

He ignored me, and we exited the closet into another part of the studio with different items. These set pieces were familiar to me. As soon as we approached the trough, I knew the next recurring activity. This was when we would say hello to the unlucky general audience children merely watching the show at home, their little faces displayed in the photos their moms sent to the station, hoping to be in my place.

As for these "magically transforming pictures," there was a water trough, like the one where a miner would pan for gold on the cowboy *Roy Rogers* TV show. What I saw at home: blank rectangular pieces of paper floated in the basin, and Sam would speak some proclamation words, and the next thing you knew, after a commercial, the kids watching would see their very own photographs appear!

In the studio, that fantasy bubble burst when the man with headphones came up and, with no magic employed and without so much as an incantation, replaced the blank papers with actual pictures of children, using only his hands. *What in the hell?*

I could see my dad in the background of all the equipment, and I knew he never watched this show with me, so I could not plead my case with him. He had to have seen Sam and his short fuse with me in almost every scene, but with this being live television, even an anger devotee like Dad would not pop on camera, *would he?* I had to put that horrid thought out of my mind and stay focused. We had only had a TV in our house for a few short years, and its extraordinary powers had even the adults in awe. Its stars were to be admired and gazed at. They were special people, even when drunk. Dad stood down.

Sam innocently asked me if my mother were watching at home,

probably hoping to redirect my Sherlock Holmes-style queries and knowing she was not with us.

"No, she's at the beauty shop," I answered, which was true.

This made Sam's sizeable round head jerk, much like the cartoon character Yosemite Sam experiencing a revelatory shock regarding the shenanigans Bugs Bunny would thrust upon him. TV Sam could not know that *nothing* got in the way of Mom's pretty parlor appointment. I could see evidence building up that Sam might turn into hothead Ralph Kramden, Jackie Gleason's mercurial role on the TV show *The Honeymooners*. But no, his big shoulders slumped. Sam was temporarily defeated and had to take a beat of time to recover.

Following my beauty shop comment, Sam's patience ran out. His hangover must have blossomed like an atom bomb mushroom cloud in his brain, not helped by my dad off camera watching him like a hawk (and news to Sam, my dad probably battled within his mind whether to ambush the goings on). By the time sobering Sam got to the end of the show and the awarding of the birthday gifts to me and my non-curious, and thus favored, fellow guest, the pin had been pulled from Sam's patience grenade. The moments ticked off.

My six-year-old co-star was clearly from a TV-perfect family, *The Adventures of Ozzie and Harriet*-type home, and by demonic chance, this pallid angel-child had been teamed with me, a decorated veteran of domestic warfare, hellbent on uncovering the secrets of the business called show. The boy received a football, which he quietly delighted in and thanked Sam for with the most admirable manners, in as few words as possible. They were, in fact, the only words he uttered during the show: "Thank you."

My prize was next. *Oh! What could it be? Did Sam wish it were a kick in the crinoline?* Sam pulls out from behind him a pink metal doll case, about two feet tall, with hinges, clasps, and a leather handle.

What? A doll case? For a girl who plays "war" and Cowboys and Indians (I preferred being an Indian so I could shoot a bow and arrow) with all the boys in the neighborhood, one who does not need such fluffery? I spoke up to the fading and quivering TV host, emitting his liquid lunch from his forehead. I recognized the unmistakable smell of pine trees at Christmas and Dad after a gin infusion.

I firmly yet politely said, "I would like a football, too. I don't play with dolls." (And didn't until Barbie came onto the scene later.)

That was the breaking point. Sam, with white hair and pale countenance, turned as red and flaming as a fire engine racing to a tragic scene with babies being tossed from windows. He said something like, "Just take it!" And he signed off the show and herded me back to my dad in a huff. *Was there a little shove?*

Sam's show was my first TV performance, and I have had many more since beginning my one-woman humorous memoir shows in the late 1990s. That maiden showbiz voyage was a rough one, but it taught me a lot.

I saw how television worked and that the people on a show were not *inside* the TV, which was my initial theory. Also, in person, they were different from the people we saw on the screens. The duality of watching it at home and what happens at the TV station offered me a big *aha!* It illuminated that show business is not what it appears behind the scenes, just like life.

Perhaps some DNA from the Gwydir Wynn kings, princes, and royal ladies activated early on in my veins, bestowing upon me the eminence grise to dare. Author Judy Corbett describes her Welshman neighbor as: "He has grown out of this landscape like a tree that turns its back against the wind and grows in spite of itself."

I was growing my spirit despite some genuine fears and anxieties. Two faces had I, one of adventure and one of self-doubt. So, I came to make room in my life-saving quiver of protection and stability, the powerful new arrow of my Faith, even though I sometimes misconstrued that, too.

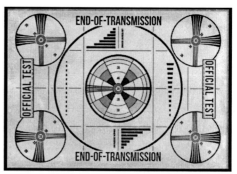

In the past, TV programming ended for the day at a particular hour around midnight. The test pattern stayed on TV all night until the morning shows.

Chapter 9

Catholic School: Women in Black

LEARNING TO present myself properly on the stage of life came from a source some abhor, but I salute. These influencers regarded deportment, proper grammar, posture, manners, values, and an emphasis on serving society through leadership as lessons as crucial as any academic subject. They all formed the *Sister Act* of the convent school that I attended.

Despite a few run-ins with the Good Sisters when I was older, they were the ones who helped me pull the sword from the stone so that I could quest across the land with decorum and at least the façade of confidence as I explored new worlds.

Mom and Dad attended Catholic school. Mom spoke very little about her education or the teaching nuns. I think she did not feel she excelled at school.

Dad always had his truculent side, so he collided with the nuns in school, I gathered from his comments, except for one, his favorite, Sister Francesca. She had his number and knew how to reach him.

When they closed St. Aloysius in the 1970s, Dad went there to scavenge souvenirs from his old school. He took four coat hooks from the "cloakroom." Post-heist, on one of his subsequent hospitalizations at the VA, Dad brought along those hooks and had a fellow patient paint pictures of the four Wynn kids with our nicknames. It is on the wall next to my front door. So, perhaps the school meant more to him than his stories conveyed.

St. Aloysius School and his teaching nun, Sister Francesca, had to have held a special bond for him. Was this nun the only adult in his life to understand his true nature and needs? Was she the one who fostered his unique singing talents as a child? Was she even-handed, using no hands for discipline, unlike his father?

I was five years old when I saw my first teaching nun. I had to take

Trishy (me), Ricky, Buggie (Kathleen), and Robby,
all in Irish children's clothes, with shamrocks.

a school entrance exam with her. I thought she was a man in a veil. Maybe it was her makeup-free face with no hair showing. It was very confusing. Having come from Miss Violet's kindergarten class in public school, this heavily draped, dour figure as a teacher took me by surprise.

Miss Violet wore brightly floral day dresses, with bare underarms swaying like a bag of frisky kittens. Standing before me was the opposite: this human figure covered in severe black and white flowing veils. She sported a vast Rosary for a belt better suited to a state fair sideshow giant.

Mom said she was my teacher. I smelled trouble.

Where Miss Violet had smiled and thought my Show-n-Tell performances were just about as spectacular as a runaway hit Broadway musical, this nun held a somber and disapproving visage the entire time I was there in the classroom alone with her and my mother. It felt more like a dental appointment than a school.

Catholic school charges tuition, which was a hardship for our home finances. I don't know if the fees were fully met because I know sometimes Mom would pay what she could, as she could, for some bills. All financial obligations and challenges were Mom's to cope with. Dad always appeared unconcerned.

Mom must have needed to reduce her kid manifest at home, so I started kindergarten at four. Maybe because I was only five years old going into first grade, I needed to do the entrance interview with the nun named Sister Angela. I remember her telling me I would need to stop investigating the classroom, sit properly, and answer her questions. I learned in that one session that nuns mean business, and you cannot pull the veil over their eyes like you could a bedraggled and overburdened mom. Still, they must have thought there was hope for me because they let me in.

The school year began. I liked school but was timid. We raised our hands to be called upon. We sat with two feet on the floor and hands folded on our desks. We stood to answer Sister. We were not to say "yeah" or "nah." If we responded to Sister with a "yes" or "no," we would need to say, "Yes, Sister," or "No, Sister." The unwitting child who would say, "Hey, Sister," would be met with, "Hay is for horses, not Sisters." I thought that was clever.

We sat and stood straight. We opened doors for each other. We were to be quiet. If Sister pulled a straight pin from her habit, dropped it onto the linoleum floor, and couldn't hear it *ping*, indoor recess punishment would ensue. If a visitor, like a priest, came into the room, we would rise *en masse* and greet him with a sing-songy, "Goooood Mooorrrning, Faaaaatherrrr." He would answer, "Good Morning, Children."

All this regimentation did not thwart me. It made me feel happy, stable, and secure. The rules were clear, and the atmosphere was like a movie storyboard—it allowed me to anticipate and prepare. It was the opposite of home life. I knew my lines and stood in lines as "forward march" as any military battalion. When we entered the church for Mass, Sister had a "clicker." One click = genuflect. Two clicks = rise. I welcomed the static structure.

In my young mind, discipline equaled focus and accomplishment. Discipline is what winners like athletes, actors, and Annette Funicello, who had to practice all of that singing and dancing to be the star she was, have.

One young James-Garner-looking priest was a favorite of ours. The flippant label for these handsome priests was *Father-What-A-Waste*. One day, Father brought in a record and a record player, which in the mid-1950s was a positively shocking thing for a priest to do! *A priest having records like ordinary people?!* It was as if a zebra had entered our room to dance the Andalusian folk dance, Fandango. And the song was not in Latin, like our Mass songs. It was a modern song!

This was second grade. Sister St. James must have had a private chat with Father and told him about some kids being utterly cruel to an extremely low-income student in our class, Sandra. I realized what was being thrust upon Sandra using my well-honed room-reading skills. I did not know how to help her stand up to the bullies at age six.

Sandra always looked sad, tired, and unkempt. Sandra's skin appeared grey as if she needed outdoor recess sunlight, and her eyes had dark circles under them. She smelled like a child who slept with younger siblings who were not toilet trained.

We all wore uniforms, but some of our togs were bright and crisp as a June morning, while a few others were disheveled, wrinkled, and like grey melted snow in March. I was somewhere in the middle of this sartorial spectrum. Sandra's look was at the bottom of the laundry pile.

Sandra was absent the day Father came into our classroom, becoming Dick Clark with his own American Bandstand 45.† He set up his record player and told us to listen to this song.

It was "The Little Blue Man." This strange song is about a woman being stalked by a little blue man whom she repeatedly rejects until she pushes him off a roof. He stops saying, "I wuv you to bits," and finally gives up and says, "I don't wuv you anymore."

The good Father's musical prop.

To this day, I marvel at how Father obtusely intended to help Sandra with this weird song. But it did. He discussed hurting others, and we comprehended the rejection part of the cryptic song. I do not remember how Father handily sidestepped the rooftop death of the Little Blue Man.

Along the way, various children met with verbal and physical projectiles of ridicule, and it always angered me. Bullies deserve a fair parry in my book. Later, I would talk back to bullies and put them in their place to defend others or myself, and I still do. As recently as yesterday, a "mean girl" adult woman was actively trying to body-language bully

† A record disc with a big hole in the middle.

me in a ballet class. My piqué arabesque in our center combination came precariously close to her personal space.

That same second-grade teacher, Sister St. James, came to my defense when I became the bully target, not by other kids, but by the cafeteria monitor nun with her Eat-Everything-On-Your-Plate-Because-of-The-Starving-Children-In-Korea philosophy.

The nun on guard duty, well, lunchroom duty, noticed I had not eaten my lima beans. I was mere seconds from nasty food freedom, but I had not been quick enough to stuff the vile legumes into my milk carton like the other kids had.

The bell rang, and the students lined up to return to their classrooms. The guard sister made me stay behind. It was a stand-off. We were not to defy the nuns or even look them straight in the eye with a scintilla of rebellion. I tried to explain my documented nauseous history with lima beans. I told her I would not eat them. She said I would. I had never gone head-to-veil with a nun.

Unbeknownst to Sister Power Hungry, a child who has firmly established sanity-preserving boundaries in her own home is a match for lima beans, whether fresh or past their prime. I pulled out that stubborn as Grandpa Mitchell's mule behavior card . . . with a nun! Sister Cold Beans, eventually defeated, released me, and I returned to Sister St. James' classroom.

That's when the miracle occurred, and two new lessons were learned. The first was to hold my ground against forced feeding. And then came the second.

Sister St. James asked, "Patricia, where have you been?"

I said, "Sister Michael made me stay to eat the lima beans, but I cannot eat lima beans, so I didn't. I throw up when I eat them. You can call my Grandma *Caddy-aw* and ask her." (A lima bean vomiting event occurred after the birth of little sister Kathleen and Grandma Cavanaugh's stay with us. We Wynn kids could not pronounce Cavanaugh. It came out as Caddy-aw.)

Sister St. James took in this information, fumed a moment, and looked pissed off, *but not at me.*

She exhaled and said sternly, "I will have a word with Sister."

With this, the heavens parted, and I heard heralding trumpets; *aha!*

Sometimes, authority figures differ! Even at this young age, I tapped into the palace convent intrigue: Sister St. James *did not like* Sister Michael. Also, I wondered why they both had boys' names.

In another notable incident, we were warned not to play with the clay sculptures we had created that, in my imagination, preened enticingly, singing their seductive siren song to me on the windowsill right next to my desk row.

I could not resist the clay allure and played with one of the pieces. Tom M. raised his hand and tattled on me (I also know, Tom M., that you stole my cherished key chain with an attached locket containing fold-out tiny pictures of the Seven Wonders of the World from inside my desk, you rat). Busted for clay infractions was I, and Sister Marie, third grade, said I had to stay in for recess.

Later, the recess bell rang, and the children lined up except me. I remained seated at my desk with my hands folded on top.

Sister Marie said, "Patricia, line up!" I reminded Sister of my *clay-fraction* and that I was to stay in. She now recalled her previous punishment decree. I remained at my desk, within reaching distance of the scintillating sculptures. I did not yield to another temptation, much to my credit.

The next day, Sister brought in some maroon felt badges that she had carefully fashioned into a diamond shape with pinking shears. There was a sea-blue medal of the Blessed Virgin sewn in the middle and (is the world ending or what?) some potato chips and Cokes on her desk. This was a mirage, I supposed, because nuns only ate communion wafers and lima beans.

Sister said she was starting an Honesty Club, and I was to be the president. Then she gave about six students felt-backed medals, and

President of the Honesty Club with my badge and errant Toni Home Permanent cursing me again on picture day.

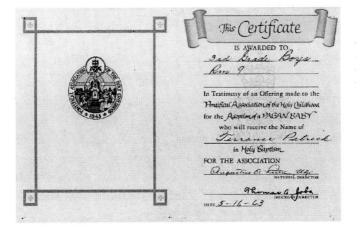

An "adoption certificate" for a "pagan" baby.

we had pop and chips. Our class consisted of approximately fifty kids, so clearly, it was filled with a bunch of lying, sneaky third graders. The telling of the truth was instilled in us early at school. Dogs never ate our homework.

"Acts of Mercy" were not just expected; they were golden tickets into heaven, and "how to" lessons were part of our day. These acts included assisting those unfortunate foreign "Pagan Babies."

We would collect money in a milk carton for the Babies. According to the Maryknoll missionaries, these babies resided in Korea and needed to be converted to Catholicism. With a mere five dollars, you could adopt a Pagan Baby and provide them with food and clothing for a year—or so we were told. If you brought in the most money, Sister would name the Pagan Baby after you!

God knows my mom did not have money to spare, but she gave me the dough, and I was a triumphant Pagan Baby Big Spender. Baby Patricia Ann lives in Korea. I hope she is happy.

We performed our holiday shows in school and orchestrated the elaborate May Queen coronations of the BVM (Blessed Virgin Mary). We sang the beautiful Mass in Latin and sometimes even sang the Requiem Mass for parish funerals. We sang with Sister Agnes Clare, fourth grade, who began our March St. Patrick's Day song practices the afternoon after February's Valentine's Day.

I was in my element, but sometimes, home rocked the smooth sailing school days boat. During a Good Dad Day chat many years later, my dad recalled the following event.

Since he was on disability, Dad was to get me ready and drive me to school. However, we arrived late, and I was steaming mad. Dad was unreliable in many ways, and "No Show Wynn" could have been his confirmation name.

I dreaded that tardy-to-school perp walk attention.

But Dad saw a different theme in the story. He called it "determination."

"You were about seven, and when we got to the school late," Dad related, "you just sat in the front seat beside me. You didn't get out of the car. You turned toward me and glared. Then you opened the door and huffed out of the car. You scared the shit out of me with the angry look you shot at me."

I thought, *Good. Not on my watch, Mister.*

Sister Regina Assumpta possessed a nun name that made me assume *she* could assume into heaven, like the Blessed Virgin Mary, had she wiggled her nose like on the TV show *Bewitched*. She was our young and vibrant art teacher in eighth grade. She could have played Maria Von Trapp in *The Sound of Music*. Her teaching philosophy was to focus on each student's personality and talents.

I loved her art sessions with us. I could draw a little, which I learned from Dad. He would draw pictures, and I would watch how he did it. Grandma Aggie would paint with watercolors, and I would watch her in her atelier (a.k.a. garage). She would let me paint with her.

Perhaps Sister Regina Assumpta had too much of "a Problem like Maria" under her wimple. A few years later, she made a dramatic and much-whispered-about-by-the-adults exit over the convent wall and into the arms of a former priest whom she married.

Parents then were so "on the nun's side" no matter what, that in high school, when I was too shy to sing a solo in the spring show, the director, Sister Clarette, called my dad and told him I was leading riots in the hallway at school (which was *absolutely* not true. Telling funny stories, yes. Leading riots, no). I arrived home that day, and I was slapped across the face by Dad: judge, jury, executioner.

A pencil drawing by Dad, c. 1954. Titled *Wynn Color Guard*. Labeled on the left, "General Wynn" (Grandpa Wynn), and on the right, with the bugle, "1st Sarge Aggie Wynn." My brother Rick and I are saluting.

I imitated Sister Clarette, who had a fevered devotion to pianist Van Cliburn, in a parody skit during a school performance. I had all her many mannerisms down, including her stacking conducting baton, which she once tapped and collapsed into her arch-enemy student, Thomas A., in Sophomore Chorus. By my senior year of high school, I wanted to be done with school. I was beginning to reveal my comedic talents and act the class jester. Also, I was busy. School by day. Two jobs by evening. Cheerleading. Boyfriend doings involving travel.

When I asked our principal, Sister Jean, for permission to work at my high school jobs in the afternoons so I could save more money for college, she said no. I had finished all my required classes, and I tangled with Sister Jean for a few more contentious meetings in tears and with a runny nose. She finally gave in. The fury of "determination."

Sister Consilia, my senior year French teacher, told me one day when I had a whole circus of laughs going on in my corner of the room that I would end up in a women's prison. I did, but it was to do my volunteer projects, and they let me out at the end of the sessions.

a)

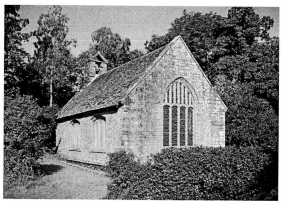

b)

c)

d)

Gwydir Chapel: a) interior, ceiling b) exterior
c) pulpit d) gallery Photos: Judy Corbett

Chapter 10

My Adultery

WE ALL HAVE our haciendas of happiness. For Dad, it was that temporary watering hole, Ye Olde Grogge House. His Happy Hour haven. When he was not hospitalized, it seemed he was at the bar every day and, most often, into the evening.

For Mom, her oasis was the beauty shop, m'lady's chamber: The Pretty Parlor. Mom's hair appointments were sacrosanct by her royal decree. Immediately after her breast cancer surgery, her very first directive to me was to reschedule her canceled weekly hair appointment because the doctor said it would be acceptable to keep it.

My primary calming place, my keep, is a church. It's always a site where I can find serenity and stillness. I visit churches in my travels and always say a prayer of thanks for the opportunity to find solace and see beautiful stained-glass windows and flowing-robed saints.

Although I remain a rebel cradle Catholic at this writing, I still use the teachings, namely my Rosary, to help me meditate and breathe in peace. I say prayers for myself and others. I know which of my saints specialize in which earthly needs, as though they were vitamins and additives from a health food store.

I have St. Anthony, patron saint of lost objects, on speed dial. St. Jude, Mr. Impossible Tasks, is always at the ready: no problem too big or too small for this heavenly host. I met my guardian angel in a dream (he appeared as a mafia don). The Blessed Virgin Mary (BVM) is my BFF.

When my husband and I discovered the ancient Wynn ancestral home in Wales, it became another soothing touchstone. For whatever reason, learning of the "illustrious" Wynns of Wales repaved the neural pathways of my brain. I felt reprogrammed with a possible ancient home base I never knew about.

The Welsh word for this discovered connection is *hiraeth*: a deep longing for somewhere, a home, sometimes even a place you've never been, or a place you dream about. At the Wynn ancestral home, Gwydir Castle, the small stone chapel is a hop, skip, and jump from the main house, and on our 2011 stay there, it drew me to it like a pilgrim to Lourdes. During my psyche-restructuring castle stay, I ambled up the hill to the chapel one day.

The building began in 1693 under the direction of Sir Richard Wynn. Richard Wynn happens to be my father's name. The interior of the spacious Gwydir Chapel combines both Gothic and Renaissance styles, featuring a pulpit adorned with intricately carved wooden figures.

According to the Welsh government site, one should "Look upward to lift spirits." When you do this in this chapel, you see a heavenly field of angels, cherubs, doves, and symbols of the sun, moon, and stars. I sat there for a good while. Spirits duly lifted. Self-perceptions shifted.

In the musical *A Chorus Line*, they sing about how beautiful everything appears at the ballet, no matter what mayhem occurred in the real life of the dancers. With all the disappointments they endured, in the ballet, paradise was found.

When I was young, paradise meant peace in the valley. This is not the case for many, but Catholic school provided a sense of predictability, logic, and orderliness that I craved. The nuns dressed in solemn black and white like Coco Chanel-inspired spiritual Rockettes. Their habits were meticulous, unified, and austere as a royal's ceremonial robes. They seemed to float down school hallways. We were not to touch them. No baby spit up on their shoulders.

I knew exactly what would happen at school, when, and how. There were no surprise attacks. It was quiet. Arguing and fighting were *verboten*. For me, school was a daily safe landing away from the island of my family cacophony and strife. When we arrived at school every morning, Sister was on duty; she suffered no chaos. Sister never went away.

By second grade, the nuns decided we were at the "age of reason" and knew right from wrong. Which we did, for the most part. There were just a few vague areas. So, Sister prepared us to make our first Confession and our First Holy Communion. Our recitations, answers to dogma questions, and deportment for these solemn sacrament ceremonies were taken very seriously as they reflected on Sister in the eyes of the priests, our parents, and the parish.

Preparation for confession had us reflecting on the areas where we fell short of grace, focusing on the Ten Commandments and church teachings as outlined in the Baltimore Catechism, our Catholic Children's owner's manual. We knew how Eve felt in the garden when she received the news that she could not eat apples. Our eyes were opened to the world of sinfulness.

Sister's pedagogy ace was imagery. Sister informed us we had an angel on one shoulder and the devil on the other, both vying for our attention. Another recommended precaution was to leave room on the right side of our desk's bench-like seat for our guardian angel, thereby having a good behavior coach with us throughout the school day. As it says in the angel prayer, "to light, to guard, to rule, and to guide. Amen."

Sister explained sin to us through milk bottle illustrations on the blackboard. She drew three milk bottles on the board because our milk came in bottles delivered by a milkman in a truck to our door or inside our homes to our refrigerators.

The pure white chalked milk bottle exemplified no sin. Sister let us know none of us had a pure white milk bottle for a soul.

In our bottles, more than likely, she explained, we embodied venial sin: "A slight offense against the law of God in matters of less importance, or in matters of great importance, it is an offense committed without sufficient reflection or full consent of the will." This garnered a slightly spotted milk bottle and was pretty much my gig.

With actual sin: "any willful thought, word, deed, or omission contrary to the will of God," added some additional spots on the bottle. The milk bottle darkened on the board with less white chalk as the sinner inched closer to hell.

Finally, the big Kahuna, Mortal Sin: "a grievous offense against the law of God!" Here, we have chocolate milk and eternal hellfire consuming you for eternity. Woe be the chocolate-milk-bottle people. However, loophole! If you confessed your sins—Ding! Ding! Ding!—you were sprung from the incendiary sentencing.

Confessing our six- and seven-year-old sins with the priest was a scary exercise in faith for us and, I am confident, potential comedy material for the priests at dinner. After our intensive confession training with Sister, we finally entered one side or the other of the dark confessional booth alone. It smelled of polished wood, lingering incense from a church service, and blown-out candle vapors. We took up our supplicant positions on the kneeler, little feet suspended in the air, and waited for the priest residing in the center cubicle to open the sliding wooden window on our side. Mercifully, the mesh wire screen obscured our identities.

The window casement slides open with a *clack!* Nerves ignite. Quick, think! What color is my milk bottle?

We began each confession with, "Bless me, Father, for I have sinned. It has been [length of time] since my last confession." Then you laid out the worst of yourself: what you did and how many times you did it. This was my usual list:

1. Talked back to my parents (a daily sin).
2. Fought with my brother and sister (I had only one brother to fight with so far).
3. Talked during Mass (I made this one up so I would have something to say if I ran low on sins).
4. The seasonal sins, e.g., I took my brother's Halloween candy/ Christmas gift/Chocolate Easter Bunny/July 4th sparkler.

Once we were purified, it was time to receive the body of Christ at our First Communion. Our First Holy Communion was a sacred and Met Gala-level sartorial event. We girls were dressed in stiff white dresses puffed out with crinolines, veils, and gloves, and we looked like baby brides. We carried small white purses holding nothing but a handkerchief and a white pearl-like material-covered missal of the mass, with its tiny crucifix shrine embedded inside the front cover.

The puppy-dog-tail boys were a bit less fashion-careful and Big Holy Day behavior-conscious. Some of them looked like little drunk and disheveled grooms with shirt tails out and ties askew. But once we stood ready at the church's vestibule to walk down the aisle, Sister had them all tucked and straightened, their hands folded in prayer formation, as if she were training obedient penguins at a circus.

∗

To make our First Holy Communion, we little sinners needed to learn about sin and make our first confession.

My First Holy Communion was soon besmirched by a chocolate milk bottle of sin. Standing with St. Agnes, the virgin martyr.

I continued going to confession regularly. But one day, an innocent girl's confession-fun-and-games went to hell in a handbasket. I inadvertently hit the big-time chocolate milk bottle. What happened to this second grader was this.

The year was 1958. I walked home from St. Agnes Church for a candy bar at the neighborhood carry-out store. The proprietor, Fred, always seemed a bit sleazy and nosy to me and was forever smoking a cigar and chatting with his cronies at the register. I probably appeared to be a midget adult to him: a little person with weekly adult requests, listed on a scrap of white envelope from my mother to fulfill her domestic needs. For instance, one typical visit had me bringing him a list from Mom that included a pack of Winston cigarettes and a box of Kotex the size of a dorm room refrigerator. This cracked Fred up, which irritated me.

However, on this occasion, after my rote confession of my cooked-up transgressions with the good Padre, I rewarded myself with a Snickers candy bar at Fred's. Just a few minutes before, I had possessed just a couple of polka dots on my soul's milk bottle. Now evil lurked and caught me unawares. I inadvertently glimpsed a girly magazine with a naked lady on the cover stashed in a stack under the counter.

My shoulder angel thundered! I thought, *Oh no! Gotta go back to confession.* I was not sure how I had sinned, but I was certain I was not supposed to see a naked lady posing like Marilyn Monroe, smiling like it was Christmas morning.

I knew I needed to confess . . . something.

As I walked back the few blocks to church, I took a quick inventory of the Ten Commandments and the milk bottles while snacking on the Snickers bar.

Father Schmidt, who had just heard my confession, was our parish priest and pastor at St. Agnes. He was aware of our many family problems and counseled my parents. I recall my mother telling me once that Father Schmidt advised her that she would need to stay married to my father no matter the abuse and financial neglect he subjected us to. It was expected in the Church's teachings. She needed to help my dad, Father said.

As for this second-grader's naked lady boomerang return to church, when I arrived, I tip-toed into the confessional booth to take my punishment. The wooden window shutter opened wide—*clack!* The silhouette of Father's profile appeared like a ghost. "Bless me, Father, for I have sinned. It's been twenty minutes since my last confession."

His usually dispassionate tone rose an octave as he sputtered, *"What did you do?"*

His mind must have raced to hear that a child could sin in such record time. He was not aware of my attempted murder with the butter knives. *Omertà!*

I remembered the commandment that Sister was so squeamish and vague about in school. It was a mysterious sin involving adults, perhaps naked. Since mine had naked lady overtones, I said,

"I committed adultery." The sixth commandment.

Adults, and now I, had committed big sins that made nuns blush! Fr. Schmidt paused as if to reflect or, more likely, to think, *I gotta hear this one and share it with the boys,* and he replied,

Father Schmidt, the priest on the left top row,
and our gigantic baby boomer class of children.

"Did you touch yourself?"

He flummoxed me with this confessional curveball. I had not an inkling what he was referring to.

Stumped, I answered, "No, Father."

As I was a child with a low voice and the confessional screen partially camouflaged me, Father gently presented his considered penance with a warning, "Say three Hail Marys and *be a good little boy.*"

More confusion.

I exited the booth, walked to the altar rail, knelt, and silently said my three Hail Marys for the second time that day. I just pretended I was Peter Pan for the "good boy" penance part. After all, I reasoned that Mary Martin was a girl, and she played Peter Pan, a boy, on TV.

After high school, I didn't go to confession again until decades later. Fr. Klein, a young priest and family friend, mentioned during dinner one night that attending would be a healing experience for me. He was familiar with the highlights of my *Familia Membra Vitae.* He recommended our city's King of Confessions, Monsignor Cody. I made an appointment.

This confession was like no other I had experienced. We were in his office, face to face, in daylight, he at his desk, me in a chair facing him—no mesh screen. No kneeler. No church fragrances. No filtered disguise.

Monsignor said, "Do you remember how to start?" I said I did. His eyes widened when I got to the multiple tens of years since my last confession. He knew he had his absolution hands full.

He inhaled deeply and said, "OK, so that takes us back to about 1969. Let's begin."

I thought back to 1969. Man landed on the moon. The Beatles had their last performance on the Apple Records roof. The first Concorde test flight was conducted in France. We shuddered at the Manson Murders.

I told the monsignor, "Well, I am still mad at my dad for not letting me go to Woodstock." Monsignor roared with laughter.

He decided on a new confession tactic. Monsignor said, "Tell me what has given you the most pain in your life." I told him that it was my dad's mental illness. I gave him an unsparing *Cliff Notes* synopsis. He listened carefully. I had never spoken like this to anyone on earth. No one had asked. He talked to me about Dad, Mom, and our family life. The bad-bloodletting conversation gradually transformed into a balm of healing.

Then he spoke my penance, which was a way, he explained, to extend this gift of being understood. My penance was to do something kind for my mother, who he said "had inevitably suffered greatly." I took her roses.

According to the *Castles* book, the river near Gwydir was so clean and clear it produced pearls. In 1636, Sir Richard Wynn, the previous Richard Wynn of Wales, presented pearls on bended knee to his queen.

From a young age, I would conduct investigations into my mother's wooden jewelry box with the three little doors (some might call it pillaging). I would lift each door by the small round gold knob, inspect the shiny costume jewelry from her humble royal treasury, and try on the pieces.

Among the rhinestone bracelets and colored glass necklace strands,

Mom/Dorothy, and her four kids. L-R Rob, Kathleen, Mom, Rick, me.

Sir Richard Wynn (1588–1649) of Gwydir Castle, 2nd Baronet.

My dad, Richard Wynn (1920–1980), on a good day.

worn when Mom and Dad went out on the town before the whole flock of kids arrived, I discovered two pins fashioned of pearly white shells affixed together to resemble little turtles. Attached to one of the pins at the back of a turtle was a note in my dad's left-handed penmanship, which consistently appeared as though he had his hand in a short-circuiting toaster while printing it. The words on it spoke of the two of them being "these loving little turtles."

My mother kept these pins throughout her life.

There ought to be a commandment abolishing mental illness, represented by a smashed milk bottle with shards splaying out and piercing all those circumstances that cause it to be. The iridescent pearls of proper treatment, compassion, and community support are the start of mending.

Inside Gwydir Chapel. Soul nourishing. Photo: Steve Brown.

Chapter 11

Little Sister

I WAS SO in awe of my teaching nuns that I, and many of my classmates, wanted to become one. These holy women glided across our classroom floors in their flowing veils and habits like ballet dancers. They knew all about the ins and outs of heaven and hell. They seemed to possess the secrets of success in life, which involved exceptional manners they imparted to us: ways to walk and sit that probably resembled how the royals were also trained, we agreed amongst ourselves.

They had extraordinary hands—smooth and white. Those hands did not work in dishwater or diaper pails, nor did they bake and wrinkle in the hot sun poolside. Those hands were for praying, tending to the sick as nurses, or writing with chalk on chalkboards as teachers. Those hands never had to defend themselves from abusive husbands.

These, I thought, were free women.

Nun couture

white habit, forehead, skull wrap, neck cover

white bib collar

black veil

black gown

silver crucifix on chain

black or brown rope belt

black bead rosary & cross

I was enamored of the nuns' clothing as much as their vocation. My nuns were in full sail: in a habit with all its dramatic add-ons—layers and layers of protection from worldly influences and people. Every student had a personal goal to see somehow what was under that veil and if, in fact, they had shaved off their hair. This was a daily goal of mine.

Like many Catholic school girls at the time, I felt I had what the nuns termed "a calling"—a yearning to become a nun influenced by unseen yet felt celestial advisors.

My chance to test the convent waters came in sixth grade with pre-nun information classes. The wee Munchkin-sized nuns leading these preparatory sessions were in the order of the Sisters of the Poor Child Jesus. Their mother house was based in the Netherlands, and they became my recruiters. Our Lady of Bethlehem Convent was on the other side of town. Attached to it was a boarding high school for girls planning to enter the convent upon graduation. I had my heart set on doing just that.

Nuns lived neatly ordered lives with clearly defined hours of work and prayer, which we, as students, were forbidden to ruffle, leaving them to their higher thoughts. They wore dramatic costumes that caught your attention and respect. Nuns had authority and controlled the classroom, with even the most gregarious and nefarious among us becoming loyal subjects. Nuns were smart. Many were refined and from "good families." They were close to Jesus because they were married to Him, the Brides of Christ, as they are called. Jesus must have had His hands full with all these Sister Wives.

Some of my nuns had a special devotion to the little boy Jesus, known as the Infant of Prague. The original Infant of Prague statue was a wedding gift from a Spanish princess to her Austrian royal cousin. Once lost, it was found in Prague, where, in 1637, a priest praying before it heard the infant statue speak. Miracles occurred. Many developed a special devotion to the Infant of Prague, whose peculiar power was, and this drew me, protection. This Lil' Jesus was also a dress-up statue with gorgeous gowns of the finest silks and satins.

My school had an Infant of Prague statue on a piano. The church ladies reverently changed his little outfits monthly, a fashion show I cherished. The Barbie doll had nothing on the Infant of Prague.

A group of girls from Our Lady of Perpetual Help School car-pooled from our parish with a "Driver Dad" to this convent-nun high school for Sunday sessions to discuss our religious leanings. My dad was never one of the drivers. I never knew him to volunteer for anything at any of our schools. I am confident Dad would have preferred sticking needles in his eyes than ferrying a carload of giggling girls.

The Sisters leading the discussions would talk to us in their sunlight-filled sitting room about vocations and helping others through teaching or nursing. They mentioned that we could eventually go to high school there. Then, they would serve us tea and cookies. My guess was that no prom or homecoming queen frivolities were allowed for girls attending "Holy High."

After our Sunday afternoon chats, a group of the girls already attending "So-You-Wanna'-Be-a-Nun High School" would come into the room, and we would go outside and play baseball, which I loved doing in my neighborhood, too. As I write this, I stop and look out of my home office window. If the trees were removed, I could see that convent from my desk, just across the Olentangy River.

One person who was part of our vocation day at the convent was neither a nun nor a student. She was a distinguished and classy-looking woman who would participate in the sitting room program by playing a song on the piano for us at one point in the afternoon.

She walked like a model: straight and poised—très soigné. She dressed as if she came off a 1940s movie set, with a greying chignon hairstyle. She was introduced to us as Miss Gillars, who taught music, French, and German at the nun-to-be school. She never spoke to us. She would swan in, play a song, and then glide out of the living room like an unsettled ghost on a cloud of superiority.

On one of the Sundays when I was getting ready to go to the convent for pre-nun class, my father had programmed himself into a ranting temper setting, stomping around, yelling about something or other to my mom, with all of us hoping his anger would dissipate before landing on a target. It was anyone's guess where this roulette pill of rage would settle.

Then, whuh-whoh, angry Dad turned on his heel away from Mom, charged toward me, and burst out, his face steaming mad red,

"Is there someone at that convent named Mildred Gillars?"

"Yes. She plays the piano for us. She teaches French and German at the school," I said warily.

Dad blew his top, "That's. Axis. SALLY!"

Then he sputtered out the history of her treasonous war crimes. His neck's jugular vein pulsed with rushing blood as he spat out his words.

I was unclear about the whole treason deal since I was only about twelve years old. But I thought: Holy Mother of Christ, is he going to go to the convent as a vigilante in his never-ending war days and kill her?

Verbal jujitsu ensued. I employed my increasingly deft communication skills (which some call malarkey, but I call a family asset) to hoodwink Dad into believing that Miss Gillars was being deported to Germany. She would no longer be on the scene. Dad finally calmed down, and I vamoosed to the convent with that week's scheduled "Driver Dad" when I heard the honk outside.

Henceforth, in our convent sessions, I used my lookout skills, and from my parapet, I surreptitiously focused on Axis Sally and gathered intel. I did not share my top-secret findings with anyone. Had I shared it, I would be drawing a connection from my dad to Gillars, and if he *did* act on his anger, that could be potential evidence; that would suck me into the quicksand of the legal system.

I honestly thought like this as a child. As an adult, I researched Axis Sally, and I have a file. Axis Sally, her radio nickname, was Mildred Gillars, who grew up in Belleville, Ohio. I was to learn that she was the Tokyo Rose of Germany, a radio propagandist during WWII. Gillars was the first American woman convicted of treason after the war and was sentenced to Alderson prison for twelve years (Martha Stewart's prison alma mater).

There appears to be a connection between Eunice Kennedy and Gillars' placement in this convent, where she lived after incarceration. It was a sanctuary for her because people like my dad wanted to kill her. When I requested information about Gillars from our Catholic diocese many decades later, none was forthcoming.

The *New York Times* covered Axis Sally's trial. She had attended

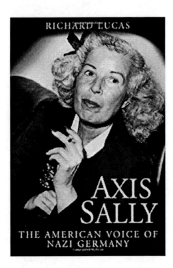

RICHARD LUCAS

AXIS
SALLY

THE AMERICAN VOICE OF
NAZI GERMANY

Axis Sally, a.k.a. Mildred Gillars.

Oberlin College, and the trial's feature stories from this era uncover this "vital fact": she was one of the first women at the school to wear knickers. They wrote that she was a dreamy actress who went to Germany before the war to expand her chances of stardom. She became a radio host during WWII through events that stranded her just as the war broke out. Her love interest with a ranking German officer came into the narrative. It would make a great movie.

The *Times* wrote many comments about her hair and clothing and how soldiers were disappointed to eventually see trial photos of the woman behind the disembodied sexy voice they heard on the radio during the war. They thought she looked old and unattractive. The trial records accuse her of telling the GIs their sweethearts were dating someone else and naming American soldiers while describing their injuries (she vehemently denied doing this). Part of her defense was that there had been several "Axis Sallys," and she had not used that type of dispiriting propaganda on her show.

The possibility of someone angering Dad, especially someone related to the military, and their destruction by his hand was an eventuality lying over our lives like a grey London fog. The Big Ben of peril continued to ratchet through the hours. I worried that the endpoint of his fuse was approaching. We were safe this time, but what about the next?

Keep in mind that this desire to attend the convent high school for four years countered the fact that I could not even stay all night at a friend's house without getting sick to my stomach and having to come home, let alone leave for the school year and only return at Christmas and summer.

My great secret fear was that if I were gone from the house, they all could be killed by Dad when he was in a fit and out of his mind. His guns were so close at hand in my brothers' room. I believed it was my job to keep my family alive.

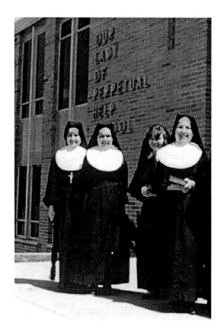

The girls who went to the nun classes got to dress as nuns for a presentation at our school, Our Lady of Perpetual Help. I drew the short straw and had to be the postulant, a nun-in-training with the less dramatic partial habit, with hair in my face. Center. Photo: John Mountain

One night, staying at my friend's house across the street, I became so anxious that Dad would turn on our family that I became physically ill and threw up over the side of the bed onto the floor. My friend's mother cleaned up the unpleasant mess, gagging all the while. I was so embarrassed. She woke my parents by phone and took me home, assuming I had a virus. What I had was a full-blown panic attack.

I could not have girls stay over all night at our house for several reasons. First, my sister and I slept in a double bed, which was also the site of our nightly battles. Second, there was the risk of Dad's temper. If something managed to wake that angry bear, having a friend over would not only endanger her but would also let the bear out of the bag; she could serve as an eyewitness to his outbursts, exposing us all.

I had one friend whom my father liked, which was as rare as Haley's Comet. She made a few day visits to our house. Dad said she was brilliant and well-mannered. My friend was very good with my dad, too. She was able to speak with him calmly. I did not have her stay overnight at my house, but hers was the only house where I did sleepovers and felt totally at home.

Her father was a champion of mine, always uplifting me with his encouraging comments. I had never had such support from an adult. When he died many years later, I cried so uncontrollably at his funeral that the people seated around me became concerned for my well-being.

Now, back to the nun school decision.

The time came for me and my family to decide about my going to boarding high school at the convent. I brought home the stack of important fine print Nun School Permission Papers. At this time, as at so many times in our family's life crossroads, my dad was away at the VA or psych ward or escaping somewhere because my mom, yet again, handled the decision-making alone.

Mom sat at the table in the kitchen and read the Nun School Permission Papers, inhaling a Winston with a cup of coffee. She dabbed out the burning cigarette in the ashtray, emitting an exasperated tornado of smoke into our overly tobacco-fragranced abode. Mom never spoke to me about her own experiences in Catholic school. I always had the impression that the nuns did not consider her an outstanding student; in return, she was not a fan of theirs but respected their authority.

Mom's kitchen station was near the rotary dial phone on the counter where she did her best home-spun therapy, talking with Aunt Cornie, her sister, or her mom, Grandma "Caddyaw." When she was deeply engrossed in a conversation, inevitably, we kids would swarm around her like fireflies. We'd blink our lights, bombarding her with a myriad of whiny requests for snacks, playtime at a neighbor's, towels for the swimming pool visit, or materials for a school project due the next day, even though it had been assigned a month ago. We considered each need as important as an emergency kidney transplant.

Mom waved us off like a first-base coach with her cigarette-free hand. The phone, bingo, and the beauty shop were mom's life-giving oxygen in our stultifying home atmosphere. We were not to come between them and her.

I, her daughter, wanting to become a nun, had to have given Mom a whiplash moment. I was the mouthiest of her four children and cantankerous at home. I argued with my parents continuously because I did not want to play the "Let's All Live in Holy Hell" game. I fought with my siblings verbally and physically. I spent excessive time working on my hairdos, watching movies and TV shows, dreaming, and sulking.

I did not demonstrate any affinities for missionary work nor working with children as a teacher—as the oldest of four, kids were a nuisance to me, and she knew it.

At Mass, I contemplated what it would be like to live in Paris but tuned back in for the singing parts. I could not have offered you one sentence about what the priest had said in his homily—I was transporting myself into other realms. My goal each day was to find an escape. I wanted to be a nun because nuns were respected, dressed in fabulous church garb, and no one seemed to go nuts in their midst, causing the collapse of the circus tent of daily living.

My nun influences were featured in the films *The Bells of St. Mary's*, *The Sound of Music*, and later, *The Trouble With Angels*.

Mom placed the important unsigned typed white pages of convent school documents, now with a coffee cup stain on the corner, on the table in front of her. She placed her hands, which had seen an ocean of dishwater, atop the legal forms and declared,

"Trish (I go by about five Patricia derivative names; a nun name would have been an addition), you are *NOT* nun material."

No truer words had my mother ever spoken to me.

Only two years later, at fourteen, was I to meet the boy I would eventually marry. Not only did I not enter the convent, but I fell into public school the following year when we were assigned a new parish with a new Catholic school under construction. It was the year being Irish Catholic hurt the most.

PART IV

Jolted Forward and Conquering New Lands

There is a saying in Tibetan, "Tragedy should be utilized as a source of strength." No matter what sort of difficulties or how painful the experience is, if we lose our hope, that's our real disaster.

—DALAI LAMA

The connection between the assassination of President John F. Kennedy and the eruption of Beatlemania in the U.S. . . . on "The Ed Sullivan Show" has long been established. The joy in the group's new sound and look played out on the faces of Sullivan's audience full of

Beatlemania, Ed Sullivan Show, 1964.
Photo: CBS Archive

screaming teenagers, gave a grieving nation a much-needed reason to smile once again.

—*THE LOS ANGELES TIMES*, November 22, 2013

Life is uncharted territory. It reveals its story one moment at a time. —LEO BUSCAGLIA

Picture Day. Not Ready for Prime Time Player.

Chapter 12

Innocence Lost

WITH THE post-war Baby Boom, new schools and Catholic parishes were as fertile for growth as the families who populated them. Our family became part of a new church parish, but the school had not been built yet. So, I was sent to what we called a "Protestant" school (a public school) until it was. I felt like an emigrant sailing to foreign shores. I was to learn the ways of their people.

Being the official "Catholic Girl" in seventh grade, I stood out like an inexperienced, directionally, and rhythmically challenged dancer in a polished Broadway chorus line. I was way out of step in all areas. Having worn uniforms until this year and on a family budget running in the negatives, my 1963–64 school year wardrobe was limited, determinedly demure, and side-eyed by the other hipper students.

My Pollyanna attire was one thing. The way I sat in class, ramrod straight, as previously demanded by the Sisters, fooled the other kids into believing I was either an aristocrat on the lam or sporting a back brace while recovering from scoliosis surgery.

I had entered another territorial sea. The relationship between student and teacher was shockingly informal. Instead of obedience to the teaching Sister who, when she entered the classroom, heralded the rapt attention and laser focus given to a deity, what did I see? The relaxed students hardly noticed when the teacher arrived, sometimes requiring her to call the class to order!

Already, these public school girls were advancing like racing gazelles into their sexual development and boy-magnet mode. These girl-women could not have been more anti-nun protocol, donned in tight mohair sweaters and pencil skirts with a sexy slit in the back: the better to view the black textured hosiery.

Even these protestant girls' baby geisha feet spoke of desire. Their coveted Capezio t-strap *come-hither* shoes, worn with actual grown-up lady hosiery, fastened to their gingham garter belts, partially exposed their toes, and gave them a leg up on me style-wise. I stepped about in little white prissy-girl anklets and penny loafers. My entire foot was encased in cotton socks, like a burn victim.

The sweeping and swirling habit-wearing nuns and their black angel wings shielded us from the many creeping vine sins of the mainstream. These dark angels used a strictly enforced cultural time machine to maintain Victorian-era guidelines for dress and deportment. From the land of my "Nearer My God to Thee" plaid jumper "uniform," I landed smack dab onto the set of the real-life play *Grease*, West Side Columbus style. Look at me / I'm Sandra Dee / Lousy with virginity.

While I engaged in hopscotch prowess, the public school girls already going steady wore boy's rings around their necks on a chain. They methodically wrapped the ring band with angora yarn that they would brush *during class* into a furry Himalayan-Persian cat's fluffiness, and the teachers allowed it! No hands folded in prayer atop desks for these 1960s pop star Dusty Springfield look-alikes.

The young ladies wore bras and heavy cat-eye makeup and ratted and sprayed their hair in the restroom. I still wore an undershirt. I attempted a Jackie Kennedy flip hairdo for my class picture (sporting a red jumper, such a sizzling couture act of rebellion against the plaid jumper). Still, my flip flopped, resembling the ends of Dali's mustache, without the pizzazz.

I did not like going into the restroom at that school for fear of the brutal eighth-grade warrior, Olga Foley. I once witnessed her pulling some victim's hair out by the roots and slamming her head into the sink. Although I had learned to fight with my sparring siblings and neighbor kids, Olga was in a weight, height, and ability class all her own. Also, Olga had issues. I did not want to share them. I developed bladder control instead.

I was not interested in boys yet, but as I now seemed to be a freak show, a rare museum piece, a curiosity, if you will, the boys were curious about me, as one would be about a panda bear that happens to be juggling grapefruits while pushing a grocery cart. Up to this point in life, I had chosen to be invisible.

An eighth-grade boy was enamored of me (fascinated by my panda bear act?) and invited me to the drive-in restaurant with his parents for dinner. My dad must have been in treatment because I was allowed to go.

It was a Friday. The nicely dressed and very polite mom and dad of my "date" sat in the front seat and discussed their orders for hamburgers. I began to crumble in the face of sin. I had to tell them I could not eat meat on Friday. Jimmy's parents had not realized I was Catholic. The surprised look on their faces informed me their hopes and dreams for this young scion did not include the Latin language of the Catholic Mass, discussions of pagan babies needing salvation, or consuming the body and blood of Christ. They hurriedly ordered a grilled cheese for me.

One saving grace of mine was that I was a good dancer. I had watched the best of the best in movies and on TV and then practiced the moves in my room. We had dances at school that year. The kids admired good dancers. During one song at a school dance, my dance partner, the basketball team star, and I cleared the floor with our fancy twisting, monkeying, and frugging. I shelved my shyness.

This was my first time in school with Black students; three became my friends. I was invited to a party at Tony's home (Tony was the little brother of the fabulous jazz singer Nancy Wilson), but my dad would not let me go because I would be the only white kid. On this, there was no wiggle room whatsoever. My parents still used the n-word in everyday conversation.

One school party I attended that fateful year was my very first boy-girl house party. My outfit was yet another fashion faux pas unless I was planning to appear in court to convince the jury of my complete innocence in a murder case. I wore a school uniform in disguise: a grey jumper with front inlaid pleats and a little white Peter Pan collar, a signifier of purity. Affixed to the top left front of the jumper, my chest still as flat as a multiplication flash card, was a veritable neon sign of incorruptibility, a pin of red cherries made of papier mâché with green felt wired leaves.

I was the first to arrive at the party, dropped off by Dad. There were no parents around as I scoped the scene. *This can't be good*, I thought. I got a clue about how things were rolling when the host told me to come into the bathroom with her to wait for others to arrive. Her older sister, an actual in-full-flower high school teenager, was in the bathroom in her bra and underwear, smearing on make-up, curling her eyelashes, playing a radio, with a lit cigarette burning on the sink edge. She would take puffs in between beautifying measures. She looked like gorgeous and beguiling actress Yvette Mimieux, a minx of a girl at that time.

I had entered the gates of hell.

My discomfort alarm sounded a low buzz. The kids began arriving and then immediately started slow dancing and making out to music crooned by Johnny Mathis. I decided to run up the distress flag. I made my way to the kitchen wall phone and called my dad to pick me up. Dad was good about saving me from potential disaster when he was in residence.

Despite these awkward moments swirling in the seventh-grade vortex, I did something that changed everything about school in one brave act. As shy as I was then and as new as I was to the school and the ways of its prurient, Gina Lollobrigida-girls, I took my ability to dance and went out for cheerleading . . . and made it. I have no clue where this confidence came from, but I had always yearned for dance lessons, and maybe I figured this was as close as I would get.

I began to understand that I had a "me" inside, separate from my family, someone who wanted out. I always felt like I was in the wrong movie. Couldn't anyone see that there were things I could do and wanted to do if given half a chance?

At twelve, I decided to engage in life on my terms. I began throwing off the bowlines to sail freely. I reimagined my real life for the first time. Any talents or skills I might have possessed had yet to be recognized, encouraged, or supported at home. The reason: Maslow's hierarchy of needs in our house listed extra-curricular school activities and talent-nurturing as No. 6,890.

After cheerleading, I began signing up for the swim team, theater stage crew, student council, and synchronized swimming performing troupe at our neighborhood pool. My parents had no clue what I was doing and asked no questions. I could easily have started a gambling and drug ring on the sly, and they wouldn't have noticed a thing—until one infamous day, they did. It was a singular moment in our family history.

It flabbergasted me that my parents and paternal grandparents visited the pool to see one of my synchronized swimming shows. All of them were there just for me and my solo act. What next? TV series character Gidget inviting me to surf with her in California?

How far is California, and could I hitchhike there?

The story begins like this. My next-door neighbor, WWII German War Bride Margaret, had albums and a record player, and she would let me select my swimming routine music from her collection. I chose a song cut from David Rose and his orchestra that summer. Wikipedia describes it as having "a jazz influence with especially prominent trombone slides." It screamed for white elbow-length gloves and a leap from the high diving board, according to the choreographer (me).

After a torture session with Grandma Aggie the morning of the show, as she fashioned my hair into a bun by hammering bobby pins into my skull, *everyone* headed to the swimming pool. The thought of this right now has my head swimming. What had made this single event such a family crowd-pleaser?

In the end, I shocked the hell out of them.

My number was next. Gloves on, I climbed to the top of the high board. As my music started, I slowly took off one glove and tossed it off one side of the diving board to the audience. Then, I removed the other and threw it off the other side of the diving board toward the rest of the crowd. Arms denuded, I took a swan dive, and, with my best Esther Williams moves, I proceeded with my swimming routine to the song "The Stripper."

I had never seen a stripper. My knowledge of the World Entire had gaps as if it were flat, and I could fall into a random pit of dragons at any time. I had the notion from God-knows-where that the strippers only took off gloves.

I swam my act and climbed the ladder out of the pool. The look on my family's faces informed me I had transformed before their eyes into Gypsy Rose Lee.

My dad was horrified and huffed like a struggling locomotive. Mom acted like nothing had happened: no show, no witnesses, nothing to see here. My grandparents probably figured they made the hour-long drive from their house only to be met with swimming smut. And here was Grandpa, once captain of the vice squad, who had busted real strippers.

No one said anything to me about it. Not a word. We just got in the station wagon and drove back to our house. Silence is the loudest rebuke of all.

But it did not stop me. I continued with synchronized swimming and swim team competitions and faced one of the most jarring and inexplicable events in my life and the nation's. I did it in less-than-neutral waters.

It is still my protestant school year. One day in late November 1963, in Mr. Wasilik's seventh-grade English class on the second floor, we could hear a garbled announcement echoing through the hallway, but our classroom PA speaker was out. The teacher asked me to go to the office and see what was happening.

I walked into our hallway, proceeded down the staircase to the school office, and encountered a bewildering sight. Mrs. Freda, our exemplary and kind school secretary, was weeping and being patted on the shoulder and consoled by Mr. Mills, our principal, a stern but amiable man who always wore a suit.

I slowly entered the office, and my mood detector silently sounded, "Scary danger ahead!" Mr. Mills and Ms. Freda saw me, so I could not escape. They asked me what I needed. I told them I was running to learn about the announcements because we could not hear them.

Mr. Mills looked me in the eyes and gravely told me that I needed to inform my teacher that President Kennedy had been shot and was dead. Also, I was to say that new announcements would follow, and we would need to return to homeroom, where we would be dismissed from school.

Gulp.

I took in as much as I could absorb, and being trained to carry out orders, I turned and walked back up to our classroom laden with my

John Kennedy at our Ohio State House. Oct 17, 1960.
Photo: John F. Kennedy Library

shattering message. I entered the room. I told Mr. Waszilik the horrible news. Shocked, he told the class.

At this point, we needed to return to homeroom. I was crying by now. The Kennedys were family to us, in our minds. They were Irish Catholics. They were OUR royals. They were from the same county in Ireland as my Cavanaugh family, County Wexford.

A significant contention during the run-up to the election was that Kennedy was Catholic, and his detractors said he would answer to the Pope. The anti-Catholic bias became a significant part of the campaign.

As we returned to homeroom and teacher Mrs. Lassie Phillips, my thoughts immediately raced back to seeing JFK in Columbus when he ran for president in 1960. My dad had taken us to hear the presidential candidate speak at the Ohio Statehouse during his campaign. That had been a momentous day for us.

Standing on the sidewalk downtown watching his motorcade arrive,

Columbus, Ohio, Kennedy supporters during his visit.

our family friend Dorothy Hayes swung her ponytail like a lasso as Kennedy passed by, and he made the same motion back to her.

In her fine book, *When We Were Kennedys*, memoirist Monica Wood, whose Irish Catholic working-class family also identified with the Kennedy family, writes of how Kennedy's assassination affected her. She, too, was so attached to the Kennedys that she experienced "a profound dislocation, a feeling like slipping on the shifting surface of my allotted scrap of God's earth."

I'm with you, Monica. I might add to your spot-on description that I thought they would be gunning for us *Mick Papists* next.

Now that I had returned to Lassie Phillip's homeroom at West Franklin School, I started crying almost hysterically. Lassie, the teacher, not the TV dog (the dog would have shown some compassion), reprimanded me for my emotional outburst by saying, "Calm down. That's enough. Stop crying."

I angrily shouted back at her, "I can't help it, and you must be a communist!"

I had never liked this teacher, who was Southern and repeatedly attempted to discourage my friendship with a Black girl in my class. I guess in my house, the worst thing you could be called was communist, so I hurled that insult at her. That retort led me to my second trip to the school office that day. I was suspended from school by Mr. Mills.

But no one went to school for days because we were all in front of our TVs watching Walter Cronkite as our "good uncle" newscaster, helping us through our national tragedy, which continued assaulting our emotions and our sense of safety.

We watched the Texas Rangers and G-men on TV, trying to find the shooter still on the loose. The assassin killed a police officer. When they found Lee Harvey Oswald and took him to jail, we watched as Jack Ruby, dressed in a business suit and a gray fedora hat, shot and killed Oswald. Oswald was wearing a sweater over a collared shirt and was surrounded by police officers and sheriffs in cowboy hats.

We were choked up with tears seeing Jackie Kennedy in the funeral march bravely processing down Pennsylvania Avenue, wearing a long black veil (although you could still see her face, which was puffy from crying). And then there was darling John-John, saluting his father's casket as it passed, wearing that little blue coat that matched his sweet sister's. Our living rooms across America were one big funeral parlor.

I understood then that terror was part of our lives, both inside and outside of our homes. This was a revelation. The whole country was traumatized.

In November 1963, I thought that if something this brutal and raw could happen to the beautiful Kennedys in the middle of the street on a sunny day, it could indeed happen to us. I was not wrong, considering the many danger signs within our family pointing towards the red "locked and loaded" zone.

As the years passed and I progressed through each school grade, advancing into adulthood, America and our family navigated through a murky era of grimness and violence.

Chapter 13

The Calvary Has Arrived

TO SAVE US from our national misery and distract us from the tragic loss of our own handsome and charming US prince, God sent a special delivery CARE Package to us (young people, anyway) from a place we had never heard of before: Liverpool, England.

Until then, England only meant that Queen with a tight perm and the funny way of waving, royal guards costumed like the flying monkeys in *The Wizard of Oz* (but tail-free), Robin Hood in Sherwood Forest, and teen movie idol Hayley Mills, who landed at the Disney Studios.

This place, Liverpool, had all of us becoming cartographers first to determine its location and, second, whether we could swim there.

The four life-restoring traveling troubadours, who called themselves the Beatles, stormed our shores and sang of courtly love to a rock and roll beat. They later went on to pen more profound lyrics, leading a generation on the trail of discovery and introspection that lasted only ten years.

The media and parents across this great land paid as much attention to their mop-top hairdos as they did to the irritating din of their music. The four lads' sleekly styled bespoke suits gave them a winning edge in our parents' eyes over the slightly mangy Rolling Stones, who continue to roll *en groupe*.

When the Beatles appeared in America, my dad was disappearing more and more to the Keg Room, the VA hospital in Chillicothe, Ohio, or to psychiatric wards. His fight turned inward most of the time now, taking the form of deep moaning and sighing depression.

A condition I now know as "malignant normality" descended on our house. Dad's destructive behaviors—yelling, storming out of the house in anger, hours of sullen throne time in his La-Z-Boy recliner—felt like the order of the realm, to be skirted, diverted, or converted philosophically into understanding. I knew that, paradoxically, this was Dad's dungeon.

I made peace with his internal war. *This is how he is. Stop fighting it. Start living a parallel life.* I would run up to the "astronomy tower" of my room over the garage overlooking our front yard hill and settle into reverie, my sights on other lands and my compass pointed east to England.

New York had never seen anything like the young people's response, with 3,000 people showing up at the airport to welcome the Beatles to America.

Vince Calandra facilitated the first Beatles performance in the US on February 9, 1964, on America's beloved Sunday nighttime variety program, *The Ed Sullivan Show*. Calandra was the show's associate producer and later reported on the young musicians, "They were four of the nicest people I've ever worked with, not just nice, very professional." There were 50,000 requests for only 728 seats. I did not see this in-person performance in NYC with those fortunate golden ones in the audience. I watched it with my neighbor Colleen Fishinger in her basement rec room on her TV in Columbus, Ohio.

Colleen and I sat on the linoleum floor in front of the television with Colleen's collie, a Lassie look-alike, nearby. No grown-ups were present to judge our Limey boys (my Irish dad's title for them), not even Colleen's ever-harassing two older brothers. This was between us and the four singing and head-bopping guys. It was our world. Adults need not apply.

Ed came on the TV to introduce the Beatles and began with the announcement that they had just received "a wire" [telegram] from Elvis Presley. Colonel Parker congratulated the Beatles on their premiere performance in America. *Good form, Elvis*, I thought. Ed also acted as school headmaster, calming the screaming girls in his audience with a wave of his arm, whipped out from his stiffened back like a wind-blown ship's yardarm, delivering a stern reminder to the erupting teens to calm down, and then with an arched brow adding, "You promised!"

"Close your eyes, and I'll kiss you / Tomorrow, I'll miss you," sang the

Look at their first appearance on Ed Sullivan. I still swoon. Photo: CBS Archive

Beatles as they opened their appearance. Colleen and I began screaming along with the studio audience screamers in New York. Paul quieted things down with the following number: a ballad, "Till There Was You." That's when they put their names under each singing face.

Colleen and I had yet to learn their names. The lucky-ducky ticket-holder audience members (kids with connections) reacted.

Paul! [screams] **Ringo!** [screams] **George!** [screams] **John!** Then, under John's picture, **"Sorry Girls, He's Married"** [a mixed audience reaction with some disappointed sighs]. I was not affected by John's marital status, as Paul was now my man.

The boys tore into "She Loves You."

And I do you, Paul.

Paul was so cute. He had dreamy eyes and a darling smile. He dressed modishly and neatly in his tailored suit. He had "personality." You could tell he could charm the leaves from the trees. I even loved the way he bowed along with his mates. His bow was energized and palace-level. In the interviews with reporters that followed, Paul was witty but polite, not a smart aleck like John. Paul had class, and I loved his and all their accents. My friend's mother was a war bride from England. I wanted to be near to hear her speak because she sounded like a Beatle.

Fantasizing about Paul became my drug of choice, with the total understanding that it was all whimsy. It transported me away from sad thoughts that were always with me like a heavy satchel toward beautiful, light, and airy scenarios.

I bought their *Meet the Beatles* record album. I also met the Beatles through their songs, teen magazines, bubble gum collecting cards, and TV interviews. Nothing would ever be the same. I entered an entirely new kingdom where my parents could not, nay, dared not, enter. The teenage christening waters of Beatlemania baptized me.

My mental abdication continued. The Beatles offered me a safe passage from the tribulations at home and beguiled me with their sorcery, which held the whole world of youth in its thrall.

I went out and bought black Beatle boots with something called "Cuban Heels." In a style surprise, my dad liked them because he was partial to motorcycle boots. He was the only dad I knew who wore motorcycle boots and a deerskin jacket with brown and white hide on the shoulders. In his style choices, he was "Mr. Davy Crockett Presley Brando." He didn't have a job, so there was no work clothing he had to wear.

I began a pilgrimage, walking unknown teenage pathways, leaving behind my well-trod childhood turf. I would listen to my Beatles album, my first long-playing (LP) record, a thousand times in my bedroom sanctuary. I would dream of Paul, England, Carnaby Street fashions, mod hair, and miniskirts (not jumpers in plaid patterns). I bought a small pot of white Yardley of London lipstick with its rays of rainbow colors around the base. Our white, creamed, bloodless lips made us appear cyanotic to our mothers. We cared not.

I decided to write a letter to my savior-King Arthur-star-boyfriend, Paul McCartney. I had written only one other fan letter. It was to Ty Hardin TV's Bronco Lane when I was about eight years old. I considered him to be an excellent cowboy. I think we sent it to the local TV affiliate. No response.

I did not ask my mother to oversee the international Paul letter; it was a private love affair between Paul and me. I put my letter in an envelope and addressed it this way:

Paul McCartney
Beatles
Liverpool, England

I had no transportation to the post office, so I conscientiously placed all the change I had collected from the prototype of the ATM, my dad's La-Z-Boy recliner, inside the envelope to pay its chinking and jangling transport across the pond.

So far, there has yet to be a return letter.

JFK was assassinated on November 22, 1963. The Beatles' performance was a little over two months later. I was twelve years old. It was as though our nation's mourning young people, so distressed and unmoored by this outrageous end for our charming prince of a president, were about to be rescued by knights in Savile Row armor.

Whatever the circumstances, to be a child in a crisis, or to endure the loss of a beloved president, to suffer a war (even by proxy), or weather a violent domestic situation, is to be unarmed, unprotected, unable to fight back, powerless, and knowing full well it is all undeserved. Relief in the form of four cute and talented long-haired boys from a place called Liverpool was cavalry-style deliverance. We all screamed with relief. It was primal.

My dad took my visiting cousin, Bonnie, and me to the drive-in theater to see the new Beatles movie, *A Hard Day's Night*. Dad liked drive-in movies, but I am not sure he enjoyed this movie. I do not know because Bonnie and I sat on the grass in front of the screen on a blanket so we could rapture in private.

That's when I saw the movie's extra character, Patti Boyd, and her fab hair on the big screen. Patti subsequently became George Harrison's girlfriend; later, Eric Clapton stole her from George. I wanted Patti's hair. I changed the spelling of my name from *Patty* to *Patti*. The world of choices and possibilities began stretching before me like a giant gob of Dippity-Do hairstyling gel. It grew out beyond my part of town, across an entire ocean, with song lyrics dancing in my head about love and Paul wanting to hold my hand, singing to me to close my eyes, and about his desire to kiss me.

My fervent expression of fealty found reward. The Beatles were coming to Cleveland on September 15, 1964, a mere two-hour drive from Columbus. I campaigned with Dad to drive three of us to Cleveland for this concert. I was dedicated to seeing this goal through, despite possessing full knowledge that while Dad could handle the drive-in movie, a field trip to Cleveland followed by an arena of screaming teenage girls was two bridges too far for him. Blind hope propelled me, nevertheless. I begged him to transport us. He looked at me like I had just asked him to whip up a cocktail dress with feathers and sequins on the Singer sewing machine and bake us a cherry pie. It was a firm "No."

But wait! We interrupt this dashed adventure for some breaking news! They announced a new style gig, a simulcast of that Cleveland concert in my city, Columbus, as the live concert tickets sold out in minus three seconds at the Cleveland arena! And it was only twenty minutes away. Amazingly, Dad agreed to drive us there, drop us off, and pick us up. I was gobsmacked. *What miracles lay in wait? Dad becoming a scout leader, arranging camping trips, and captaining canoe adventures?* Remember, my mom flunked her driver's test, so she did not figure into our transportation calculations when we were kids.

Our little neighborhood cohort of newly crowned teen girls, vibrating with unleashed and previously untapped teen frisson, attended the simulcast, which was packed. At the front of the auditorium was a relatively small screen. Our seats were way back in the crowd. The Beatles played on the grainy video picture. We squinted to see. Everyone stood on their chairs and screamed their heads off, and we could not hear anything. No matter. We were sated with adoration for our balladeers.

Unlike some fiercely feckless fans, I did not diss, denigrate, or dismiss Paul or his first bride when he finally married on March 12, 1969. I am my own romance screenwriter and understand the Walter Mitty overtones. Reality bows in servitude to magical thinking for me to process forward, but it does not deny me phantasmagorical thinking. It is a lovely minuet I dance.

These disappointed Paul fans confused make-believe with their personal Magna Carta and rights to Paul's real life. They threw tantrums, wept, and scorned his betrothed, Linda Eastman. I winkingly knew that deep down, Paul would truly love me more than Linda had he met me, and he had not met me, so he married someone else. How hard is that to figure out? See how this works? It's a beautiful thing.

Frankly, I was in Paul's previous girlfriend, Jane Asher's, court for his potential nuptials. I saw her as better suited for the task, being an intelligent and successful actress, seemingly reserved and mannered, and in show business.

Oddly, several decades later, at a flower show in my city of Columbus, I once passed a British street improv group, with the men in derby hats and English suits and the women in flouncy dresses and Ascot hats, there as festival entertainment. They started their routine by pulling me into the shenanigans of their conjured scene. For their act, they named me, the newly dragooned passerby member, Jane Asher.

As for Mrs. McCartney No. 2, Heather Mills, Stella McCartney (Paul's daughter) and I both knew she was not the girl for him. Stella was vocal about it. I was howling into the wind of obscurity. Sure, Heather's disability (only one leg) helped her in the sympathy department, and Paul is kind (I hope), but when she appeared in *Dancing with the Stars*, her duplicity reared its ugly head. Near the end of the competition and needing votes to stay in the game, she fell. I am convinced she faked this.

I once saw Paul and Heather interviewed on the Larry King Show on CNN, and Paul became very impatient with Heather's yammering while discussing the sad fate of baby seals and clubbing. He interjected definitively, "If I may have a word." I knew then that their time as a couple was nearing its end.

In their divorce settlement, Mills asked for $250 million, but she received $48.6 million. The judge said her claim was "unreasonable and, indeed, exorbitant." Stella and I never liked her

The magic of Gwydir (and it has magic, to be sure) spread when we were in Wales in 2011 because Liverpool was only two hours away! We traveled there and took in all the sights of the Beatles: Their child-hood homes, Penny Lane, the church where Paul sang in the choir, and Strawberry Fields. It was thrilling. My friend Anita and I went to the Cavern Club to listen to a Beatles Tribute band, exactly where the four lads played those years ago. Anita and I dabbed on bright red lipstick and added kisses to the thousands of others on one of the submerged club's columns.

It was a trip to Mecca, one of the most significant journeys of my life and one of the first foreign locations I vowed to visit in my youth. We walked the streets of Liverpool, the same streets the Beatles walked. We had tea at a shop, just like the Beatles did. We stood outside Paul's boyhood home, and like thousands of others have done, we stared at it and thought of all those years of loving Paul.

I did *not* stop at the Liverpool post office to check their dead letter file for my post-Ed Sullivan show love note.

I have seen Paul in concert three times post-Beatles. The last concert I attended, about seven years ago, was special because I came face-to-face with someone now standing between Paul and me. (My husband knows of my undying love for Paul. He also understands gambling odds.)

In 2015, our friend Danny Ansel decided to do an incredible act of kindness and bought us twelfth-row tickets at a Paul McCartney concert here in Columbus. Danny knows of my deep amour for Paulie.

Before the show, people hoisted signs expressing their love for Paul or celebrating their anniversaries, and some sported splashy Union Jack get-ups. It had become a tradition at his concerts. These signs and costumes were judged, and a lucky person would be brought to the stage. Unfortunately, I knew nothing of this custom, so I had arrived sans sign.

But what I saw before the concert made me flip my un-flipped hair. There was the third Mrs. McCartney, Nancy Shevell, walking around in our area looking at the signs and, I was to learn, making a quiet choice of who would go up on stage. No one else recognized her.

I walked up to Mrs. McCartney and asked to have my picture taken with her. Shevell slyly answered, "You don't want your picture with me; I'm not famous." I replied that I sure did want a picture with her, and as she tried to escape, I held her arm (not so much held as restrained), and my "Quick Draw Photo McGraw" husband captured the moment.

Luv, before writing these sentences today, I saw a picture on Facebook of Paul walking on a street in London wearing a long navy-blue

The third Mrs. McCartney . . . and the fourth, me.

Mac with a hood and wielding a proper black English umbrella. *Was that a scream coming out of my mouth?* Paul's mop top hair is grey now. I could barely tear myself away from the photo to return to you.

But I want to tell you about another man who gave my castles in the air another wing to dwell in, one that I inhabit to this day; and gave me wings for flight that carry my soul.

Brother, Rick, me, and my neighbor, Linda. The creek also plays a role in a love story.

Chapter 14

2-4-6-8! Who Do We Appreciate?

IN MY early teens, I set my cap toward a particular local boy. My parents' daily living scripts did not have pages containing this *mise en scene*, which possessed an exciting twist. Mom and Dad, daily at odds, had to unite to handle a teenage girl, a particularly mouthy contrarian.

From what I could discern, there was an unspoken code in our house that there was to be no hanky-panky boy-girl stuff going on until the end of time. The precise rules and matters of the birds and bees were never openly and explicitly discussed, so the terms of the transgression must first be transgressed to discover *The Mystery of Chastity Belt Expectations and Repercussions.*

As I entered my Gidget years (she was the teenage surfing TV queen at the time), Dad remained his disgruntled self, and Mom worked full-time at the phone company in the accounting department. Her workplace provided her a haven and an amiable social life away from Dad. All four of us kids went about our childhood business of living our lives, tooling around the neighborhood on bikes and skateboards, getting up games of softball in the street, or playing football in the backyard. The creek by our house became our world.

Then, when I entered high school, it was as if I had sailed into a new world of uncharted territory with its standards and hierarchies of power. Now, Mom and Dad were no longer the ruling class. The high school was commanded by Queen Bees and Jocks and, of course, strict nuns.

Away from the family fiefdom, I was keenly aware of how teens conducted themselves. I learned where my life parted ways (in every way). These rarified teenaged creatures impressed me with their glistening Pepsodent toothpaste smiles, relaxed conversations full of giggles, and perfectly pressed uniforms.

Our white uniform blouses had French cuffs that required cufflinks.

They came with white button ones that I misplaced early on. My cuffs just flipped open at the fold and covered my hands. They were always flapping in the wind as I rushed down the hallways to classes until our hip modern priest gave me a pair of his silver cufflinks.

I became one with my bedroom mirror, singing Supremes songs into my hairbrush–microphone as I dreamed of the teen I wished to be. She happened to appear as a combo of actress Hayley Mills and Beatle's girlfriend, Patti Boyd. The ultimate goal was to achieve actress Julie Christie's hair (of particular note: they were all British Mod Scene Royalty).

We all wore school uniforms, yet some stood out from the crowd. Confidence trumps anything you put on your body, including plaid. The girls' uniforms were designed to keep the female form modest. Some well-developed girls could best that intention. I was not one of them.

The nuns strictly monitored makeup. Light pink frosted lipstick was grudgingly tolerated. Bouffant hairdos became a day-to-day construction competition, though you could get Hairdo Detention from Sister if it were ratted too high. Uniforms could also be a nun magnet if you rolled up the waistband to make a mini-skirt and Sister caught you.

I worked summers and after school and saved money to buy a few things, such as records, Dippity-Do hair setting gel, teen magazines, my beloved blue Madras print jumper (stylish plaid), and my pink Bobbie Brooks wool pencil skirt with matching V-neck knit sweater.

Surprisingly, I ran for student council each year and was elected. Even though I had been a cheerleader on a small scale in seventh and eighth grades, it took *a lot* of nerve for me to go to high school cheerleading tryouts. I was very anxious, so my Pepto Bismol intake increased. But I made it and was a cheerleader through my senior year. I understood these things were early passageways to my dreams.

I recall my parents coming to a game to watch me cheer for the first and only time. They left at half-time. Seeing them sitting together at a basketball game in the high school gym was a strange feeling. It made me feel normal for half a game. My parents did not ask many questions about high school, and if you had inquired of them which foreign language I was taking for four years, they could not have told you (French).

I went to school and work and, when home, decamped to my bed-

I made those bell bottoms. I found out I made the cheerleading squad that day.

room. I had worked summers at the swimming pool since I was twelve and began a good-paying summer and after-school job at age fourteen. It was for a psychiatrist who also made a fortune having his technicians do electroencephalograms in his office and at about eight other hospitals. My job was "tearing brain wave tracings," which meant separating the marked pages the doctor circled, ripping them from the perforated stack, creating a file, and filing them. I was also the evening receptionist because my desk was at the front of the office.

My sense of independence grew with each paycheck I cashed and deposited in The Great Keep Treasury of my jewelry box. I added a second after-school job as a long-distance operator for Ma Bell, increasing my coffers. I spent plenty of time on the city bus getting to and from my two jobs, making escape plans.

I stayed on the passive sidelines of the teen love scene until cheerleading practice one day in the hallway during my sophomore year. The boys were having early spring batting practice in the gym. Before they closed the gym doors for training, I saw. Him. Stand. Ing. There. (Just like the lyrics of a Beatles song.) At bat.

The heavy pine wooden doors to the high school gym had small windows near the top about the size of a shoebox. I grabbed onto the

I loved cheer-leading. I'm top row, left.

narrow wooden trim at the bottom of the window box and hoisted all 109 pounds of myself up to gaze in.

There, with his back to me, was tall junior Steve Brown. I had been talking to him on occasion with sparkles in my fourteen-year-old blue eyes as I had been looking into his dreamy fifteen-year-old green eyes. Next to him was John Nolan, my savior chemistry class partner. John signaled to Steve to glance at the gym window.

John pointed and said, and I could read his lips and body language to see what he said, "Look up there. It's that Patti Wynn."

Steve, holding the bat, turned his head in my direction. I was hanging on by my reddening fingertips, bobbing up and down from the strain of trying to hold my position at the window. The only visible part of my face was the top half: from my snooping eyes to the top of my head.

Steve smiled at me, tipped his baseball cap in my direction, and winked. That was it. I dropped to the ground. I was sold!

The singularly stated rule my father had set, a man for whom rules held absolutely no hold, was that I was not to date until I was sixteen. Until then, I was destined to talk in the hallways with Steve or see him at a dance. Dad came from the bar to the St. Stephen's cafeteria at one dance, where we kids danced the night away. Steve and his best friend, Dave, were there.

Drunken Dad demanded I leave the dance. One of the adults chap-

Steve, center, graduated in 1968. With his dad, Bob, and his mom, Jody.

eroning, Jeanine Morbitzer (mother of nine), knew our family situation with Dad and talked my dad into letting me stay. She told him that she would make sure I was OK. I stayed, embarrassed, but I stayed.

Also, in the plus column for Steve was his family life. It was stable. There were no tears around the dinner table (a dinner that often included Jell-O with tiny marshmallows). They had cake for dessert every night. His parents, Bob and Jody, talked to each other. His dad played basketball and baseball with him and his siblings. These people were straight from the *Father Knows Best* TV show.

A man can only take so much teen pleading and swooning on her fainting couch. Dad relented. Success! I was fifteen and had been granted a special paternal dispensation to date.

It did not turn out well.

Steve and I were back from our movie date (*Hombre*, with Paul Newman, but Steve says it was *Goldfinger*). He parked his car at the bottom of the steep hill, Wynndy Knoll, leading up to my house. Steve and I then walked through the neighbor's backyard and down by the creek. We sat on the concrete bank and talked and talked and talked, losing track of time. We were both too shy to kiss then, so we just talked.

I had no idea of the hour or that a time bomb was ticking. I walked in our front door, which leads directly into the living room, to discover Mom sobbing on the couch while Dad, fuming like a water boiler about to blow, paced, his only hobby. The air was thick with anger.

By this time, Mom had finally passed her driver's test only to be in a car accident, breaking her back. She sported a back brace as she sat on the couch and bawled out, *"Where* have you *been?"* in a tone that made me think I must have been lost at sea for a decade.

I said, "Talking down at the creek."

Dad's Secret Manual of Teenage Ethics proved to have been missing pages. They had never had a child go on a date before and had not thought of mentioning a curfew.

Through gulps and tears, my mom explained that Steve's dad, Bob, had been repeatedly calling about Steve's whereabouts and kept talking about a test called an "S-A-T" that Steve had to take early the next day. They knew nothing of this S-A-T but did understand from Bob Brown that it meant everything to Steve's future, which my dad had determined by now would never, in a million years, include me.

My seething dad interrogated me about what had happened down at the creek, screaming accusations in some kind of Dad Code implying that sex had been involved, while I explained, again and again, that we had just been talking. Repeatedly, he roared, "What were you doing down by the creek?" never satisfied with the universal child's ready response, true or not, "Nothing!"

The time ticked to zero about fifteen minutes into this inquisition, and the dad bomb went off. He pulled his hand back and hit me across the face so hard that it knocked me off my feet, and I sailed a few feet across the room. At this, my mom's sobs increased in volume and frequency. I thought that if anyone should be crying, it should have been me.

I got off the floor in front of the fireplace and went to my room, my now nearly daily tower of resistance. The neighbors had to have been woken by all of this, but no police arrived . . . *that* night.

For the first time, I was grounded from social activities, only seeing Steve at school in passing. I cried the tears of Juliet Capulet while torn from my new boyfriend for days nonstop, sometimes sobbing on the

Steve's senior prom. I was a junior. I was sixteen. He was seventeen.

couch in the living room with my face in a pillow so everyone could endure my misery.

After about a week or two, and it had to be torturous for all, miracle of miracles, I was allowed to date Steve again with strict curfews—anything to shut me up. My dad remained uncommitted to his full sword-on-both-shoulders blessing for Steve. They were exact opposites.

Once Steve and I were dating regularly in high school, I made a request to him. It was Christmas time, and we were in his 1964 Biscayne Buick, which he had purchased from his grandparents. He parked the car for some stolen kisses, and I turned to him and said, "Get me out of here."

A word about angry hands, a loud family, and corporal punishment when The Law did arrive. When I was around thirteen, I got slapped by Dad so hard for arguing that the commotion led our neighbors to call the police. My screaming protests, my dad's yelling, and my mom's keening like a Banshee rang from our house on the hill.

The two officers stood inside our open front door with one hand on their sidearms, and both seemed preoccupied with more pressing matters. I sat on the couch clutching a pillow to my stomach, head down, eyes looking up at the police officers, my heart pounding.

By then, our whole family sat in our usual spots as if we were the Simpsons. One officer asked what happened. I gave a perfunctory, mumbled answer about a slap. Dad, now standing, looked nervous. A handprint was still emblazoned on my burning face. The cops asked if I wanted to press charges. I immediately answered, "No." Even as a young teen, I knew this would cause much more trouble than good.

I learned the stage directions early.

Chapter 15

When Bobby Came to Town

1968. THE WORLD pivots yet again.

The Beatles swan fetchingly in and out of London's hippest clubs. Swathed in their iconic Lord John clothing graced with ruffles and polka dots, their mod fur coats muffle the rumblings of their partnership's coming doom.

The Beatles began breaking up as the United States was breaking up with its youth. I was a junior clad perpetually in plaid in a Catholic High School. As America sizzled with tensions, I focused on politics, the national unrest, and the 1968 presidential campaign.

Boys we knew were shipping out to fight in Vietnam. My boyfriend Steve would soon turn draft age (eighteen). A draft lottery was imminent. Our classmate's brother, Chris Rains, was killed in action in Vietnam. Steve and I each had a cousin serving in this war. Newscaster Walter Cronkite brought the battles into our living rooms every night on the TV news, and his coverage exposed the horrors of this war. One cousin wrote home to his mother, "Tell the guys, don't come here."

My dad, age forty-eight, still pro-military in Vietnam, sent a letter to the Navy to enlist. Unsurprisingly, he was turned down. At this point, he and I drew up unspoken battle lines on the topic of Vietnam. To speak of it would be to fire the first shot.

Student protests abounded nationwide, which Dad abhorred and railed about at dinner. He spoke often of the "goddamned hippies." This was a new course added to our meat-and-potatoes evening meal, where frequently, war or no war, there was an unappetizing kerfuffle. Forget convivial dinner conversation. Ours was a rapid consumption of the offerings; any food complaints were met with screaming harangues from Dad.

Once, I tried to bring some decorum to the table proceedings. I raised my hand to speak because this seemed to work at school to keep things in line. This innocent gesture sent Dad angrily flying off his chair at my cheeky slam of his book, *Richard's Rules of Discord*.

Because our home was not a place of efficient and shared home management, our burdened mom carried most of the household load of shopping, meal planning, and cleaning. The delegation process seemed another stray piglet to wrangle, what with the necessary-to-the-process training, supervision, and our inevitable crabby balking at the assigned tasks. Deputizing kids merely created additional work for Mom.

I never cooked with my mother, so I did not learn to cook. She alone dealt with the basics of frying steak, mashing potatoes, and heating canned corn. I spent most of my childhood without an appetite to eat. Turmoil in the home turns a tummy. After dinner, there was more friction on the TV with the evening news of national events in an increasingly chaotic country, which greatly interested me.

Despite still living at home, I continued to have my private, dreamy, head-in-the-clouds musings separate from my family life. School added another persona, so I began feeling like I had as many different lives as Mata Hari.

Had you asked any of my family what I was interested in or capable of achieving, why I flunked Algebra I and had to retake it, or what time I needed to be at the gym to cheer for a game, they would have been at a loss for the answers. So, I began seeking ways to raise my sails, launch, and captain my ship. *If you need me, I'll be in my room. I am making plans to enlist in the world at large.*

The United States at this time had its own internal strife. President Lyndon Baines Johnson announced he would not seek re-election, shocking the country and dashing my assigned, in progress, Problems of Democracy paper on LBJ's reelection campaign. According to some on both sides of the aisle, Johnson had become the face of the country's many issues.

Onto the political scene came one of slain President John Fitzgerald's brothers, Robert Francis Kennedy, a.k.a. Bobby. A fresh face. A glimmer of hope for better days. He had risen from the ashes of his brother's heinous assassination. He girded his loins to fight the good fight.

The nuns at my Columbus West Side Bishop Ready High School positively adored Bobby. Yet, no one other than Ethel, Bobby's fertile wife, idolized RFK more than Sister Anthony Marie, who taught journalism and oversaw the school newspaper, *Excalibur.*

Sister Anthony Marie, a short nun, was originally from Chicago. During my high school years, the nuns shed their old habits and were now in partial veils, and we could see their hair. Sister Anthony Marie's hair was black.

She knew the eight nursing students in Chicago whom Richard Speck brutally murdered. She spoke to us emotionally about this horrible event. This made her not only compassionate but *in the know* and worldly in our eyes. She did not suffer fools gladly. She had us call her SAM, the "I'm hip with the kids" acronym of her nun-name initials.

SAM would give my classmate Janet and me the nun-tested and proven life-stopping evil eye because of our temporary affection for presidential hopeful and major anti-Vietnam war candidate Eugene McCarthy, who was also running in 1968. SAM needed not have fretted over our misguided infatuation because Bobby was coming to town.

Four of us from school planned to hear him speak on May 13, 1968. That is officially when Irish Kennedy overtook Irish McCarthy in our hearts.

Our merry little band of high schoolers arrived at the Columbus airport to see Kennedy and his contingent land at the then-named Port Columbus. Bobby Kennedy exited the plane, and senatorial candidate John J. Gilligan was there to pick him up. Newspaper reports quote Gilligan as saying, "I never saw anyone who was gathering that kind of excitement," and he added that Kennedy's message was one of "justice, compassion, and the obligation we have to help other people."

I saw an additional benefit to Bobby's run: maybe we could return to the days of Jack and Jackie Kennedy's *Camelot* feeling in our country. Jackie immortalized her husband's time in office as reflecting *Camelot.* She told his biographer that JFK listened to the happily-ever-after Broadway show's soundtrack every night.

We four Bishop Ready High School students got back in the car and left the crowd on the airport tarmac, welcoming Bobby. Next, we traveled downtown to the site of Kennedy's speech. Bobby, Ethel Kennedy, and Gilligan traveled in a convertible, along with others in the motorcade, to the old Neil House Hotel in downtown Columbus.

Thousands greet RFK in Columbus

by Kathy Moore, 86

Several Readylites were among the thousands who cheered Sen. Robert F. Kennedy of New York when he made an overnight stop in Columbus, May 13. Kennedy, accompanied by his wife Ethel and their dog Freckles, stopped here to speak to Ohio delegates to the Democratic National Convention at the Neil House Hotel.

Among the "dignitaries" waiting to greet Sen. Kennedy at Port Columbus International was Mr. Bob Cromwell, social studies teacher, who represented the Rev. Richard Endres, Father had a religion meeting here that night.

Excalibur photographer Ivars Vilums and I rode the press bus, which took us directly onto the runway, to greet Sen. and Mrs. Kennedy personally.

At the airport

Many other Readylites, mostly backers of Sen. Eugene Mc-Carthy, were scattered throughout the crowd, bearing signs. A dozen signs reading "Unity—Humphrey for President" were also visible among the crowd, which numbered between 3500 and 4000.

At the airport, the senator told the crowd that the Democratic Party "has accomplished great things in the past," and "will accomplish even greater things in the future, and that is why I am running."

"However, I do not run on the record of what we have done, but what we will do," he announced. He called for an end to violence and lawlessness in the nation's cities and promised to fight for "equality and justice for the people of these United States." Kennedy was mobbed several times during the motorcade from the airport to the Neil House

downtown. The seven-mile trip took two hours.

'Tremendous' reception

A member of the Kennedy staff, riding in front of us on the bus remarked that, compared to other cities, this reception was one of the biggest and wildest. Later at the hotel, Mrs. Kennedy expressed the same idea, saying that it was a "tremendous" reception.

The motorcade stopped in front of St. Charles Borromeo Seminary, where scores of seminarians, several carrying signs, "We want Bobby!"

Mixed in with the crowd were many well-dressed people, people in pajamas, several young men in baseball uniforms, one boy in a track suit, and hundreds of confused-looking children. One young lady became so excited she literally lost her wig.

Enthusiastic welcome

Kennedy received his most enthusiastic welcome along Mt. Vernon Ave. where thousands of ecstatic, nearly hysterical, Negroes surrounded the car in an attempt to get near him. Hundreds of them, cheering and screaming, followed the parade downtown. There was one tense, silent moment when a firecracker was set off in the crowd. Kennedy made several impromptu speeches along the way. He told the crowd that "Peace and understanding, not violence, are what we all want—black and white together."

Negro reaction

From the press bus immediately behind the senator's car, I talked to several people walking alongside the bus. One young Negro cried emotionally, "He's a wonderful man! Violence is the

fool's way, but he's doing it the man's way! He's gonna win—no doubt about it!!" A small boy named Dennis, when asked his opinion of Kennedy, declared enthusiastically, "I think he great!!"

Another Negro man shouted, "I like him better than—what's his name?—Wallace." When asked if Kennedy would win, one enthusiastic young man replied, "You bet? I'm gonna vote five times!!" I asked one teenage boy his opinion of Kennedy and he replied solemnly, "I don't know—I can't vote."

Ready's band

The Ready band, with also 1000 other people, was on hand outside the Neil House to greet Senator and Mrs. Kennedy. In a short talk from the band platform to the crowd, the senator again mentioned racism, saying that rioting has no place in our society.

He spoke about Vietnam. "I am against unilaterally withdrawing our forces from Vietnam," he said. "But I feel we should have the Vietnamese take over the major portion of their own war."

The senator closed his speech by quoting George Bernard Shaw: "Some people see things as they are and ask 'why'; I see things as they never were and say 'why not?'"

Uninvited guests

Shortly after 11 p.m., Kennedy moved inside for a closed speech to the delegates, who had been waiting over two and a half hours.

Among those waiting inside were seniors John Canney and Elaine Ballmer, who walked in and joined the delegates in a buffet dinner. How did they manage that? "We just walked in!" Also present at the speech were Bill Lager and Terrir McClaine. They had more difficulty getting in. Terrie claims they were kicked out three or four times.

First they tried hiding in a phone booth; next they tried to appear inconspicuous by standing in a corner with a bunch of brooms.

While a policeman was kicking them out for the third time, a lady, whom neither Bill nor Terrie had ever seen, stopped him, saying, "Why are you kicking them out? Those are my children!!" The

policeman let them through. Junior Tom Applegate, with Ivars' camera and press card, tried unsuccessfully to get past three policemen. Finally, he walked up to Mayor M. E. Sensenbrenner, introduced himself, and presented the press card. The Mayor turned to a policeman and said, "This young man is with the press—let him through."

Speaks to delegates

Kennedy asked the delegates to reserve judgment until after the primaries in Nebraska, Oregon, and California. He said that he was encouraged by the victories in Indiana and the District of Columbia, and he hoped to return to Ohio to "look at the record" and see if he could help the people

of Ohio. One man in the audience led the applause, calling out, "It's a deal!"

Kennedy received another round of applause when he declared, "I am not asking your help on the basis that you were friendly to a relative of mine a few years ago. He claimed all he is asking for is a "fair shake."

He also mentioned Richard Nixon. "They say he's the one... One what?!" Kennedy emphasized the party. He said he was very proud to be a Democrat and proud of what the Democratic party has accomplished. "The Democratic party as a whole means something. I mean nothing as an individual."

Senator Kennedy emphasizes a point in his airport speech, May 14. Photo by Vilums

Ready's band, behind Mrs. Kennedy, welcomes the presidential candidate who is still lost in the crowd outside the Neil House. Photo by Vilums

Freckles watches from the plane's portable staircase. Photo by Vilums

RFK laughs it up for the crowd. Photo by Vilums

All Kinds of People say,

Our high school student newspaper, *Excalibur*, covered the event. Some feistier students used creative ploys to get into the late-night delegate dinner.

    In an interview years later, Gilligan said that when they got off the main highway, they entered a neighborhood where the people went wild surrounding the car. Bobby stood on the trunk, and the crowd could not get enough of him. They started pulling him into the throng. A security guard held Bobby's waist, and Gilligan said he stabilized Kennedy by grabbing the security guard. They ended up grasping Bobby's ankles to keep him tethered.

    We teens arrived downtown, parked, and decided to circumvent the crowds in front of the hotel where Bobby would soon speak. The site was on downtown's main street, across from our Statehouse (where Lincoln laid in state in the rotunda in 1865).

We cooked up a plan to arrive at Kennedy's speech by a different entrance than the one in front of the hotel's main doors. We surreptitiously came through the back hotel door entrance and *through a kitchen.* Cooks and dishwashing folks were all around us. No one gave us a moment's notice. We bounded in and passed through the workers to reach the hotel lobby. Now, knowing the wretched fate about to befall Bobby just weeks later, on June 6 in Los Angeles in the kitchen of the Ambassador Hotel, this scene has become an eerie memory for me.

We then proceeded through the lobby amid gathered dignitaries awaiting RFK's arrival, and no one there batted an eye (being white kids in school uniforms, hell, we could have been Kennedys). We waltzed out through the front doors of the venerable hotel to a great vantage point: we were a few rows of people back on the sidewalk by the flatbed truck that would hold our featured speaker. The dignitaries took their places atop the facsimile stage, then Bobby and a pregnant Ethel (carrying Rory), always game she, were hoisted up onto the makeshift podium.

This day, in that year of years, 1968, had dynamic Bobby breathing renewed aspirations into this Columbus audience and the country at large. A beaming Ethel, standing proudly beside her husband, was wearing an orange, above-the-knee, white belted coat dress with large white buttons and a rounded collar. She looked put together in her ensemble, featuring white kid gloves. Her tan glowed in contrast to her outfit's modish, bright tone. It favored her.

Mr. and Mrs. Kennedy were the most handsome and glamorous couple I had ever seen close-up in real life. They were bronzed from the Hyannis Port sun and beaming, displaying nearly a corncob full of white teeth. They had each of us convinced they were as happy as clams to be in Columbus, the same way they would feel frolicking on the beach and playing football with their nearly a dozen kids in the yard at their Hyannis Port compound.

The message I, a sixteen-year-old, took away from Bobby's talk was that *one person can make a difference.* Each of us has the power to start changing the world for the better for ourselves and others, and not only that, but we can and must. He spoke with such a connection

Bobby with Ethel Kennedy, Columbus, Ohio, May 13, 1968. My gang was just to the right, out of camera range. Photo: Columbus Dispatch

to his audience with his Boston accent, and he wowed me with his delivery (and no notes trembled in his hands, as I had experienced giving dreaded oral reports in school).

I have a picture of Bobby Kennedy in my home office. His vision and oratory skills inform my work, daily interactions, goals, and this memoir. He is why I never give up hope, even in the worst situations. He wanted us to "contribute in some way to make things better."

Of that night's venture: I never told my parents about the permanent impressions Bobby scrimshawed into my bones, nor did they ask. And anyway, my pie-in-the-sky talk about changing the world would be pushed away like an annoying gnat. I was now an active agent on my personal secret mission: creating my own life, no patronage sought.

Bobby's running for president and its effect on my parents are unknown to me, but he did not receive the adulation in our house that his brother Jack did. Bobby was a Democrat, so he would have had their vote had he lived.

A few weeks before this May 13, 1968, Columbus stop, Bobby Kennedy had the arduous task of announcing Martin Luther King Jr.'s murder in Indianapolis to a shocked and hysterical crowd. In Kennedy's quickly reformulated remarks, he said of King, "He dedicated his life to love and justice between fellow human beings. He died in the cause of that effort. On this difficult day, in this difficult time in the United States, it is well to ask what kind of nation we are and what direction we want to move in."

Bobby Kennedy, who suffered a terrible loss and resulting depression due to the soul-crushing cold-blooded murder of his brother, inspired a particular regal obligation in anyone gifted with even a fraction of faculty, humanitarianism, and communication skills to work for good. That included me. As Bobby towered above me on High Street, a few feet away, he seemed to say right to my face that I embodied agency and possessed power, and life's circumstances need not stand in my way. Bobby himself had fallen into a clinical depression after the death of his brother and risen again. So could all of us.

The stories we tell ourselves about our ancestors have the power to shape us.—MAUD NEWTON, author of *Ancestor Trouble*

Bobby endeavored to carry on his brother's legacy and vision. It was in his blood. Then he too was murdered, his blood spilled in that attempt.

The Irish Kennedys' service to the country, vigor, attractiveness, and humor offered me a new sense of pride in my Irish Mitchell and Cavanaugh family lines. I felt connected and emboldened.

I learned about Gwydir Castle many decades later, and the same transformation occurred. I learned how influential the Wynn family was for two hundred years in Wales. I may be trespassing beyond my DNA, but after learning about them, legitimate or not, I tapped into that wooden bung of their genetic code keg to empower me.

The Gwydir website describes the Wynns as "one of the most important cultural and political powerhouses in Wales." Just this morning,

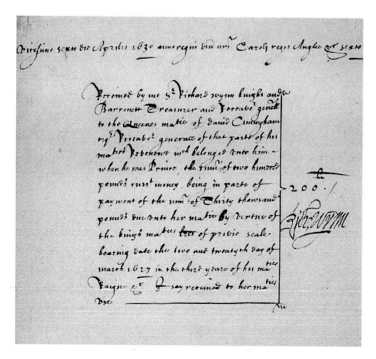

Sir Richard Wynn's signature of receipt of taxes is on the
right side of the page. Photo: Gwydir Castle Archives

Gwydir posted on Facebook a document from 1630 they obtained at
an auction. It was a monetary note submitted to Sir Richard Wynn for
payment to Queen Henrietta Maria, Queen of England, Scotland, and
Ireland, from her marriage to Charles I. Sir Richard was her Treasurer.

Still at home in the summer of 1968 and heading into my senior year
of high school, I would come home from full-time work and go to the
swimming pool to relax in my treasured aqua world. One night in
August, when I returned to our house on Wynndy Knoll Hill, fresh and
cool from the pool, Dad was in a *Good Dad* mood, and we sat together
on the screened-in porch with a small TV and watched the Democratic
Convention in Chicago.

We were both slack-jawed to behold all hell break loose.

Cops were beating demonstrators, and young people were covered in blood and being dragged away to jail. Dad and I watched in disbelief. I could see Dad was torn between his patriotism, due to his service to his country, and his sense of injustice at the sheer brutality of the cruel powers that be, whose motives he always found suspect.

Mayor Richard Daley of Chicago ordered the savagery. Later, a trial occurred with the arrested and jailed male demonstration organizers who became known as the Chicago Seven. They were charged with crossing state lines and inciting a riot. Some men were acquitted soon after, and the other charges were later reversed on appeal.

My own sense of injustice ignited watching those brutal Chicago scenes. Bobby and Martin Luther King, Jr. had been assassinated. The Vietnam War raged. I experienced significant unsettling of my spirits that carried over into school. I began using my humor in slightly subversive ways to counteract my boredom or tweak any instructor I found overly authoritarian or inept. This led to after-school detentions and papers being written on the topic of respect.

As is the case for many students in their senior year, I was done with high school. I put in my time. I ended up in the principal's office a lot for disrupting a class with my idea of comedy or for talking back. I was sad and missed my boyfriend, Steve, who had gone away to college the year before me. I would visit him there, missing days of school. I still had cheerleading and worked after school, but I felt like I was living the *in-between times.*

I wondered how I could balance this new sensation and infusion of potentiality to make a difference in the world and become a visible girl with a voice despite my ingrained fearfulness of public speaking and performing.

The first step toward following Bobby's message of changing the world was to speak out as my true self, not in the form of shouting and jumping as in cheerleading. My sense of inferiority, because I perceived myself to have come from a family of damaged goods, and my debilitating stage fright both needed to cease.

Sixteenth-century table with the lion and eagle carved on the legs. Built by John Wynn in 1590. Sold a hundred years ago and purchased by William Randolph Hearst in an auction of Gwydir items. It was bought for a five-figure sum by an anonymous person and donated back to Gwydir. It is said to be the most important piece of Welsh furniture to survive from that date. Photo: Judy Corbett

Chapter 16

Stage Fright

Nec Timet Nec Tumet
(No Fear, No Vanity)

THE EAGLE and the lion from the Wynns of Wales coat of arms are carved into their furniture and grace other adornments. *Nec Timet Nec Tumet*, I learned in the *Castles in the Air* book, is the Wynn family motto. At this point in my growing up, I needed to get these bold concepts into my life, not just as a protective persona but more profound, into my very being. If I were to stand up for myself and my dreams, help others, and lift spirits, I needed to soar like an eagle and roar like a lion. I needed to conquer a specific fear.

So instead of remaining in a blighted state, overwhelmed by emotions and perceived obstacles, overtaken by darkness and *fear of speaking in public and performing*, I picked up my metaphorical sword, climbed on my metaphorical steed, and gave it all I had. I had to squire through the experiences to knight myself and create my new fiefdom. This bold campaign had unsuccessful and troubled beginnings. It would be a "mouse" that set me back.

Fear has been my ride-along interloper from the start. He is ever the whiner. I must constantly discipline and wrangle him into submission. He controls my body as well as my mind. My "resting" temperature gauge is set at red hot *hyperalert*. My *modus operandi* is to expect trouble and embarrassment if not total annihilation. Blushing is my rouge. Who needs Cover Girl when you're Duck and Cover Girl? An overriding sense of inferiority can bring me to the point of hives. Those growing up in a PTSD-wrought household are more comfortable with the fight or flight impulse than a hug, and we live on high alert, all senses racing at maximum RPMs.

In grade school, we were required to stand to answer the nuns' questions in class. In the scant instances I would volunteer an answer, I would nearly faint as I rose from my seat, a wooden surface smoothed by decades of young Catholic school kid bottoms, to offer a response. Our heavy oak desks had hinged tops you pulled up to store your books, pencils, rulers, notebook paper, and, later, ink cartridge pens inside. They were complete with abandoned ink well holes in the upper right corner. My brain would go blank standing there while I answered on automatic pilot. I would sit down breathless and dazed, wanting to lift the desktop and insert my head.

Even supposedly relaxed surroundings had no positive effect on my uber-buzzed system. One summer, when I was about ten, I went to day camp. On the sole morning I had been assigned to raise the flag and say the Pledge of Allegiance in front of my fellow campers, I called in sick from the resulting distress.

I believe children who grow up in chaotic homes, especially the eldest child who assumes imperious responsibility for the troubles with a faux brave front, often have an inadequate sense of self.

A case in point was high school cheerleading tryouts, where a swashbuckling flamboyance of physicality and charm disguised my utter sense of chickenhearted timidity. My body knew the ruse.

Year after year, tryouts had me captive in the restroom until it was my turn to execute my cheers. I was zippy and peppy on the outside, but on the inside, the stress was coagulating in my intestinal tract. I always made the squad, but my weeks of debilitating self-doubt were nothing to cheer about. Imodium, the diarrhea medication, was my loyal tryout mate.

Let me set the scene for the tryouts. Cheerleading judges, who were teachers chosen by the Phys Ed teacher, sat at a table on the gym stage with score sheets. I am sure they surreptitiously glanced at their watches, hoping to end the spectacle fast and get to Happy Hour.

We contenders awaited our turns in the bleachers, which I would leave to go to the restroom about every five minutes. When called by name, we would come down onto the gym floor two by two and execute the required cheer and a cheer we created ourselves. I would have practiced both more times and with the same intensity as a pianist readying for a Carnegie Hall concert debut.

Our glass kitchen French doors were a perfect reflecting mirror in the evening for my rehearsals. No one in the house seemed to take any particular interest in the jumping, strutting, and gesticulating accompanying my chant of "S-U-C-C-E-S-S / that's the way / we spell success!" all followed by a cartwheel into the splits. By this time, my family assumed I was living on my own planet, and my visiting transport just happened to be docked at their house.

Once I was down on that gym floor, pressure mounted under the focused gaze of the judges and all the other girls sitting in the stands, critically assessing their competitors. Some girls succumbed to nerves and would fumble their routines only to trudge off the floor in defeat. The air was filled with the aroma of unwashed teenage girls, Right Guard deodorant for women, and chalky blue gym uniforms, extra ripe with flop sweat. These baggy outfits, with silver snaps up the front, lived in our gym lockers, often without the benefit of laundering. The garb was a style suitable for prison life.

I had practiced my cheers so often that my muscle memory always kicked in. My mind would enter a performance mental zone. I put on a mask of radiant happiness, the likes of which might appear on a Broadway chorus girl's face despite her fiancé leaving her at the altar the Saturday before. "Presto change-o" visage magic!

Tryouts complete, we would wait a few days for the names of the chosen cheerleaders to be posted. I was always on the list. I loved cheerleading. My uniform remains with me under glass in my home office.

Cheering and executing the movements (which in those times were dance moves, not the Cirque de Soleil

Uniform immortalized.

death-defying antics of today) was a therapeutic release of pent-up energy. I performed in a primal style that resonated deeply with my emotional makeup, moving and shouting without inhibition, transforming internal chaos into bursts of joy. But talking to a crowd as one small, self-worth-doubting girl was a different matter altogether.

From childhood, I had longed to be an actor and performer, and I saw a way to take advantage of this yearning—to turn it into something that might conquer my timidity. Show business had always been my North Star. I decided to swallow my fear and try out for a manageable part in our high school play: the secretary role in *The Mouse That Roared*, which was perfect for me as she only had one line. Baby steps.

Despite my excellent choral and pageant experiences under elementary school teacher Sister Agnes Clare's tutelage, anticipating being on stage brought up cascading anxious thoughts, as though I were in trench warfare in the fields of France in the WWI Battle of Somme, fighting for my life. Years later, I witnessed famous, experienced actors with the same jitters and have learned that this is not uncommon. That knowledge helps me bring fear along like an old pair of socks.

However, I was not privy to this knowledge, which might have helped me on the opening night of this high school play with both of my parents in the audience making an uncharacteristically lengthy visit to the school, something rarer than catching a shooting star in a butterfly net.

I entered from the wings to deliver my single line: "The jet planes are overhead, sir."

As secretary, I wore high heels for the first time. I wobbled as I waited in the wings, stage right, to enter on cue. There it was. I started walking, nay, clomping to center stage. It was taking an eternity to reach the student playing the president. Every step seemed to echo into the darkness beyond the lights.

Finally, I arrived. He was seated at a desk. My tummy began speaking to me about the disaster to come. It gurgled. My breathing ceased. I looked at him. He looked at me. This went on for what seemed like ten years. Abject terror took center stage. My mind was a complete blank—tabula rasa.

Finally, in complete unscripted exasperation, as if he were some big-shot star actor whose underling had dashed his Tony Award hopes, he blurted out his adlib with the exasperation of a coddled and spent Barrymore, *"Well, are the jet planes overhead?!"*

I did not utter a word as I had no words in my mutton head to offer this angry man. I just nodded up and down a few times (acting out an idiotic "yes") and turned on my sliver of a heel, propelling myself forward on what now felt like six-foot-tall stilts, and exited. I think I heard my dad moan out loud in the audience.

The senior boy who played the president ended the scene and came backstage to find me. He gave me, a sophomore, a tongue-lashing. It was devastating. I went out of the back of the theater and cried. Another senior boy in the show, named Tony Policaro, found me and calmed me down. He said, "Don't worry about this. In twenty years, you'll be telling the story and laughing." I doubted his words but appreciated the thought from this handsome upperclassman.

I apparently got the line right the next night of the performance, but I did not know if I had or not, as I had conveniently left my body to deliver it.

I eventually worked out a deal with stage fright. I still have it, but my intricate paper planning for public events, as if I were Captain Sully Sullenberger doing the pre-flight checklist that enabled him to land a plane in the Hudson River, doing many rehearsals to prepare, visualizing success as Olympic athletes do, prayer, and feeling an appreciation for the audience being there, all work to help me perform.

Many years after my inauspicious high school play opening night, I was giving a speech to the senior class at my old high school about where life had taken me and how I had overcome some tough things, particularly with my family life. I also mentioned that some in the audience might have had difficulties at home that they did not discuss with their friends. The silence that befell the space was like snowfall in the forest. It was a soundless nod of energy signaling that some shared this situation.

These students listened to an adult who understood what some were living outside of school and what no one else might know. I explained that their counselor, who organized my visit, could help if they met with her to discuss what was happening. Some did just that.

I could stand up and give a public talk about home problems, the likes of which I had never heard as a student, a talk my younger self had desperately needed. I had picked myself up after that awful opening night and took the next steps.

To lighten our moment for my talk at my high school, and because I was on the same stage where *The Mouse That Roared* had been performed when I was a student, I told the boys and girls the story of my one-muffed line in the play. I acted it out, making the same entrance and playing the president's part, too. The kids got a kick out of it. All high school students know what it is to be mortified at some point in their young lives.

Then, one student raised his hand. He was a handsome and sturdy football player, and he surprised me with his request. He said, "Why don't we do the scene again? I'll play the president, and you could get your line right this time."

I liked the idea! *Reprogramming* then and now is part of my personality repair kit. It is like uncrossing the wires in my brain.

This student came up on stage, and we took our places. He sat at a desk, center stage as the president. I entered from stage right. I walked up to him, and he looked at me. I looked at him, and I said, "The jet planes are overhead, sir."

The audience of seniors who were about to leap into their futures in life erupted in wild applause. The gossamer threads of calm and renewal they wove from their home-spun "trauma therapy" settled over me like a soft blanket of security.

I want to tell you next about another gift I received. This one, from the US government, became my golden ticket into my dream life. This gift helped me combat fear via success and set the stage for future victories. Chasing after a boyfriend led me to it. But I would never have received it if my dad had not been what he was.

In a poem from her book *The Uses of Sorrows*, Mary Oliver writes of receiving a strange gift, "a box full of darkness." She later realizes this, too, was, in fact, a gift.

Judy Corbett's posts about Gwydir inspire me and give me peace. She writes, "I am here alone today, and it's perhaps when the house is at its most mysterious. The portraits sigh: a fly knocks against a windowpane. I'm held in a stone embrace." Photo: Judy Corbett

Co-ed. No more home perms.

Chapter 17

GI Bill Girl

I'm gonna broaden me outlook.
—PAUL McCARTNEY
A Hard Day's Night, film

MANY OF OUR lives enlist scaffolding to make that constructive leap into new and improved futures. By that, I mean that scaffolding is employed to reach the other side to support the crew and equipment when they build bridges. Scaffolding is also a term in education where a teacher offers support with information or demonstration as a student learns a new skill.

From the 1500s to the present day, the many repairs and renovations of Gwydir Castle often required scaffolding to revive its glory. Scaffolding supports our daily lives and kicks the "bootstraps" theory of success into the moat. A person might have contacts to achieve their goals: scaffolding. A person might have privilege that bumps them ahead of the line: scaffolding. A person might have a mentor: scaffolding. A person might have financial help: scaffolding.

What is invariable is that we do not build bridges to the future in a solo act without some means to extend or suspend ourselves. We can't make a pyramid of cheerleaders with only one person. Life requires buttresses. Life requires support. My scaffolding came from the war.

Shifting gears here to reverse. My parents once told me that at the first parent-teacher conference of their lives, kindergarten teacher Miss Violet told them I was exceptionally bright and should go to college. This bridge was so far that it could have been equated with a super space highway rocket ship ride to the moon, and it was nowhere on their radar. It was a vast journey alone to make sure I had a clean pair of socks, received my school vaccinations, arrived home at some point in the evening after a day of playing, and avoided polio, which was rampant then.

Years later, Mom and Dad told me about that day. They said they looked at each other at the conference and wondered how a person would determine this about a four-year-old. They found this information to be as suspect as if Miss Violet had told them I would one day sprout wings or had announced they had given birth to Judy Garland.

This was in 1955. Women represented six percent of the college student body. No one in our extended families had graduated from college. Before research for this book led to discoveries about their lives, I was not sure whether my parents had completed high school.

I had never given college an iota of consideration until my boyfriend Steve said during his junior year that he planned to go away to school. That's when I decided I would go to college, too. It was a dual motive; the other was that I wanted to relieve myself and my family by offering a four-year mercy pass to my parents on the jousting field. It never occurred to me to simply move to Athens, the home city of Ohio University, where Steve was going, and get a job there to be with him. I felt the need to be on the same level playing field as a college coed, even though not many girls in my high school graduating class planned to go on to college.

My all-of-a-sudden higher education zoom-zoom-zeal confounded our high school guidance counselor/football coach, who advised my parents against sending me away. He said, "Don't send her out of town to school; keep her in Columbus at Ohio State because she will likely flunk out, and you will just have to move all her stuff back home." To his thinking, my scheme was a fruitless endeavor.

The counselor undoubtedly had statistics and gender bias in mind, with the cost to our family's socio-economic strata playing a big part. Out of my 1969 graduating class of about 210 students, I am guessing ten to fifteen girls graduated from college. A handful of girls married right out of high school; usually, pregnancy played a role. We had quite a bumper crop of girls get pregnant while still seniors. They married or were "sent to their aunt out of state for the summer," which was the code then for a home for unwed mothers where babies were given up for adoption.

Birth control pills were just starting to be part of a woman's health care. In 1960, the first birth control pill was approved by the US Food and Drug Administration. In 1965, Planned Parenthood won a Supreme Court ruling that rolled back state and local laws that had criminalized the use of contraception by married couples. Frisky teens were expected to remain chaste. Fat chance of that.

When one relative became pregnant during her senior year of high school, Mom came into my room in the morning, sat on my bed, and woke me up. This was atypical behavior, so it set off all kinds of alarms in my head. Mom announced that the wedding of said girl would take place the following weekend and told me, "If you get pregnant, I will kill you, and you'd better come home."

I asked her, "If I am dead, how am I supposed to come home?"

Mom's tried-and-true response to any levity on my part regarding her misguided decrees was, "You know exactly what I mean." I did know.

One high school girl had given birth to a baby and then moved from another school to ours. As the word spread, the rumor mill went into full-tilt boogie. She was doing well at our school with several notable achievements, and her beauty was movie-star quality. Her blond bouffant flip could not be bested. She drove a snazzy, fast car.

One day in religion class, no less, a girl I had always detested outed the transfer student in front of our class, exposing her out-of-wedlock baby secret. The mortified student ran out of the classroom in tears. I followed her to the restroom and tried to console her. That was the meanest mean girl meanness I have ever witnessed to this very day.

Surprisingly, Dad offered assistance when I said I wanted to attend Ohio University. I accepted his helping framework through the Veteran's Administration and the GI Bill: as his daughter, I qualified.

Mom was unhappy to hear that Dad discovered during one of his VA hospitalizations that the children of WWII disabled vets could receive tuition money the same as military service people. Mom's goal was to keep me strapped to my after-school job at the phone company switchboard for thirty years, bubble-wrapped in job security, tied up with a retirement-plan bow, independent of a man.

My decision to go to college cold-cocked Mom and shook her world-view, draped as it was in perilous uncertainty and struggle. Joining the circus would have made more sense to her because I would be paid, given costumes, and provided all the cotton candy I could eat.

Uncharacteristically and startlingly, my newly announced life goal intrigued my father, who had never taken much interest in my education. He also inexplicably shed his paternal armor. He had ever been *en guarde* against marauding boys, who were eternally up to no good in his thinking—and at college, they would be out of shotgun range.

I was attending the same school as his nemesis, my boyfriend Steve, a fact that also received a pass through his front line of defense. (Any boy who dated his two daughters was guilty until proven innocent, a verdict none ever achieved.) Following my boyfriend was, at this time, my never-spoken primary collegiate goal.

Dad pursued this college tuition opportunity like a mechanic drawing plans (a brief job he held after the war) with unusual attention to details, timelines, forms, and required information. Did he want me out of the house to eliminate a sparring partner? Did he remember what Miss Violet had said in 1955? Did he always see me as smart as well as a smart-ass? Did he want to do something good for a daughter? Was he doing it to spite Mom? Who knows? But as I had observed over the years, he was a master at working the system. His specialty was the art of malarkey and finding a way around bureaucracy and authorities. It was his sport.

The scaffolded base from which to spread my wings and build a life was ready to reach new heights as I traveled with Dad to meet my destiny. I did not talk about Miss Violet or her kindergarten-era prediction during the drive to Cincinnati in 1969, late in my high school senior year. There, I would have my GI Bill interview and take the accompanying required test at the Veteran's Administration building. Still, I was thinking about her: Miss Violet's abilities as a seer occupied my mind.

In addition to kindergarten-memory-lane thoughts on the drive,

I could have continued working a switchboard for the next thirty years, awaiting my gold watch.

I wondered what questions would be asked and what sort of exam I would have to take to gain these tuition benefits from the VA. Written essay? Multiple choice? A physical? Push-ups with a drill sergeant? Would I have to jump out of an airplane?

Interestingly, by the late 1970s and 1980s, women surpassed men with bachelor's and master's degrees and continue to do so. I did not realize I was bucking the system when I went to college. What I was doing was chasing my boyfriend. Wherever he went, I would follow. So, I planned to continue working through the summer, save money, and then detach from the switchboard at Ma Bell.

President Franklin Delano Roosevelt signed the GI Bill or "Servicemen's Readjustment Act" in 1944. The benefits for veterans included low-cost mortgages, low-interest loans to start a business or farm, one year of unemployment compensation, and tuition to attend high school, college, or vocational school. My GI Bill benefits would be based on the Survivors' and Dependents' Educational Assistance Program (DEA). My dad was classified as 100% mentally disabled by the VA. His four children could apply for tuition benefits.

Dad set up the appointment for the test and then drove me to the VA offices, about two hours away from Columbus. It turned out to be an interview and aptitude test conducted by a lovely lady, maybe a

FDR signed the GI Bill in 1944. Photo: United States Department of Defense

social worker or psychologist. Before I entered her office, Dad said he needed to go in alone to speak to her. In he went for about fifteen minutes. In these situations, he seemed to become Sir Richard Leo Wynn the Lion-Hearted and exuded the "leave all of this to me" attitude. He would rule the day.

Dad came out smiling, looking pleased as punch with his royal self. I then went in, wondering what lay ahead. Pages were placed before me to complete, and the lady went about her own business in the same room. I took the test. It was an interests and aptitudes survey, with some intelligence-type questions and multiple-choice sections. I finished it in about forty-five minutes and handed it to the presiding female representative of the VA. I joined my dad in the reception area and awaited my results.

The testing lady came out and had me go in again alone.

She was in her late twenties or early thirties, stylishly dressed in a pencil skirt, with modern hair, tasteful make-up, and a pretty smile. She seemed interested in her work and tuned in to me. She had presence. She rested her arms on the desk in an "I'm gonna level with you, Sis" position. I must have flunked the aptitude test because of *what?* Having no aptitude for anything? Is that a thing?

The woman looked me straight in the eyes and began. She was direct but empathetic.

"Your father is very concerned that you are going away to college *only* to be with your boyfriend, but he believes you would do very well in school."

Oh, so that was what his private audience was about.

I, of course, skilled in my own measures of malarkey, assured her that solely going to school to follow Steve was not the case, even though it precisely was.

She added, "But you are intelligent and would be successful in college. Your dad thinks so, too. Do you know your number one vocation on the aptitude test?"

I did not have a clue.

She said, "A Catholic nun." (*Well, that ship had sailed.*)

I asked, "What was number two."

She answered, "A speech therapist."

Bingo. Speech therapist it was.

At seventeen, I would go away to college. During the first quarter of my freshman year, I made the Dean's List. The university mailed the good news to my parents in very formal language on fine, quality university letterhead, signed by the Dean of the College of Communication. I was the first in my family, including nineteen first cousins, to go to college, so the university practices were new to all of us.

Upon receiving the letter but not quite comprehending its actual message, my mother splurged on a long-distance person-to-person call to me. Naturally, I assumed someone had died. She began the conversation by admonishing me for whatever college misdeeds had brought me to the Dean's attention, requiring him to write to her in the form of this regal letter. She was gravely disappointed but not in the least surprised.

I had to give her a "whoa, Nelly" and explain the letter's true intent. She had assumed the Dean's List consisted of people who misbehaved rather than those with excellent grades.

I liked college, which was a good thing, too, because when I arrived there, my boyfriend was having such a blast that his time with me was limited. In a year, he broke up with me at lunch one day, saying, "I want to sow my wild oats." He used those exact words. We remained broken up for a year. Someday, we can discuss this over a beer. I dated a couple of other men during this hiatus.

I had plenty of time to study, which I learned to do for the first time. My dad bought a book about studying from Reader's Digest. I read the book. It made sense to me, and I adopted the techniques. It also helped me with my prep work later for my one-woman shows.

I worked tirelessly to become a standard bearer of academic excellence. I was a slow reader, so with pages and pages of reading assignments, I would need to study for about four hours daily. I took copious and meticulously outlined class notes that I would practice writing from memory repeatedly, one of the *Digest* study book's suggestions. (I remain a "slow study.") I outlined the chapters I read, too, and practiced those notes. I always told people who wondered about my good grades that I started studying for finals on the first day of class. I never procrastinated. I did everything the nuns had taught me, at long last.

When I returned to high school for a football game, I ensured my high school guidance counselor received the good news of my freshman-year academic success. The language I used to inform him was, how shall I put it?. . such that both Miss Violet and the nuns would have blanched.

However, my first year at Ohio University would end prematurely, abruptly, and violently, and the world was watching.

Chapter 18

OU Is Not Your Mother

THE WORST thing that could befall me in my late teen life, according to my parents, was *pregnancy,* which, in Mom and Dad's minds, hung over my head like a guillotine blade. On the methods of how to become pregnant or, much more importantly, not to become pregnant, they remained mute. I was playing Maternity Roulette.

We had no sex education at home other than observing the more fertile assortment of relatives becoming pregnant. Considering the fruitfulness of just my maternal line, Mother Nature views our lot as prime real estate.

The Cavanaugh side of the family. Not all the cousins were born yet.

At school, the only sex education I received was the day Sister Alex-anne, an Algebra teacher, herded all the female high school students into the school gym. This Vague Event was proclaimed to us in home-room . . . Be there! NO BOYS ALLOWED.

The reel-to-reel film projector threatened enlightenment in the mid-dle aisle of riveted girls in rows of folding chairs on the gym's wooden floor. We flanked this soon-to-be-revealed mystery in hushed platoons. Sister flipped the switch on the side of the grey metal machine, and the rat-a-tat-tat of the unspooling plastic and silver film began to chitter out its volumes of misinformation, whirling in a ray of light teeming with little specks of dust. Our single high school sex education class was a movie solely about the gross and putrid diseases of syphilis and gonorrhea. Not helpful.

Steve and I had entered the forbidden zone of chocolate milk bottle-level sin (see previous chapter on sins explained with milk bottles), a.k.a. in this case, sex, and although I had no clue about the prescribed procedures, I was a natural. I was following his lead and even ad-lib-bing. From where his knowledge was derived was unknown since we were both in virgin territory.

The nuns taught us to be good researchers, so Steve purchased a book about sex at the drug store to bring me up to snuff and to sort through his own trove of unreliable playground gossip. He picked me up in his family's car with this paperback book on the dashboard. We drove to the park. This was the same park where my dad had taught me to swing on the giant swing set and ride a bike. Steve and I sat in the parking lot and read the book. It was enlightening.

A couple of years later, on my first gynecologist visit, the doctor asked about my sexual activity; I replied, in all honesty, "Only on spe-cial occasions."

With my newfound carnal wisdom derived from a celibate nun and a dime store paperback, I cast off for college in Southern Ohio, seven-ty-five miles away, at age seventeen. I had never been out of the state of Ohio. I was still afraid of the dark. But I'd already arranged it so that my home hours were minimal and my interactions with Dad were few.

I had worked summers since I was twelve; I had gone to school, worked my junior and senior years of high school, and been with my boyfriend Steve at other times. I had become Her Ladyship in my personal Age of Enlightenment, navigating by the seat of my pantaloons.

Goodbye, Columbus. Goodbye, Mom and Dad. Undoubtedly, my departure came as some relief to them, as they were no longer responsible for rebellious and obstinate me. They entrusted my care to the university, which possessed the legal authority in loco parentis. That is, legally, the university became our parents.

"Mom and Dad" Ohio U. was strict in the Fall of 1969, which might confound readers who assume everyone was a hippie. Female students still had what was titled "Hours." Women had curfews and violations, which resulted in detention on dorm weekends. On Sundays, they were to dress nicely for lunch in church clothes, for instance, an A-line skirt and blouse or a shift dress, à la Jackie Kennedy. Men were not permitted upstairs into our rooms. They called from the lobby for ladies to swan down the stairs like princesses headed to the ball. Women and men could sit together in the "parlor" area of the dorm, but No PDA (public display of affection).

The university had guidelines regarding ladylike behavior. Ladies were not to complain. Ladies had to sign out for the weekends and, God forbid, never to a motel. Destinations had to be specified and approved. A live-in Resident Director oversaw the woman's "dorm family." That person doled out detentions for infractions.

According to Ohio University's *Arts and Sciences Forum*, due to severely limited library curfews, women were prevented from accessing the benefits of a whole education. They were also not allowed to participate fully in student government. Females were deemed "not quite adult or able to make their own decisions."[†]

Then, this started happening: The article states, "But while women students participated in these demonstrations, their dress and movements were strictly circumscribed by university rules."[‡] Women on campus began to engage in civil disobedience: breaking the rules.

[†] "OU Is Not Your Mother," The College of Arts and Sciences Forum Newsletter, Ohio University, October 1, 2013, https://www.ohio-forum.com/2013/10/ou-is-not-your-mother-oct-24/.
[‡] "OU Is Not Your Mother"

Most of the people in this photograph are male students who are standing up for women who would be punished for participating in this type of protest. Photo: OU Post

By the 1969–70 school year's end, from the battlements of cultural and political change, those old ways died in skirmishes, fights, fires, and shootings on picturesque college greens and in the takeovers of hallowed halls of administration buildings. The war in Vietnam, armed soldiers on campuses, protests for civil rights, the destruction of property by rioting students, and gunshots fired by the US National Guard spread discontent and rebellion across University Land, USA. The era of university-enforced Victorian manners and propriety ended its reign in public schools.

Here is how that fateful freshman year started: September 1969, Athens, Ohio. My parents drove me to Athens in the station wagon, with my stuff in the back of the car. I would exchange my blond wood desk control center for a metal desk next to my dorm window, the better for dreaming of new lands to build.

The custodial baton pass from parents to the university for this woman-child coed began on a bright morning under a sky colored Mediterranean Sea blue. I lived in an apartment in Columbus all summer with my high school friend. I had escaped home early while working my phone company switchboard job.

I still had a foot in each world, but even with my declaration of teen independence from the fiefdom of my home, my parents took the traditional turn of moving me into my dorm. Upon arriving on campus, we drove by the central college green and beheld a contrasting confluence of hair and fashion.

Traditionally dressed students with books and spiral notebooks in arms (no backpacks then) walked the crisscross sidewalks of the central college green in the fashions of the time: women in Bermuda shorts or slacks with bobbed hair, men in Madras shirts tucked into chino khaki pants. But relative newcomers were mixed into this rite of passage wearing their ceremonial garb: rag-tag hippies.

Dad took one look at the hippies in torn and patched bell-bottom jeans, with long straggly hair, lounging about on the war monument, smoking pot, and sporting t-shirts with peace signs emblazoned on them and had a volcanic conniption.

He wasn't going to allow me to leave the car. After much shouting, I finally won the day with, "Dad, I *promise* I will NOT become a hippie!"

College moving-in day was a breeze compared to these times with TVs, refrigerators, coordinated home décor, bed-desk IKEA constructions, mounds of clothes, shoes, and microwaves.

Our dorms had one TV in the lounge, which required the highest order of persuasive skills for negotiations over the three available channels, especially for soap operas of choice. Any food needing to be stored cold wasn't purchased until winter, so it could be placed outside on the windowsill.

Mom, Dad, and I unloaded everything into my spartan dorm room that could double as a nun's cell. I gave my goodbyes. I did not cry, but I did feel something like a release from my old home to my new one. When Mom and Dad poured back in the station wagon, my mom shouted out the car window, "I never did get to see the school!" Of course, "the school" was the collection of buildings around her. This was news to Mom, who had never looked at a brochure, let alone attended college. I could hear Dad's last words through his open window, which billowed Camel cigarette smoke as they pulled out of sight, "Goddamned hippies."

Fall of 1969–70 of my first year at Ohio University—Tiffin Hall with girls on our floor.

Classes began, and the time came for my first ordeal: standing in line at the office for my GI Bill tuition check. On this occasion, which was a pivotal day for me, I had on a yellow scooter skirt (half skirt/half shorts), a matching yellow triangle-shaped head scarf (tiny daisies lined the edges) that was tied at the back under my hair, a white t-shirt, and blue strap Dr. Scholl's wooden sandals. I weighed about 109 pounds and was 5'6" tall. I still ratted my hair at the crown of my head. That Supremes bouffant hair trend would soon pass.

All these silent men engrossed in their thoughts were lined up with me for their GI Bill checks. They were rugged-looking guys, like TV cowboys who rode the range, and older than the average college students. Some wore army jackets with their last names stenciled across the front pocket. A few had long hair, and one sported a red bandanna, but it was rolled and tied around his head like a crown.

The group's dead silence struck me: they were worn from tilting at windmills in the fog of war and, in the way of knight-errant Don Quixote, withstanding suffering each in his own manner and with varying levels of success. Their vibe filled me with empathy. It was familiar.

There were no other women in the line that day. I was still a teenager, a girl surrounded by men who had seen things I hoped I would never know. Most of them were home from the Vietnam War. I felt unworthy of receiving this government money in their presence. They had earned their tuition money, whereas I was one step removed. It felt like nepotism.

I silently surveyed the men and wondered if they suffered as Dad suffered. At that moment, one of the men in front of me in line turned around with a puzzled face, and he hesitantly asked, "Uh, hi, my name is Stan. Were . . . were you in Vietnam?"

My answer was rehearsed, "No, my dad is mentally ill from WWII, and I can have the GI Bill too."

I had created this pat phrase because I knew I needed to collect my compensation in public and possibly even explain this resource to my dorm mates. I knew I would look out of place in the check recipient line. I knew I would need to explain why I qualified for this money. I considered that sentence was all anyone needed to know. The check helped me attend school but also kept me chained to shame.

This former Vietnam War soldier understood precisely what I experienced from those few words. I did not need to say anything more than that for him to grasp an entire epic and panoramic family drama. He asked no questions. Tall and rangy Stan Rooney took me under his wing on check days. His comprehension sheltered me as though he had thrown his body on top of mine in a missile attack of my imagination.

It was a comforting connection, one I've never forgotten. Some months later, the government office started mailing our checks, so I no longer needed to line up in person. Stan's friendship was temporary at school, and we both went along our own paths. Did you know that angels sometimes wear khaki green?

I went merrily along my first year, attending "afternoon teas" (beer blasts), studying religiously, and never missing classes. I attended football games and reveled in the terrific OU band's half-time shows (during those times, known as the "110 Marching Men of Ohio." Six years later, women were allowed in). I was nominated as a candidate for "Sweetheart of Sigma Chi" (and lost) but found a new world in which to thrive—academia. Mostly, my venture was going well.

Mom + Dad
I'm starving!
PLEASE
SEND
FOOD!

[hair falling out]
[baking eyes]
[Sallow cheeks]
[ribs]
[skin & bones]
[GRAND GIRL PICTURED]
[HAS EATEN A RAT]

I need food to make it
through the rest of the
quarter. Send all proceeds.

Too dramatic?

I had trouble adjusting to dorm food. I was a notoriously picky eater to begin with and wrote this note home. "Miss Independence" still tapped into her parents' assistance in those days. Mom kept it. It was in her things when I went through them after she passed away at age eighty-nine.

Soon, though, clouds began to gather at the edges. There were 17,000 students on our campus. On Dec. 1, 1969, the men faced learning their number in the draft lottery for the Vietnam War. The heavily peopled and orchestrated production aired live on television. I gathered with my boyfriend Steve and his buddies in their dorm lounge to watch the men in dark suits draw the numbers.

One person at the nationally televised event would pull one of the little blue tubes out of the bin. This tube would be handed to a woman in a prim fitted suit who would twist open the container and read the birthdate. That date would be placed on a giant board beginning with the number 001. The men born on that day would be the first eligible to be drafted.

There was more an air of incredulity, with jests and jokes, in the college lounge than fear. Their birthdates would determine who would go to war first should their college deferment be eliminated or used up—the first birthdate was September 14. The room went silent. That white paper was placed on the board next to 001. April 24 was 002, and December 30 was 003. All three birthdays belonged to men in this very room. They were friends of Steve's. Steve was 021 in the draft.

They had likely all played Army Men as boys. Most of their dads had served in WWII, and the war had come home to their dorm.

The men were safe while they were enrolled in school. If they flunked out, they would be shipped out. Before the draft lottery, unmarried men not attending college had simply been drafted. Now, with the lottery, all men would be called to action in order of their draft number once any deferments ended. Thus, many of the men with low numbers began a search for any possible medical conditions to prevent them from serving. The National Guard became a safer military haven than Vietnam. This would change dramatically for some men in the spring of 1970 in Ohio.

Steve faced that "flunking out–shipping out" fear his first year, even before the draft lottery, with all his "sowing of wild oats" and little studying. Someone who shall remain nameless wrote a couple of papers for him, elevating his grade point average and keeping him on campus and out of the rice paddies and jungles of Vietnam. It was an act of civil disobedience on her part. She has never regretted this decision. Steve then pulled himself together, settled down, and began to study.

Spring quarter arrived with the lilacs. We took to the outside like frolicking lambs. But it was now 1970, and campus unrest clouded our days. The conflicting moods had everyone feeling like they lived on the tipping point of a lance. We felt the impending shift toward imbalance.

Demonstrations and rallies against the Vietnam War coexisted in an unholy alliance with everyday college life and frivolity. It all unfurled like the feathers of the perennial majestic peacocks of Gwydir Castle, dramatic with sweeping military action and laid-back teenage repose in a terrifying dual.

The Ladies of Tiffin Hall, Ohio University, tanning, before all hell broke loose spring quarter, 1970. My dorm friends. We had no idea what lay ahead.

OU peace rally, 1970. Photo: Ohio University, University Libraries,
The Peter Goss Photograph Collection

Chapter 19

Kent State

"Four, and how many more?"

THE FATE THAT my parents feared would place me in the stocks of societal shame, pregnancy, did not befall me: no neonatal head crownings for the Wynn royals. Instead, new maneuverings in manorial court brewed. Soon enough, Mom and Dad had more significant worries: life and death. The spotlight fell onto college campuses, including mine, Ohio University, at the cross-section of Court and Union streets in Athens, Ohio.

Demonstrations with crowds, bullhorns, speeches, posters, and chanting occurred nearly daily in the spring quarter of 1970 on our campus in Athens, Ohio, and across the nation. Rumors flew. Reports from the Pentagon appeared to all of us to be deliberately set smoke screens obscuring the truth of Vietnam.

I was taking a speech class that spring after the draft lottery, and I was still in my freshman year. A friend had taught me a trick with a banana: You stick a pin into the banana without piercing the skin on the other side, move it back and forth, and do that same thing repeatedly down the side of the banana so that when you peeled the banana, you had immediate slices!

Public speaking remained a supreme ordeal of torture, but it was a mandatory core class for my speech and hearing therapy College of Communication major. I had to give a speech. The banana prop and the act I concocted helped me.

I wrote a speech, lying for effect, about a tiny insect in South America that burrows into bananas in a straight line. When you peel the banana—*voilà*! You have convenient slices for your morning cereal. I showed the little burrow, a.k.a. pin marks. At the end of my deceit, I peeled the banana with a sorcerer's flourish, much to the astonishment of the class and professor.

Then I admitted I had lied to them. I explained about the straight pin. Our daily student lives, amidst campus upheaval, included many voices and opinions. I cautioned them that in our troubled times, we must be careful in discerning what is true and what is not. As they just witnessed, sometimes we are easily fooled.

I received an A.

During the daily demonstrations, I participated in a peaceful rally against the war in Vietnam. One such demonstration was called a "sleep-in." I went by myself, walking up the hill from Tiffin Hall toting a sleeping bag.

Hundreds of kids sat on the college green, listening to the speakers. A minister was one of the orators, and the message was "No Violence, Protest Peacefully." I have always been a person who requires a lot of sleep, so at about 10:00 p.m., I went to sleep in my sleeping bag under the stars amid a sea of my fellow students.

When I awoke at about 8:00 a.m., I was shocked to behold that I was the only one left on the expanse of the heavily traveled college green. I must have misinterpreted "sleep-in." Alone on the ground, I rolled up my sleeping bag, trying to look cool and nonchalant. I trudged back down the hill to the dorm for breakfast.

My parents were unaware of my exploits. It was like I had moved to France and led a completely foreign life to theirs. Days and nights went on at home, and I was not privy to any problems Dad might be causing. It was a huge relief for me. They did, however, see the TV and newspaper stories about college campuses heating up and students rioting and protesting. This caught their attention.

On May 4, 1970, the Ohio National Guard fired their weapons into the crowd of Kent State students. Four were killed. Nine were injured. Two of the four dead were demonstrators. The other two were bystanders. Over the next nine days, tensions flared, and our Ohio University students and outside people coming to our campus to protest became increasingly violent. Most of us did not follow that path, however.

Students started to avoid traversing the central green, which had been the hub of activity before. Our campus became militarized with

The National Guard on the Kent State University Campus, May 4, 1970.
Photo: Kent State Library

police and National Guard soldiers, complete with bayonets on their guns. It was a stunning and compelling sight. We were all drafted into a war zone just walking to classes.

I returned from class one day loaded with books and spiral notebooks in my arms. I ran into Steve and his roommate, Jan. The National Guard had arrived in full battle gear. Steve and Jan stood on the sidelines with me, incredulously watching the line-up of combat-ready soldiers in front of the administration building.

We were not afraid. Instead, we were amazed at the foreboding riot gear, shields, batons, and automatic rifles. The warrior men had their Gwydir insignia lion and eagle game faces on. Conviviality absented itself. There were some shouts of protest from passing students at the soldiers, but it did not feel dangerous.

Suddenly, at a signal from the guard commander, the guardsmen began to rush the students, though we had not observed any substantial provocation. Shockingly, a couple of soldiers headed directly toward our threesome, and it appeared they were randomly targeting me.

I could not possibly have appeared as a threat—I had yet to say a word. We three began to run and quickly scattered. Jan happened to

Steve is on the far left.
I am next. Jan is second
from the right.

dash in the same direction as me. He scooped me up in his arms so we could get away faster, and we scrambled to a safe distance.

Then, we turned around and looked. We had become separated from Steve. We could see that he was safe but too far away for us to get to him. The soldiers had diverted their attention from now-absent me to a student who had been next to me and beat him with a baton. I am still baffled and chagrined by this indiscriminate aggression.

As our OU campus rallies increased, anger and tension rose and exploded like an atomic bomb, like the kind for which we had rehearsed so assiduously in grade school by uselessly crouching under our desks. The rioting escalated. Students began throwing rocks and beer bottles. Some bottles had burning papers stuffed into their necks and were tossed at the uniformed men. Buildings burned. Rioters smashed storefront windows.

The 1,500 National Guardsmen lined our college green and now also our streets. Bricks were excavated by rebelling students from the quaint Athens streets and thrown through windows and at guardsmen. Guardsmen attacked students with tear gas. Canisters were lobbed back at them. Broken glass became the new street surface.

The *New York Times* wrote about Ohio University, remarking that "National Guardsmen, bullets in chambers of their M-1 rifles, began moving onto the campus and the streets of Athens at dawn after the

Guardsmen on a main street in Athens, Ohio University.
Photo: 1970 OU yearbook

second straight night of skirmishes involving tear gas and rock throwing between the police and students."

Late into the night, riots raged, but I was back in my dorm room studying for finals. Student rioters were arrested, but so were innocent students just hanging out away from all the turmoil. University president Claude Sowle closed OU at 3:15 a.m. on May 15, 1970, eleven days after the Kent State murders.

We were directed over the radio, our only communication source, to be out of town by noon, or we would be arrested. Everyone scrambled to decamp. The *Post* newspaper offered instructions under this headline: "Your Rights If Arrested."

Some of Steve's friends were arrested that night because they were on a hill overlooking town watching the fires. On the radio, I heard their names among the many jailed. It was a long list.

Phone service had been destroyed in the riots, so our parents had to follow the story on the news and could not contact us. If you were a student without a car, your parents had to rally from wherever and enter our combat zone. They had to be fearful that their son or daughter would be killed like the Kent State students and the two Jackson State students killed the night before.

The OU rioting had been quelled during the night. The aftermath required us students, many of us teenagers, to organize ourselves, employ creative problem-solving, remain calm, and think through a plan. Sunbathing and afternoon beer-guzzling teas were the things of our aborted youth. About face! Welcome to the Ides of New Times.

Packing boxes were scarce, and having no car, I started walking to the grocery store, which was a distance from my dorm. It was as quiet as a Sunday in the country, with the mourning doves cooing. It was a white clapboard church bell-chiming morning despite the all-encompassing wafting and choking tear gas cloud from the night before. I continually wiped my irritated eyes with a Kleenex.

A National Guard jeep with two young guardsmen stopped beside me on the road. Their faces were relaxed and smiling. They offered me a ride to the store, which I accepted. We remained quiet *en route*. We were all stunned by the events. Many of the guardsmen were our age. It was an untenable situation for everyone.

Radio announcements in the dorm warned us that the noon deadline to leave Athens, Ohio, would be strictly enforced. We were now under martial law, under the military's control. Ordinary civilian rights were being suspended. *In loco parentis*, meet the new warlord, the US Military.

I remember a song on the radio that morning as we all skedaddled to assemble and pack our worldly goods. The women on my floor started singing it: "Na, na, na, na. Na, na, na, na. Hey, Hey-ey, Goodbye!"

My dad showed up, miraculously, in the brown Chevy station wagon before noon. The local TV news alerted parents to get their kids. I wasn't sure what would happen when he saw the guardsmen in riot gear, standing everywhere at the ready, with rifles on their hips. *Would he be incensed at the guard? Would he ask them if they needed his help? Would he start his own riot with the hippies?* Military Dad might appear, and all bets would be off.

Dad barreled into our college town, filled with gag-inducing tear gas and debris from ruined buildings, smoldering downtown building fires, destroyed storefronts, spent canisters, ripped-out class notes scattered all over the place, and smashed beer bottles. I watched him screech to a stop in front of our dorm from my third-floor window. I tried to gauge his mood with my well-honed assessment internal magnetometer, an ancient device, and a human instinct for survival.

You would have thought it was a happy Father's Weekend visit on campus. Martial law put no damper on this gang.

I did not know the terms PTSD and "triggers" then, but I did understand that the military plus hippie protesters, Dad's war experiences, and men in uniform spelled potential tragedy for his mind. It might engage his red alert siren. It could immobilize him in anxiety and depression. It might inflame him to fight.

Instead, he flew his alternate standard colors of charm and take-charge spirit and seemed to be in his coming-to-the-rescue element. He communed gleefully with my dorm floor mates. And notice he's in the photo while I am charged with snapping the pic. Hero Dad.

As you may recall, my dad could morph into take-charge Superman in terrible situations, provided he hadn't been the cause of said terrible situation. My dad, Richard Leo Wynn, rose to the tragic occasion like a true descendant of Gwydir's, Maurice Wynn, the sheriff of ancient Caernarvonshire, Wales, there to save the day.

I can cite many instances when Dad broke through his depression to swoop in like the classic movie hero Errol Flynn on a rope with a sword.

My younger sister cut her heel off in the spokes of a bike. Dad did not even flinch, put it back together, and off to the hospital they went.

Mr. Eddy, our neighbor, tipped over his riding lawn mower and nearly cut off his leg. Dad ran across the yards to rescue him and applied a tourniquet, saving Mr. Eddy's life.

One instance involved a neighbor who was in his twenties. I had heard gunshots when I was "laying out" in the sun in our backyard at home when I was in high school. My dad would take us hunting, so the *puh-puh-puh* sound of a gun was familiar to me. I rose from the lounge chair and walked across two unfenced backyards to our neighbor Miriam's house. I looked in the back glass French doors. There was a pile of money on the kitchen table. I walked around the house and looked in the open garage. A spray of bullet holes filled the door.

I ran home barefoot in my bikini across the two backyards to tell my dad what I found, and he called the police.

The police came, and Dad and I waited at the house outside the garage. The police saw the bullet holes and had me clear the area. They broke into the house and discovered that neighbor Miriam's adult son, Chuck, had killed himself. My dad stayed with the police until Miriam came home. The ambulance took the body but left the rest. My dad cleaned up the bloody remains so Miriam wouldn't have to.

Did the mundane life of a family man not do it for him? Did he need to be in war-like life-and-death situations to feel alive and worthwhile? Did he have to prove something to himself or others? Was he seeking redemption?

So, there in Athens, Ohio, after the riots, Dad came and conquered. He won the hearts of my floor mates. He expertly helped me carry all my stuff down three flights. He loaded my boxes and clothes into the car and bid a fond adieu to my friends, and the two of us headed home on Route 33. Dad seemed buoyed and confident. In these elements of tragedy, destruction, and outright discord, he became a knight of the realm.

Driving back to Columbus, he just kept shaking his head over the thousand battle-geared National Guardsmen, the destruction, the heavy blanket of tear gas, and the fact that I could have been a victim. We students almost took it all in stride, having lived the past weeks in the student battleground against Vietnam. I also felt somewhat battle-ready from life with Dad, where war became like a daily dose of vitamins to toughen up. In hunter parlance, I had been blooded.

It seemed like all my life that I had been prepared for war conditions with Dad's Hit the Deck drills in our car, Dad's outbursts and violence, the war TV shows and movies Dad liked (the TV show *Combat* was among his favorites), and those parachute seat rides when I was a kid.

Athens had been warlike, but I endured it without much terror alongside 17,000 other students.

Dad had been in favor of the Vietnam War until the Kent State shootings. After Kent State and our riots, he changed his mind.

My mother now doubled down on her bold promise to ferry my one brother, now sixteen, to Canada to avoid the draft when he came of age. We're talking about a gigantic commitment (and a break from reality) on her part as Mom could not even drive a car from the west to the east side of town to her own mother's house, even though she had her license.

"We were killing our own children, and we were killing them in support of a secret policy of slaughter on a mass scale," Graham Nash, of the band *Crosby, Stills, and Nash,* is quoted as saying about their group's song recording, "OHIO," written in response to the Kent State shootings. It is said Neil Young wrote the song immediately after the murder of the students, and it was released ten days later. It hit number fourteen on the Billboard charts. Some reports state that David Crosby cried at the end of the recording take.

My look had changed from freshman year to later in my college career. Some of our friends. Boyfriend Steve as a belly dancer. Friend, upper right, in a Kent State t-shirt.

The evening the university closed, some of us had gathered at a friend's apartment. Two guys with their hands on the Ouija planchette (sometimes titled "The Wonderful Talking Board") were blindfolded. I was the recorder of the letters. I stand by the accuracy, and some affirming witnesses, including Steve, vouch for this happening to this very day.

When the planchette dial had affixed the letters and finally went off the board, my transcription read: "A dying nation weeps here tonight."

Gwydir wedding set-up. Photo: Judy Corbett

Chapter 20

Wedding Bell Blues

I TAKE A break from writing and gaze at a photo on Facebook of the setting within present times: Gwydir Castle, my soul treasury, amulet, and royal inspiration. The space is decked out for an intimate wedding in front of the enormous stone fireplace. Light streams through the lead-lined glass windows. The room is also lit by the fire in the hearth and a five-candle chandelier. Loyal Barnaby, the pet dog, keeps vigil until the love-filled ceremony begins.

It is a welcome vision. *What might happen in this day's bride and groom's lives leading up to this tranquil scene?* As I turn my thoughts inward to my own wedding and all that led up to it, tranquility gallops off like a maiden on a runaway horse. I bid the stillness and serenity of the Gwydir Room to be my Castle-of-Honor as I tell my tale. I could have used the emotional support of serene Barnaby the night before our wedding.

Dad's depression remained, and it would thrust him into his recliner for hours in his boxer shorts and no shirt. I witnessed his entombment in the chair during my summer breaks from school. Still, we no longer stood in for his windmills; we were no longer the uncomprehending targets selected by his wounded mind, and his one-man jousting exhibitions subsided. The Lion in Winter became increasingly weary and psychotic. He still had hospital stays from time to time. He had voices in his head, tales of enemy plots. Dad was known to the FBI by this time, as he would contact their offices with his "inside scoops." Espionage became his mission.

Steve and I got back together at the end of my sophomore year at OU. We announced our marriage plans to our parents on Christmas

Day, Steve's senior year and my junior year. We wanted to be married on March 17th of the following year, during my senior spring break. By then, I would finally be back in Columbus, doing a speech and hearing practicum until my graduation.

We had no money. Steve gave me an opal necklace as an engagement gift. Our engagement was met with subdued congratulations from our parents. They wanted us to wait until I graduated. Waiting, I would not do.

By my senior year at Ohio University, Steve had already graduated the previous June and returned to Columbus to work. I remained seventy-five miles away at school. I missed him like I'd lost a limb. I would need to finish my winter quarter at Ohio University in Athens and survive it. That became a hurdle.

I was in an apartment that year with two other women from a small Ohio town who were a couple of years younger than me. They were frisky girls, no strangers to mind-altering substances of that era (of which I did not partake). They kept them hidden in the egg compartment of our fridge, under each egg. They turned our flat into Studio 54.

I remained a diligent student with excellent grades. This achievement transformed my sense of self-worth. I felt proud. My academic success was the crown of glory I needed, having shouldered shame for so long. I eventually graduated *summa cum laude*.

During my senior year, my grades sizzled, but my body became frazzled. I developed pneumonia and mono from my roommates' endless noisy all-nighters; their friends were sacked out on our apartment floor until morning. On top of this was the stress of finishing courses and planning a wedding where the cake appeared to be a powder keg—the ornament was a fuse, and my dad held a lit match. He was experiencing more psychosis.

I was fatigued. Grandma Cavanaugh advised consuming "eggnog" for strength (milk, egg yolk, sugar, warm it up), an ancient remedy some call guggle muggle. (Recipes vary. Allegiance to respective recipes remains resolute. Ashkenazi origins. Grandma Cavanaugh lived for years in a Jewish neighborhood—it was where my mother grew up.)

My mother, at the helm, managed all the wedding arrangements for three hundred guests in Columbus in consultation with Steve's mother.

I was relieved of duty, and the entire affair started to feel like it was none of my business.

On a visit home in the months before the wedding, my friend Megan and I hopped a bus downtown to a *trés chic* dress shop where the fancy ladies purchased their finery. Choosing my dress would be *my* assignment, I decided. (*Say Yes to The Dress* group voting had yet to be invented.)

Coming from an era and culture of bell-bottom jeans and flowers in your hair, my friend and I settled on a long, slim gown with narrow see-through sleeves, simple in design, ivory, and a square Elizabethan neck edged with little ivory flower trim. Think garden fairy. No veil. No train. No billowing fabric. No white.

My mother paid for the dress sight unseen, and I left it in my closet at my parent's house and returned to college. I don't remember showing her the dress, but Mom must have seen it. In my absence, she agonized over its . . . *unsuitability.*

I now harken back to 1973, when I participated in the eventual *Say No to the Dress* tandem phone call.

One day after class, I returned to my apartment—the Den of Iniquity —and the phone rang. We had rotary dial phones then. My mother was with Steve's mother on the extension phone† at my house.

The mothers were enraged, and my mom was sputtering, like a car accident witness, something over the telephone lines that included the word "dress." Both mothers ranted. They had taken the dress from my bedroom closet to appraise it together. The phone conversation with me went something like this:

Mom: That is not a wedding dress! It is not even white!

Jody: You can't wear that.

Mom: Jody tried on the dress, and it looks like shit! [I have *never* since heard of anyone's future mother-in-law trying on their wedding dress. Never. Ever.]

† Telephone History Lesson: This involved two landline phones in the same house. One person could call out, and once the call was connected, the other person in the house could pick up the second phone's receiver and join the conversation.

Me: [Ambushed and pissed by this abrupt dismissal and violation] That's because Jody is old; that's why it looked like shit!
(Jody was about forty-two or so then)

Mom: We are having your father return the dress, and *we'll* go shopping with you.

Jody: And you need a veil.

They chose my dad for this assignment because neither of the mothers wanted to do the deed since I had purchased the dress a couple of months before. Nor did they wish to face telling me to return it and having me refuse point blank.

Why did Dad accept this task despite his busy work schedule as an unofficial FBI informant revealing reprehensible underworld undertakings? Maybe because Mom knew full well that he knew how to work a system. He would employ the finagling that was his true art, which, with his on-call personal charms, was often an irresistible force. (Going in and out of the Navy and an assortment of institutions is crackerjack training for finagling.)

My friend Char worked at this dress shop and was there for my original purchase. Char called me when my dad came in with my dress, and she sounded as if she were wondering what the hell was going on. I indignantly spilled the story about the extension phone call and my new mother-in-law-to-be modeling my dress. Char said, "Who *does* that?"

The dress was returned. I was dethroned. The mom's wedding production was out of my control. I was sentenced to the dungeon of Athens with no clemency, no vote, laden with mono, and bearing the pressures of pending final exams, coexisting with cellmates still going strong with nightly Lynyrd Skinyrd concert cacophony. I had no stamina. Steve had no fashion inclinations to speak out on my behalf. We had no Barnaby the Gwydir dog beside us. The dress battle was an ivory dragon festooned with daisies too great for us to conquer.

The next time I was home, the Mothers dragged me, the POW (Prisoner of Weddings), to JC Penney's. I tried on three dresses because they made me put on two more after I said the first one was okay just to get it over. I gloomily agreed on the dress they chose. I felt like a meringue pie, all wrapped up in ribbon and brocade with billowing sleeves and

THE CHAPEL, LOCKBOURNE AIR FORCE BASE, COLUMBUS, OHIO

The church on the base.

empire waist. I did not want a veil, but Jody insisted, and she generously paid for it. I raised the white wedding veil flag of surrender.

Dad had access to the Lockbourne Air Force base and their NCO club for the wedding and reception site. Mom and Good Dad would dine at the club often. Dad was a Navy man, not Air Force, but he was a mastermind of schmoozing and connections and leaping over any velvet ropes in his way. The wedding would be on the military base in their little white clapboard church, and then the reception would be held at the NCO club, which had a spacious great hall. The rates were favorable, but Mom still took out a loan from her sister, my Aunt Cornie.‡

I now look over at the photo of the Gwydir wedding scene, the stillness of that room, as though there would be calm by royal decree. It contrasts strikingly with the high tension of the backstage family scene of our wedding day. While most weddings have some loose ends or last-minute emergencies, our "loose end" was an electrically charged wire snarled with family secrets that threatened to zap right through

‡ Mom paid Aunt Cornie back in full for the wedding loan.

the curtain of our silence to the innocent public waiting for a simple, joyous knot-tying on March 17, 1973.

The intricate organization of the *known* and *not-to-be-known* in our home would have caused the Dewey Decimal system at the library to burst into flames with its files, sub-files, and cross-files. The increasing episodes of Dad's mental illness were one chapter; outsiders were not supposed to know but did anyway. My engagement to Steve and the wedding planning, with Dad teetering on the precipice of total combustion, became a new edition.

Maybe if I tap danced down the bridal aisle with a rose in my teeth, I could distract everyone from the Father of the Bride's loopy delusions and potentially chaotic behaviors.

A week or so before the wedding, Dad was back in a local general hospital's psychiatric ward for his depression, anxiety, and schizophrenic tortures. The night before the wedding, Mom received a call from a psych ward staff member. Dad had escaped. Bride or no bride, Mom knighted me in the quest to find Dad. *Where to start? Likely a bar.*

Bars were familiar territory for me because Dad often took me with him when I was little when Mom needed a kid care reprieve. Once I received my driver's license at age sixteen, Mom designated me Miss Pickup for Too-Drunk-to-Drive Dad. Following a call from the barkeep, I would be dispatched and walk into the establishment with the bartender announcing, "Rich, your kid is here to take you home." Barstools swiveled with all eyes on me.

The saloons smelled of spilled beer and cigarette smoke. They had glowing, come-hither lights over the bottles of many shapes and sizes in front of the mirror. Patsy Cline singing "Crazy" might be on the jukebox. There were predominately men there, but they never harassed me. They stayed hunched over their drinks in one hand, a lit cigarette in the other, launching a genie of smoke ascending to the ceiling-beamed heavens.

I would pull Dad off his bar stool, walk across the tossed peanut shells that crunched as we shambled out the door, and load him into Mom's Chevy Corvair with the choke cable knob that I expertly modulated. I would drive him home, get him from the garage, up the basement stairs, offer a push toward their bedroom, and go back to bed only to rise in a few hours to attend high school.

On one *Saving Private Wynn* foray, when Dad and I had wobblily tangoed from the car, I got him as far as the bedroom hallway when he broke down and started crying. He said, "I'm sorry, Trish" (his nickname for me when I was a little girl). This sent an arrow through my heart, and I straightened my spine and refused to comfort him. I commanded, "Just keep walking and go to bed." Nothing was said the next day about any of this at home. We were conquistadors of unknowing the known.

Back to the night before the wedding: Where should I begin my search for Dad the night before our wedding? I called Steve, the groom-to-be, in about sixteen hours, and he went with me, always the gallant knight. We decided to cast around near Dad's hospital. My parents had booked a room for our wedding night at a motel near that hospital. The choice of location was baffling; it was a distance from the reception, but maybe Dad made the reservation while he was hospitalized, having seen it near his psych unit stay. §

Steve picked me up at my house for the Dad Search and Retrieve Quest, and we decided to try the honeymoon night motel bar within walking distance of the hospital. Lo! and behold, there was Party-on Dad, chipper as can be. Giant green cardboard shamrocks were taped to some wooden dividers between the liquor bottles against the wall for St. Patrick's Day.

St. Patrick's Day was Dad's favorite holiday. He would march yearly in the downtown parade in his derby hat, shillelagh walking stick in hand, within the ranks of the Shamrock Club, even though he was *not* a member.

Dad's shillelagh.

§ That was part of our wedding gift, the room for the night. We also received a sewing machine from them. Grandma Cavanaugh also gave Mom a Singer sewing machine when she married in 1947.

Steve and I tried talking him into returning to the hospital. He resisted. He was having a hunky-dory good time chatting with the other patrons and strongly suggested we should join him and celebrate our wedding, which would occur in (checks watch) fifteen hours.

Mercifully, he eventually relented. We drove him back to the hospital and dropped him off. *Would Dad be able to come to the church, as planned, the next day for the wedding AND walk me down the aisle?*

He did. The next day, he showed up, drove our family of six to the Air Force base, and participated in the wedding. In the same brown Chevy station wagon from the day of the university riot escape, the radio played the Tony Orlando and Dawn song "Tie a Yellow Ribbon Round the Old Oak Tree." I sang along at the top of my lungs—more primal emissions.

Dad, wearing his tux, and I, in full meringue, left the side room where we had gathered and walked to the back of the church. Aunt Cornie was in the vestibule for the final check of the bride to calm my nerves and set things in motion.

My mom's cousin, Paul, began playing the wedding march music on the chapel organ. Dad took my arm into the crook of his arm. We were both shaking. In that day's silent 8 mm home movies, Dad grinds his teeth and works his jaw from nerves.

The wedding went without a hitch; only the immediate family knew we were processing precariously. I just did what our family did best: I denied that the night before had even happened. "Alakazam!" Dad was out of my head. I focused on getting married to my boyfriend.

Pushed to the side altar were my worries of the moment-to-moment possibility that Dad might ignite, fresh from the hospital to which he would return still in crisis mode. Added to all the stress weddings typically bring, a blizzard of snow swept the city. The boxes were ticked for fireworks. I rose above it in the billowing cloud of a dress I wore.

Steve and I were the last to leave the reception.

I was a nervous wreck in my JCPenney dress and veil before the wedding. Bridesmaid and soon-to-be Sister-in-law, Becky, with her back to the camera.

Left: Aunt Cornie settled my nerves and inspected my face.

Right: He made it.

In my zone. My sister Kathleen, right, maid of honor.

Left: I danced with my little brother Rob, who was ten years younger than me. I once treated him like a Cirque de Soleil performer, but he has since forgiven me. *Right*: Dancing into our new lives.

After my wedding, Dad went even further downhill, and Mom was done with him. She made money at her phone company job, and Dad spent it. The beers went to him, and the bills went to her.

I had been married for about two months when Mom called and said she and Dad were getting divorced, and again, she summoned me to a quest. She bid me to become the guardian for his finances and veteran disabilities checks. Also, Dad was in debt, and bill collectors would be calling me, Mom said. This new role was non-negotiable. When it came to serious family matters, I remained servile.

"Everything was fine with your mother and me until you kids were born," Dad told me in one of his many angry calls to me during this four-year guardianship, which he resented vehemently. However, I was able to get him out of debt. As a result, he convinced the VA he could handle his finances. It was another grand performance.

Dad started to become more and more despairing, and psychosis increasingly crept in with his depression and anxiety. He left the state of Ohio for a time.

I became pregnant with our only child six years after the wedding. One night, waking me from my sleep, I received a late-night phone call from Dad, now back in Ohio living with his elderly parents, saying someone was trying to kill me and Dad had the name and number of a special FBI agent I should contact immediately to help save my life. He spilled forth this life-and-death information. I cried as I sat on our entry steps, holding the phone, eight months pregnant.

I broke with Dad at that moment.

I told him, "I can't take this anymore."

I hung up.

PART V

Let the Truth Be Known

As long as you keep secrets and suppress information, you are fundamentally at war with yourself . . . The critical issue is allowing yourself to know what you know. That takes an enormous amount of courage.

—BESSEL VAN DER KOLK, *The Body Keeps The Score*

I considered skipping this part . . .

—JUDY CORBETT, *Castles in the Air,* about the section that involved an angry ghost that she thought no one would believe. She decided to tell the tale.

Fear of breaking family loyalty is one of the greatest stumbling blocks to recovery. Yet, until we admit certain things we would rather excuse or deny, we cannot truly begin to put the past in the past and leave it there once and for all.

—RONALD ALLEN SCHULZ

With our son, Wynn Robert Patrick Brown.

Chapter 21

He Fought the Law, and the Law Won

COME BACK with me. One Sunday, when I was maybe six, our pastor, Father Schmidt, had been trying to help my dad get back on the straight and narrow again after another breakdown. Father Schmidt's solution was to have my dad do a couple of readings during the Mass to become part of the Church community through the liturgy.

I was very proud of Dad for getting involved in something normal like the other dads. Our family of five sat in the church pew. Dad rose and went onto the altar to the lectern to perform his task. He began reading the passage in a good, strong speaker's voice, then stopped abruptly and looked up in terror. He said something like, "I can't do this," and rushed out of the church.

I could not figure out what was happening because Dad and public speaking were new territory in my observations. Still, I understood this: Dad had another broken moment in public that would bring him judgment and shame. We knew we would be the collateral damage.

After our wedding, Steve and I made a home for ourselves and had our son. We named our baby Wynn Robert. This was many decades before I learned of the Wynn ancestral home, Gwydir, where Robert Wynn (a name shared with my grandfather, uncle, and brother) once lived. Steve worked in business finance, and by then, I had received my M.A. and became a teacher of students who were deaf.

We regularly attended gatherings with our immediate family. We saw our exponentially growing extended family at weddings and funerals—the only times we could fit everyone together unless we rented a park shelter house.

That was one life track: Normal World. Then there was Dad World. When Dad eventually broke off with our family after my parents'

We are at Grandma Aggie and Grandpa Wynn's cottage in Millersport, celebrating Christmas. This is the December before Dad returned from Florida and moved in with them.

divorce, he headed to Florida to do God-Knows-What. When he eventually returned to Ohio, he moved in with Grandma Aggie and Grandpa Wynn in their small white cottage surrounded by corn fields near Buckeye Lake, where Grandpa floated.

Dad and Grandpa Wynn had an invisible rampart of silent, seething anger between them, which must have created friction. But at age ninety-three, Grandpa was fighting dementia, so perhaps he forgot what all the angry commotion was about. Lately, I had observed Grandpa Wynn being sweet and solicitous instead of stoic and stern. But if there was tension, no one spoke of it. They were walled up in a fortress of silence about Dad.

In the crumbling Dad World, I sat deep inside the stormy fiefdom, listening to the foreboding tick-tock of the clock in the Tower of Inevitable Calamity. But the clock had no hands on its face to tell me when. The clock had no mouth to tell me where to look out for danger. It had no inscriptions to tell me how the crisis might occur or who might end up in the line of fire. It just ticked off the minutes and hours until it quit. And when it did, the giant powder keg upon which we had built our lives, my castle, our fortress, finally ignited.

So great was the anguish of that day for my family and me that, to this day, if asked about it, I'd rather say, "It's too hard to explain." And, when doctors ask me for my family health history and, expressly, how my father died, I still turn the question aside and give a half-answer. "His heart just stopped," I state perfectly truthfully.

It was a dancing-round-the-May-pole-with-bright-ribbon-streamers kind of day. The pink flowering magnolia was in full unfurled peacock-feather bloom in front of the brown brick public school building where I taught a small class of deaf middle school children. I had pedaled my bike to school the short distance up the hill of my street, taking in the fresh spring air and passing the houses fronted with jubilant tulips.

Too often, though, when this thing they call happiness sweeps over me, I automatically pick up my shield of self-protection because it could not possibly last. My happiness scene always has an accompanying gloomy-gowned-in-grey Lady-in-Waiting of Peril.

I entered my classroom that black letter day when dark forces danced their morbid jig and began teaching. As the morning progressed, I was writing a lesson on the blackboard with white chalk when the principal came to my classroom, knocked, and entered. That was highly unusual behavior, and my nervous system kicked into a gallop. He was a former marine with a lower lip in perpetual firm and pursed attention. He looked grim and told me my husband was in the guidance counselor's office and needed to speak to me.

A heavy red velvet curtain closed in my soul. I knew, right then, I understood. Somehow, I knew the dreaded day had come. All the walls had finally come crashing down, and Dad, the siege engine of our lives, had done it. It was as clear to me as that day's fanciful sky sprinkled with soaring robins and as ominous as a crawl through a castle's sewer, the garderobes. The principal's words were searing through me.

I felt like a spellbound, wafting ghost walking the hall toward the rubble of my life. The everyday sounds of school that came through open classroom doors—teachers instructing, desks moving, students laughing—halted. All sounds were remote, from another world. All sights dimmed, blotted out by my heart, now beating so vigorously that it might have been mistaken for a charging cavalry.

Was this how prisoners felt walking to their execution?

Any extra weight of external emotions never burdened the expressionless, duty-bound principal in any school circumstance, including this one. He walked me to the guidance office door. I saw Steve and the school counselor, Mr. Smith, directly inside. The principal, without words, stepped away.

Now, my body began to react. Every nerve awakened, and my adrenaline surged. My body went on high alert, warning sirens blaring in my brain: Protect! Hide! My neck seemed to collapse into itself, down through my shoulders, as though I were ducking from a hail of arrows. I clenched my fists and made my breaths short and shallow as if that would make me disappear.

I braced my arms in the doorway, the safe space. I knew if I went inside, my life would be taking a horrible turn, one there would be no coming back from. The two messengers, Steve and the counselor, were trying to gently persuade me into the room as if I were a feral cat being wooed with a saucer of milk. Steve's face was contorted with agony. The over-six-foot-tall guidance counselor was professional but thrown off his axis. These two muscular men felt powerless when facing me at this hard-stop demarcation.

Eventually, they prevailed. I believe Steve pulled me in by my arm. The door closed behind me. Before a word was said, I collapsed to my knees, losing all my strength. Years later, when I saw the movie *Saving Private Ryan* and the mother collapsed on her porch when the military messengers arrived with their bad news about her son, I felt that gut-punch and the tears again, alongside all those who have opened (or stepped through) those doors.

Steve delivered the news, "Your dad is dead. He committed suicide. We need to go home to your mom's."

In my ghostly trance, I returned to my classroom to get my things. I do not remember telling my students anything. I left them to my colleagues, good-souled teachers, seemingly magically conjured. In situations like this, there is always a backstage crew making plans, whispering stage directions, acting as supporting players, moving scenery, creating character roles, and revising scripts. Mr. Rogers was correct. In tragic times, look to the helpers.

Steve and I walked out of the building, cowled in worry, to the parking lot. He drove his car up to the front of the school doors. He unchained my bike from the rack and picked it up to place it in the car trunk.

I stood outside our car. I clung to his side because otherwise, I would have become weightless and untethered and could have ascended into heaven, body and soul, just like the Blessed Virgin Mary. He hoisted my bike up and into the trunk of the car, then tied the hood down with rope that, in forethought, he knew to bring. We could not speak. What could we say? Steve had delivered the story my mother gave him when she called him at work. Her information was based on initial reports that were phoned to her.

The car radio was on as Steve transported us the few blocks to our house in our single-car cortege. We would grab some things at home to take to Mom's. A news bulletin interrupted the quiet music on the car radio. A male voice sonorously announced a special report.

The man gave Dad's name, Richard Wynn, and reported that he had been in a shootout with the local sheriff and his two deputies in Millersport, Ohio (where my Grandma Aggie and Grandpa Wynn lived). The announcer, having no idea that he was talking to the man's daughter, said that my dad was shot dead by the police after he shot and wounded the two deputies. The news shattered my newly assembled construct of suicide. Now, there was horrible collateral damage.

Dad committing suicide had been the movie in my head, and now that story melted like film in an over-heated projector. New scene, upping the ante: Dad and the police battled. Dad was dead. Were the police officers who were shot dying? Where were Grandma Aggie and Grandpa Wynn? Were they shot, too, inside their house, and was there more bad news to come?

We felt like a grenade bomb had been casually tossed our way, scattering and smashing our lives again. Stunned and terrified at what news might be waiting for us, we continued our drive to Mom's on the other side of town, the house on a hill my dad had dubbed Wynndy Knoll.

I walked in the door. My mom was standing in front of the television and the special report about Dad, and she looked up with the face of the mourning mother of Christ. She, too, seemed to be working on two tracks, reeling from the new blow, and as we had always done, she was recalculating how to handle the mess.

I said, "I'm sorry, Mom."

Reflecting on that condolence, revisiting this ghost album, I see I was apologizing for failing the family after my fervent twenty-eight years of guardian vigil.

What we learned as the day went on: this tragedy played out in my grandparents' front yard, with Dad using my grandfather's rifle. Grandma and Grandpa Wynn lived in the country, and remember, Grandpa Wynn had been a policeman, and guns were very much a part of the Wynn family.

What we were told at the time was this: my dad had been staying with my grandparents since he was divorced and essentially psychotic, which rendered him homeless. A neighbor of my grandparents, a minister, heard repeated rifle shots out on the road. The minister went outside to investigate.

He said that Dad had gone out to the country road facing the cornfield opposite, in front of my grandparents' house, and started shooting at passing cars and a school bus. The minister ran back to his house and called the sheriff. The sheriff and two deputies arrived. They drew their guns, and Dad aimed his gun at them. Shots were fired.

It was two days after Memorial Day weekend, a time to remember all those who lost their lives defending our country. What is overlooked on this important May weekend remembrance is all those who lost their lives due to the fallout of war but remained living, the living dead.

The catastrophe happened in my grandparents' gravel driveway, not far from the white wood-slatted tree swing where we siblings and cousins whiled away our summer days. The two deputies shot by Dad survived their injuries. My grandparents had not been shot.

My grandfather was ninety-three and in failing health. Grandma Aggie was still going strong, having recently rewired their house for electricity. I imagine they watched the shoot-out from some vantage point inside the home.

On the TV news, we viewed the stories about Dad with chest-pounding stress. I said to my family, "I think I'm going to have a heart attack." I did not.

We collectively gasped when we saw a reporter on TV try to interview my ninety-year-old grandmother at her screen door. Seeing Aggie speak to the reporter through the screen door made me want to dive into the TV to stop this invasion.

We still needed to send one of us to my grandparents. My brother Rick drove out there since he was the next oldest of the siblings. I was considered emotionally wounded in action, incapable of continuing to fight, and shot through the heart, mind, and soul.

My dad, "the shooter," became the news of the day and the talk of the town. Dad died an appalling and sickening death. The unfortunate officers became part of this traumatic event, suffering injuries but also being forced to end a life.

Grief for Dad's hideous death competed in a sickening joust with shame for what Dad did. We were reckoning Dad being shot to death, and we were beating off the burden of family shame, a Sisyphean task. Could we rebuild our walls?

In 1980, mass shooters were not as prevalent as they are today. This event shook the corn off the stalks along that country road.

At my mom's house, the phone kept ringing. At one point, I answered it. This was a call from Steve's mother, who wanted to know what in the holy hell was going on. Because of my honed acting skills, she was unaware of the scope of inner sanctum insanity in our family. I calmly told her what we knew; my serenity only confused and upset her. I had spent the last couple of hours engaging my superpower and slowly disassociating myself from this crushing blow.

She asked, "Did your dad ever hurt you?"

I can only guess that she asked this under these circumstances out of the maternal instinct to protect, but at that point, giving her a tutorial on Crazy-Out-of-Control-Dad Times seemed like a burden. I told her I needed to get off the phone.

Even though my parents were divorced, Mom took charge and dealt with my grandparents and the funeral plans. The authorities were bringing Dad's body back to Columbus for the coroner's exam, and my brother Rick handled that. Grandfather Wynn was to stay in the Millersport area at a nursing home, as he was failing mentally and physically. Grandma Aggie would come to Mom's house until the services.

I do not know what occurred between Grandma Aggie and Mom during Dad's plum loco times, but decades of emotions surfaced during Aggie's stay with Mom. The days were not pretty, full of startling outbursts of yelling and crying. Funeral costs kept the eternal flame of hurt lit. The kitchen turned into a battleground.

Our youngest brother, Rob, was in college at Ohio University. I recently learned how Rob received the shocking news. He recounted the experience on the day we visited our mutual college campus. Rob said a woman received the message about what happened to Dad at Rob's dorm office, maybe a call from Mom, and she relayed it to him. He showed me the stone wall where he sat stunned, absorbing the news.

There was no diverting the pain and no sense of control. We were wounded. In a situation like ours, where was the protocol on the flight screen or in the etiquette book—What Would Jackie Do? In the immediate aftermath of the news, the usual casserole gifts (the food O'death) were AWOL; people were as stunned or more so than we were and did not know whether to intrude.

The tried-and-true words of comfort came out awkwardly from people brave enough to say anything because of the nature of Dad's death. The traditionally carefully chosen compliments about the deceased pressed people's creative skills. The coming ceremonies were so fraught with criminal overtones and perhaps liability that it rasped our senses raw, and we ad-libbed like bit players in response. We were a mere vapor of human functioning: a family of gauze at our childhood home, perched atop the hill, gazing down from Wynndy Knoll.

Chapter 22

Tsunami Aftermath

This is a painting by Grandma Aggie Mitchell of her cottage in
Millersport, Ohio, c. 1950s. Dad was killed in their driveway in 1980,
near the white tree swing where we kids would play and sing.

LATER CAME the breaking wave. The mental fortress I thought I had
rebuilt was hit by what surfers call a "pounder." I crashed emotionally.
I took a header. It was ten years after Dad's death. I was thirty-eight
years old. I wiped-out. I went down, and the undertow of the past
made me lose my sense of "up" in the world. The wonder of it all is
that it took so long.

The beginning mass of the wave was built by patriarchy and control.
The first hit attacked my professional accomplishments, which were
deeply embedded in my sense of worth in this world. The flood was let
loose with full knowledge of its impact on me. That much was clear.

I had been promoted to consultant for deaf classes in public schools.
This job demanded much energy, patience, communication talent, and
counseling skills. I had to deal with students, parents, teachers, ancil-
lary services, other district representatives, curriculum, and sometimes

As I said earlier, this decision has cost me a lot of pain. I would hope that you would attempt to consider my reasons and my viewpoint even though they differ from yours, but to be dishonest with you would be less than fair. Quite honestly, I could have written an insipid letter and in subtle ways let the committee feel my lack of support. Would that have been an easy way out for me? Yes. Would that have been just to a person who has merited my respect and admiration? Certainly not.

All this aptly describes my dilemma and I hope will serve as an explanation to you.

The original handwritten letter rebuke. Underlining added.

attorneys representing students' families. After eleven years in that position, I was burned out.

It had been an Ecclesiastes 3:3 moment: "a time to build." I had no idea that the next fell swoop would lead to my "time to tear down."

I had been intrigued and eager to learn more about reading and writing with deaf children, so I applied for a sabbatical to revive myself. I intended to study and write under an advisor at the Ohio State University and then teach at a deaf school in Ireland. Our new supervisor, who had just over one year's tenure, would have none of it. He demeaned my decision as disloyal and dabbled in sabotaging my leave application.

In his handwritten rebuke of my request, this mansplaining administrator spoke of knowing what was "best for me" at this time in his new administrative job, which was for me to stay in my consultant position and simplify *his* responsibilities. I had done just that, in fact, by delaying my initial sabbatical request for a year to assist his transition. It was not enough for him.

He added a threat to lie about my professionalism, saying his initial thoughts were that he "could have written an insipid letter" regarding my career accomplishments. Instead, he rejected my application and refused to sign or submit it. This shook me, then angered me. His high-handedness and his ultimate power over me were like a black thunderstorm over my head, drenching my dreams of renewal and intellectual advancement.

I was a committed professional with a spotless fifteen-year record in the schools, with such scant absences you could count them on one hand. I had worked first as a speech therapist, then as a teacher of those who are deaf or hard of hearing, and finally as a consultant to teachers in a wide variety of public schools. I also taught courses in graduate school at The Ohio State University.

I had been asked to accept the position this supervisor currently sat in well before he even applied. I had turned it down and had politely made no mention of this invitation to anyone. I needed respite, not a new struggle—my stamina vats were dry.

Then, this program chieftain scheduled a belittling in-person meeting with me. He made me feel like a chattel. He alone would decide what was best for me. Dazed and drained, I left school that day, got into my car, and started the engine to depart, but I was so stunned I just sat there staring into the abyss.

I had a *what just happened here* moment. Until this donnybrook, I had garnered only support for my innovative work with the students and teachers in my charge and accolades from my principals and supervisors. I was very conscientious. My job brought me the lightness of pride and helped ease the weight of my heavy, moldy cloak of adopted shame.

As I sat there, the Michael Jackson song "Man in the Mirror" came on the car radio. Michael sings these lyrics in a command, *"Make that change."*

Why not? Why not heed those lyrics and completely upend my career? And so, I did.

I mutinied and applied for the sabbatical anyway. I requested the required letter of recommendation from my previous long-time supervisor and received it. Based on my proposal and proper paperwork, the sabbatical was approved higher up in the school district chain of command. This circumvention of his authority and my spit-in-his-eye declaration of independence did not sit well with The Man for the remainder of that school year.

My sabbatical, the 1988–89 school year, proved fruitful as I worked in independent study with a professor who was a poet from Australia.

Part of my sabbatical took place in Ireland. Based on my proposal to Aer Lingus Airlines, I was awarded a free round-trip ticket to Ireland. I also received small donations from Irish groups in Columbus for this project. Eunice Kennedy sent me a letter supporting my work in this specialty. A Kennedy!

I set off for Ireland and stayed in a quiet, scrubbed, and polished convent on the grounds of the school for students who are deaf, which was offered by a nun, Sister Mary Clancy, the school's principal. We had become pen pals over the past few years, and she offered me this opportunity.

I slept in a small room in a very narrow bed with a picture of Pope John Paul II over my head. I wiped out of that surfboard-sized bed a few nights onto the wooden floor but then got my nocturnal sea legs. I attended Mass each morning with the nuns, and the elderly priest assumed I was a postulant, a young woman in the beginning stages of becoming a Sister. The Sisters showed me every kindness, and I took meals with them.

On my first day of classes at the Dublin school, the staff and students went out into the yard and planted a tree in my honor. The lay teachers at the school were welcoming and wonderful, inviting me out to the pub with them on occasion.

I had the honor of attending University College in Dublin and offering a session on my reading and writing research to their aspiring teachers of students who are deaf.

On my last day, the teachers organized a surprise rally in the gym to say their goodbyes and give me flowers. It was time to leave, so Sister and I loaded my baggage and hopped in her car. She began driving out of the cobblestone driveway as all the children at the school started running after the car, following us, yelling, and waving wildly. It was so very much covered with *Brigadoon*-level fairy dust and loving vibrations that it made a lasting impression.

After a sabbatical, the school district guarantees you a job. Typically, if a position is available, you will return to where you left off, which was usually the case in our program. I returned to my school for a talk

This is one of the classes with their teacher.

about my placement. The supervisor dismissively informed me that no positions were available and offered no possibility of one arising. He said I would need to seek a job elsewhere in the school system. While stonewalling my reentry, he creepily ran his index finger around the edges of his lips like he was a cartoon villain twirling a mustache, plotting against Little Nell.

I shared an overview of my work and travel over the past sabbatical year with him and offered to give a talk about it with the staff. He summarily categorized all my efforts as irrelevant and brushed it aside. He told me "no one" was "interested" in it.

Now a castaway from the program I successfully served for over a decade, I researched the school system position posts. The closest to my abilities in other parts of the school system was a reading program for young hearing kids in a tough inner-city school. It did not match my experience, training, certification, or strengths. (My certification record was inaccurate in the files; therefore, the system incorrectly matched me to this position.) I would need to swim a lake-sized moat to reach these new far-flung professional goals. Tragically, there were motorboats of misfortune in my future.

I began the school year with the best intentions but became swamped professionally and personally. We had suffered a series of deaths in our family, including Grandma Aggie and my mother-in-law (at only sixty-one, from cancer). A former student of mine, who had babysat for us, had been murdered. Our dog died. I soldiered along with my annual school year's debilitating fall cold and flu. I was fatigued.

At the same time, I was taking on a very complex and stringent reading method in this new program for children with severe delays. I was required to attend after-school classes to learn this method, and it came with hefty assignments on top of my regular class duties. I was also a wife and mother.

The staff at my newly assigned inner-city school, whose challenges would bring anyone to their knees, were overworked, disgruntled, and frayed to a single thread of professional frustration. The welcome mat never came out for me. I had no friends there—their staff had circled the wagons. The atmosphere was toxic. The students were transient, and behavior issues abounded.

One day on playground duty, I watched the ambulance medics carry a body bag out of a house across the street near the children's recess area. The school was in a high crime and drug area.

My inner fortitude tipping point crossed the threshold of my, by now, rice paper-thin constitution. The ex-supervisor's retaliatory subversion of my reentry and the resulting gossip about me (which reached me) crushed my soul. The center could not hold. Then, an event ripped me apart.

One day, my student's pre-school-aged sister errantly came to her big sister's classroom, my room. The little girl's house was only a few short city blocks away, so I walked her home.

After safely delivering the escaped child to her parents (who were unaware she was missing), I began walking back to school. The beauty of the fall day invigorated me, but then I was startled by a commotion coming from a dilapidated house up a low grade of grass on my left in this dangerous neighborhood.

Two young men crashed out of the storm door, one chasing after the other. The first man held a big wad of cash. Immediately, I understood the scene as one where a deal had gone bad. The second man saw me freeze on the sidewalk. He shouted, "Get down between the cars!"

I did as he ordered, and in broad daylight under a cerulean blue October sky, I crouched down and covered my head with my arms between two parked vehicles on the street. *Guns could be drawn.*

Then, I dropped flat to the blacktop to be as low as possible. *"Hit the deck!"* My body automatically did what Dad trained it to do years ago.

Here were my exact thoughts as I lay face down inhaling oil and asphalt: *I am going to die like Dad, shot in the street.*

I could hear the men jumping into their respective cars. There was more yelling at each other, doors slamming, tires skidding, and both zoomed away, passing my barrier car, one in hot pursuit of the other.

I cried the cry of the defeated. I knew it instantly. My survival rigging crashed on my disassociation armada. A bullet didn't get me. The entanglement of my emotional past, losses, workload, and professional denigration shipwrecked me.

When I returned to the school, I spoke to no one about the incident. I was still in shock and didn't have anyone to talk to anyway, so I taught the children.

The weeks following saw me cry every day while driving to school, a cry that Niagara Falls would envy. As I parked my car in the school lot, I wrenched my tear faucet closed, stripping the threads of my heart.

One little first-grade boy I tutored in the afternoon remedial reading session could read my emotions expertly. He said this, as if he were my elder, my fairy godfather, "What's the matter today, my little princess?" I teared up.

The October trees had been in full sail autumn colors, but now I saw them in black and white. My broken dam of spilled tears continued for a couple of weeks. Steve convinced me to take sick leave.

I called in sick and qualified for disability leave with medical authorization. I became even more depressed by my decision not to go back to school. I did not want to be a slacker.

Only one school official, a kindly administrator from human services, called me weeks into my leave to speak to me about what had happened to me. She had consulted my files and mentioned my exemplary record, evaluations, and recognitions. She understood depression, she said, because her son was a psychiatrist. She asked me to return to the schools in a more appropriate position in the program the ogre supervisor had deemed inaccessible. I told her how much her compassion and understanding meant to me. It still does.

I told her no. I could not return soon or ever. It would have been like returning to an abusive marriage. My soul had been terrorized. The teacher retirement people had informed me that after my sick leave/ disability leave, I would receive full retirement benefits if I returned to school for two years. I fully comprehended that I had a long way to go to function again if I ever could. I resigned.

I spent the next three excruciating and wearing years in therapy. I felt like I had been pulled to the bottom of the ocean by a shark, and I was drowning and being eaten alive by sadness and shame. The overall sensation that tormented me was that I was worthless, a weakling, and had failed to overcome the new challenges of my teaching situation.

I had never been in therapy before, so the cool calm of my new therapist seemed to be in such an odd juxtaposition to my soggy face, quivering hands, dour expression, and guilt-riddled slumped body position. I had lost about twenty pounds from my petite frame.

We discussed my delayed response to my dad's life and death. I recognized that the administrator denouncing my professionalism had heaped humiliation onto me. Psychologist Linda and I maneuvered me off the sea floor, through understanding the storms of my life, and into a safe harbor. She helped me acquire coping skills by reimagining my self-imposed journey charts. I was taught to reimagine my life script with cognitive therapy.

In war, there is a time at its conclusion called the "aftermath." According to the National Institute of Health (NIH) and the National Library of Medicine, the problems in the aftermath of war are tremendous and long-reaching.

Among the consequences of war, the impact on the mental health of the civilian population is one of the most significant. Studies of the general population show a definite increase in the incidence and prevalence of mental disorders. Women are more affected than men. Other vulnerable groups are children, older adults, and people with disabilities. Prevalence rates are associated with the degree of trauma and the availability of physical and emotional support.

I had spent a lifetime watching Dad fight an internal war that had occasionally spilled outward. Once I found myself face-to-face with the real threat of danger and death on the street, I had surrendered myself to a fetid quicksand swamp of mortification.

The National Military Family Association says that "PTSD affects the whole family." When I was growing up, this fact would not have been countenanced by family, friends, or professionals. It is a recent understanding. Also, on their web page, it reads, "The battle doesn't end when the service member comes home from deployment."

In 1999, ten years into my aftermath, I attended a Patti LaBelle concert. Patti entered the audience as we sang and danced to her dynamic voice. She reached where we were dancing and grabbed my hand. She took me onto the stage with her and kept singing to me. At the song's end, she told me in front of the audience, "Never ever lose that spirit, and they will try and take it from you."

I was to come into the range of more stars. I was being elevated to the peerage in my mind. All those dreams in front of the TV were coming to life.

With Patti LaBelle.

Hair Theater Beauty School.

Chapter 23

Stardusting Afterlife

*One day you will tell your story of how you overcame what you
went through, and it will be someone else's survival guide.*
— BRENE BROWN

A dysfunctional family is any family with more than one person in it.
— MARY KARR, in *The Liar's Club*

IN MY MIND, our family history had cloaked me in darkly majestic
ceremonial robes of self-doubt, anxiety, and hypersensitivity, complete
with an ermine collar of shame. I nearly made a total victory over
smothering in them. I brooded that the continuing setbacks causing
psychic immobility would haunt me forever.

In repeated phone calls, my mother voiced that thought to me, and
I anguished silently about it. Was I following Dad's psychic downward
spiral? I had not read about these studies then, but my suspicions
flowed around another *known unknown*—transgenerational trauma.

Since attempting to crawl into the back of our TV as a small child
to reach the starring characters, I have used their personas and the
people I admire as helpers to my dreams and as scaffolding to support
a calmer disposition. Because there was not a direct link from where
I stood to where I wanted to be in life: no golden ticket, no E-Z pass,
no inner circle around me to catapult me forward at this point in my
life post-breakdown, I relied on therapy and a half-baked dream of
becoming a writer and performer.

I sought the protection and guidance of my female mentors. They
did not abandon me in my woe from the beginning of my descent into
the depths. One advised that depression was like a black dog that comes
to sit with you, and as it comes, it also moves on, like Carl Sandburg's
fog. Another spoke to me of this as a time of transformation and sent
me notes that were jewels in a crown of reassurance. Still another sat
with me in my personal Dark Ages and drove me to the doctor when
I couldn't do it myself.

Naturally, the stars lit the way, too, one being Esther Williams in the *Million Dollar Mermaid*. I *loved* this movie. Drawing on this passion and my own teen-scene synchronized swimming stint, I would envision myself defying gravity and rising out of the deep with that sensation of bubbling up and breaking the surface, leaving the mossy depths in my wake.

Listening to and reading about others' life stories is one of the main ways I keep perspective and advance toward my dreams. I once attended a speech by distance swimmer Diana Nyad. I marveled at her strength and courage in finally swimming from Cuba to Key West at the age of sixty-four after four previous failed attempts.

Aging and jellyfish attacks did not stop her this time, nor did the raging sea. When I heard her story, it struck me then, years after I had quit teaching with not an ounce of strength and resistance left in my body, that I was not a failure. Like Nyad, I got back up and got back in the race. She said, "All of us suffer difficulties in our lives. And if you say to yourself, 'find a way,' you'll make it through."

One way I made it through was to ponder the writers and performers I most admired. How, I wondered, would I incorporate them into my life?

After three years of severe depression, I moved from my bed of tears to my base of operations, a home office. I gave my endeavors a company name, Edgeville Productions, as I was still feeling edgy from anxiety, but at least I was functioning.

Edgeville became my working village. I began writing essays. I started writing one-woman shows for an audience of one: me. I happily rolled along in my make-believe professional life world, being a *nowhere artist living in my nowhere land*, and still, the more I wrote, the better I felt.

Then, I entered the Real World.

One of my earliest essays, "My Life and Hard Times with a 12-Year-Old-Son," won the James Thurber writing contest. The Thurber House people told me I would need to read my story at their summer picnic series . . . out loud . . . in front of an audience of about two hundred people. I demurred. They encouraged. I softened and acquiesced to appear on stage. Then, I began my tried-and-true stage fright antidote: I rehearsed (a lot), visualized success, and silenced my jabbering negative ruminations with positive thoughts.

That Thurber night was a complete success (with the assistance of a heavy dose of Imodium). The audience laughed throughout the story, which helped me continue my quest to share stories that lift spirits and spread laughter. After that victory, I won two more times and retired from the contest.

My first one-woman show, more of a chit-chat talk than a show, was *A Woman on the Edge*. I told stories of growing up, attending Catholic school, and falling in love. I did not have a residency at Caesar's Palace in Vegas, but the little performance piece did well at libraries and bookstores.

Humor, not solely comedy, was an essential element of my stories. Even the most painful situations contain humor, and this was a survival technique in our family. It is also a very Irish and Welsh approach to living. Humorist and storyteller Malachy McCourt (brother of Frank who wrote *Angela's Ashes*) said, "The Irish mourn marriages and celebrate death."

I think of "humor" as performer Jackie Gleason did. Gleason said that if he made the audience laugh and cry, he had done his job. Humor is a combination of comedy and tragedy. My writing and performing allow me to own the hurt in my days and see the joy and laughs. The two co-exist for me as wings of the same bird.

Later, I developed and performed the *Hair Theater Beauty School* pieces for over fifteen years nationwide. With episodes tailored to the audience and themes of various events, I told stories about my life through the evolution of my hairdos. The comment I heard after every show would be from a woman who would come up to me smiling but with a tear in her eye and say, "I needed that laugh more than you'll ever know." It felt like my shows entertained audiences and emboldened them to fight on and keep their spirits in flight.

Through reading, I learned that trauma physically changes the brain.

Visualization of positive images (like I do with the noble Wynns of Gwydir), archetypes, stories, and metaphors are often used in psychotherapy to help a client let the negative go and bring her to a place of safety, gratefulness, and wholeness. These visualizations are said to create new neural pathways. I experienced that physically while staying at Gwydir Castle.

These imagery exercises tap into the right brain, where creativity is centered, and they also help us develop empathy for ourselves and others.

This flow of empathy led me to new lands.

Service to others is the rent you pay for your room here on earth.
—MUHAMMAD ALI

I was diagnosed with malignant melanoma in 1997 and again in 2013. It is a potentially lethal form of skin cancer about which I knew nothing. I just thought they lopped off the bad moles, and that was it. As I sat in the doctor's office, a nurse took my hand while the physician explained my diagnosis, and I sensed this would not be a lop-and-go situation.

I had two questions in this order.

Am I going to lose my hair?

Am I going to die?

The doctor said I would probably not lose my hair from the treatment. He left question number two unanswered until further test results were in. I eventually had surgery, and I did not lose my hair.

So, when I began the *Hair Theater Beauty School* shows, I wanted to offer up part of my earnings. I wanted to do fundraisers for a cause. I decided on a wig fund for women in chemotherapy who are experiencing financial difficulties.

The Columbus, Ohio HARMONY PROJECT choir under the direction of David Brown. Photo: Shelley Fisher Photography

Over $300,000 went to help the women. Their notes of thanks remain wind under my wings.

Even though playful sing-a-longs with the audience were part of my shows, I am not Taylor Swift. *Nevertheless, I persist.* When I heard about a community choir called Harmony Project in Columbus, *and no auditions were required,* I joined, and so did my husband Steve. The choir aims to connect people from various backgrounds and sing, share, and serve.

This led me to prison.

The warden of the Ohio Reformatory for Women was in the choir, and the choir director, David Brown, also started a choir in the prison. I had been doing an episode of *Hair Theater* called *The Hairdo Monologues* and offered to put on a show with the inmates. Warden Roni Burkes-Trowsdell approved.

I saw how the women learned to present themselves confidently on stage, so I pitched the idea of a "charm school" called Ladies of Success. It was a hit. Eleven groups of thirty women have graduated so far, learning manners, how to present themselves to others, proper communication, problem-solving, meal etiquette, and the importance of gratitude no matter where we find ourselves. The Harmony Project later began supporting materials purchases for the class.

The ORW women leave me written messages at the end of class. I have a bulging folder of these notes. Matilda wrote, "This program has helped me with my self-esteem. I feel better about myself and love myself more than I have my whole life. Thank you for seeing me as a human being and not just an inmate."

We all need people who believe in us. As the years rolled along, those stars I always looked to in the ether of my reveries started appearing in my life. Their affirmations did for me what the class was doing for the women in prison. One such instance was when I was working production with the Women's Fund of Central Ohio. I produced my shows and learned a lot by observing my cousin Debbie, a stage manager, at the big award shows in LA. The year Goldie Hawn was the featured speaker was especially dazzling to me as I had adored her on *Laugh-In*.

At the event, I took Hawn to her dressing room in an elevator at the theater, where she would appear that night before the sold-out house. I made an off-the-cuff comment regarding the song "Lady of Spain" that earned me a much-appreciated nod from an Oscar winner. Goldie looked at me for a moment, smiled, and said, "You know, you are very funny and quick."

The stardust affirmations continued big time when I worked with the Queen . . . of Soul, Aretha Franklin, on

With Goldie Hawn.

the opening of the Rock and Roll Hall of Fame. I helped with rehearsals and the live show with performers such as Bob Dylan, James Brown, Chuck Berry, Martha Reeves and the Vandellas, Heart, Jerry Lee Lewis, Johnny Cash, Little Richard, Bruce Springsteen, and that force of nature, Aretha Franklin.

Franklin arrived at the Old Cleveland stadium for rehearsals that warm September day in a golf cart with a driver. She sported a sundress and a summer straw hat with a wide brim. On her shoulder, she

At the live show with Aretha Franklin, her video camera, and my son in the Cleveland Browns jersey. Photo courtesy of *People* magazine

wielded a big video camera, 1995 edition, taking her home movies of this historic rock music event. The young man at the security gate and I greeted Ms. Franklin. I had been instructed not to speak to her unless spoken to and not to touch. DO NOT TOUCH, Ms. Franklin.

Got it!

The guard handed Ms. Franklin her security pass on a neck chain and explained that everyone needed to wear them. I saw trouble ahead: to do that, she would need to remove her hat.

Franklin said, "I am not taking off this hat."

The inexperienced guard said, "We need you to wear those."

We were at a stand-off. I needed to ferry her to the stage to rehearse.

I glimpsed the chain and asked the young man if I could look at it. We were in a crowd of onlooker officials, media people, and Ms. Franklin's ample entourage. Things were feeling electrified.

I took the tags and chains from the guard's hands, and Franklin eyed me. I had spied a tiny silver clasp. I opened it and held up both sides of the chain for Franklin to see. I asked her, "May I put this on you?" She smiled and said yes.

I just barely touched her neck, but touch her I did, with no reprisals. Instead, she offered a look of approval. She turned to me, pointed a finger in my direction, and spoke this line never to be forgotten: "You [pause] are a genius."

My SAT scores do not reflect this recognition, but if Ms. Franklin says so . . .

Writers became and still are a Holy Grail for me. Books can transport me anywhere I want to go and be with anyone I choose to be.

Humorist David Sedaris holds a special place in my mental health diet. His writing makes me laugh out loud like a child on a merry-go-round, and he also understands the "presto change-o" brain waves method to sideline despair. He wrote, "I just looked at my life, decided I didn't like it, and changed."

Another beloved humor writer of mine is Christopher Buckley. Thurber House asked me to introduce him at a huge event. My introduction was seven minutes long, and I rehearsed it for about a thousand hours. The big night arrived, and Buckley and I were seated together, enjoying a jolly dinner conversation.

Trembling, I got up to give my introduction to the smartly dressed crowd, beaming with anticipation for Buckley to offer his address. The laughter and loud applause at my intro bowled me over. It did the same for Buckley because when he rose to speak, he said, "From your reaction to that fine introduction, I believe it might be best for me to immediately return to our table and the many charms of Mrs. Brown."

I tell you these stories not for self-aggrandizement. I share them because, like Nyad, I found a way and "kept swimming" despite the raging seas and jellyfish attacks that life can bring.

Sing your song. Dance your dance. Tell your tale.
—FRANK MCCOURT, *Angela's Ashes*. My favorite memoir.

As a child, I begged for dance classes that a few of the girls at school were taking. The expenses and transportation to and from the studio were not in my cards. Synchronized swimming and cheerleading filled the bill. During my adulthood, dance became an integral part of my comeback plan, and it sustains me still. Rhythm is proven to ease trauma.

I started with beginner ballet classes. Then I went on to Irish Step Dancing, performing and competing.

After those ten years, I returned to ballet and am still taking classes. I have performed character roles in the *Matchgirl* ballet for seven seasons for Columbus Dance Theatre, danced in *avant-garde* pieces for

Under the direction of Ann Richens.

Matchgirl ballet with Columbus Dance Theatre.

the Flux and Flow studio, and played the nurse in *Romeo and Juliet.* For me, to dance is to fly.

I once spoke at the same humor conference in upstate New York as Lucie Arnaz, Lucille Ball's daughter. Lucie is a talented singer and actress in her own right and amazingly down to earth. We had lunch together several times, and I talked about how her mom and dad's *I Love Lucy* rerun shows during my depression acted as a curative medicine for me. Lucie commented that she received letters from around the world stating the same thing.

With Lucie Arnaz and Steve.

Growing up in the 1950s, the *I Love Lucy* show was more than Must-See TV; it was a cultural juggernaut. I still can't get enough of it. Lucy was always trying to break into show business and meet the big stars, and I can relate.

My husband Steve bought a Lucy doll with outfits for me one Christmas. She is presently wearing her chocolate factory pink dress and chef's hat. I look at her and cannot help but smile.

Then came that other booster shot of happiness—Gwydir Castle in 2011. I receive a daily dosage of beneficial beauty and sustenance on Facebook from the photographs and prose of proprietor and author Judy Corbett. These respite moments involve dimly lit medieval rooms with one candle burning, ancient stone walls embracing all its centuries of stories, fifteenth- and sixteenth-century Wynn aristocrats looking out from paintings on the wall, and videos of fancy pants peacocks displaying their flirty trains while strolling through the manicured gardens with pea hens toddling close behind.

When I see the posts, my blood pressure goes down, and my sense of well-being goes up. For instance, just today, Corbett posted this photo of a buckle that she found buried, shallow under the sod, and

Tudor buckle found on the grounds of Gwydir Castle. Photo: Judy Corbett

she wrote, "Just look at this beautiful Tudor belt/harness buckle found in the garden just now, a few inches below the surface. A little glimpse, a little door opened onto the past."

As I gaze back at the past, Dad's funeral rituals, allowing him to sail on, proved to be the ultimate total misery—*eternal rest grant unto to him, O Lord*, but not to us.

I knew I had to do some digging, too, into the truth about what had happened to Dad in WWII to cause his illness, which ripped through our lives as well. Or did the secret stories go underground with him for all eternity? His rites of passage require an additional life story passport stamp.

PART VI

The Revolution of Resolution

All truths are easy to understand once they are discovered; the point is to discover them.—GALILEO GALILEI

In a time of deceit, telling the truth is a revolutionary act. —GEORGE ORWELL

Nothing that lived and breathed was truly objective—even in a vacuum, even if all that possessed the brain was a self-immolating desire for the truth.—JEFF VANDERMEER

You can't handle the truth!—an improvised line from *A FEW GOOD MEN* by actor Jack Nicholson.

May the souls of all of the faithful departed, through the mercy of God, rest in peace. —THE CATHOLIC FUNERAL MASS

Chapter 24

Requiem Aeternam

V. Eternal rest grant unto him, O Lord
R. And let perpetual light shine upon him
V. May he rest in peace
R. Amen

WE ARE returned to 1980 and the rituals of death. Pity we received, but it was no consolation; pity is a soggy wool shawl of great weight that emits dank and sour odors. Sympathy aspires to an entirely different pattern with the nourishing scent of lavender and comforting understanding. Sympathy conjoins and meets us where we are. Pity separates and prioritizes. Pity surrounded us, The Wynns With The Crazy Dad, in a hideous funeral wreath of bizarre, otherworldly, and ghastly flowers tied with frayed ribbons.

This being 1980, before the rash of shooters we see now, people were rocked into literal wide-eyed and slack-jawed shock at the event. Hallmark fails to produce cards with sentiments appropriate for this type of death.

One clueless relative offered this greeting to me as a condolence when she entered the funeral parlor room that held Dad's open coffin, "Your dad is better off dead; otherwise, he would be sent to prison."

I was numb and lost; it felt like black flags flew from the Wynndy Knoll castle embrasure windows.

After the evening visitation, the next grueling day began once again at the funeral home before the procession to the church service. I found a perch sitting on a bench with its back to the wall between my uncle Tom Cavanaugh, my mom's eldest brother, and my great-aunt Corinne, my mom's aunt, to wait for the men to load the now-closed coffin into the hearse.

None of us spoke. I sat there and cried soundlessly, tears spilling from my eyes like a dreary, persistent Irish rain. My relatives' powerful presence wound around me like ivy up a pillar.

We piled into our cars, including the immediate Wynn family in the lead limousine, and crept along the city streets in our solemn procession. Other cars stopped by the side of the road to let us pass. The usual motorcycle police protection led the group to the church.

These cops knew perfectly well what had happened with my dad and the shootout, but they remained straight-faced and steadfast in their duty. We arrived at our family parish church, weaving down the driveway hill with the crunch of gravel under our tires.

To no degree did our church rival the ornamentation of the Gwydir Castle chapel, with its intricately carved figures on the wooden beams, angels adorning the ceiling, and Latin words of guidance inscribed on the walls. Ours was a working-class parish with an architectural style I would term functional.

Like every Catholic Church, we had fourteen Stations of the Cross plaques depicting Jesus's agonies attached to the walls. This is also known as The Way of Sorrows: "At the cross, her station keeping / stood the mournful mother weeping / close to Jesus to the last."

Sunshine poured unconvincingly through the windows lining the side of the church, teasing and taunting our dark clothes and lamentations. Traditionally, family members stood at the back vestibule to march in. The church was filled with row after row of people.

The priest came through a door behind the altar at the far end of the church and up the aisle from the sanctuary to join us at the back of the church. The altar boys walked on either side of him. The boys passed the thurible containing incense to the priest, who then cast the aromatic mist, symbolizing the congregation's prayers around Dad's coffin.

Dad's casket was draped fully in a white cloth pall. The exequies rites continued with the priest holding part of the long golden chain in one hand and the thurible in the other. He waved it, releasing more of the scented smoke over the coffin. It was as though he were a magician about to make the deceased reappear. The priest's incantation:

Lord God, in whom all find refuge, we appeal to your boundless mercy: Grant to the soul of your servant Richard a kindly welcome,

cleansing of sin, release from the chains of death, and entry into ever-
lasting life. We ask this through Christ our Lord.

The aroma of frankincense, a Christmas gift the baby Jesus received from the Wise Men, filled our nostrils like faulty smelling salts. The priest next gave hefty shakes to the aspergillum, making the holy water rain down on the dearly departed, briefly bedewing the pall. Now, we were all wrapped in the scented vapor and rain of death.

When we processed into the church, I cried so hard my sister Kathleen had to hold me up as we walked down the aisle. I felt like we were a spectacle on parade, wedded to an appalling headline-grabbing death. I wept for the horrific tragedy of it all. (Later at home, in genuine dark humor Celtic fashion, the votes were tallied, and I won the "worst mourner" family vote.) We filed into our respective pews in the front of the church.

The priest wore the purple vestments of mourning. The electrified tension in the air as he took center stage in front of the altar, facing all of us, could have lifted the saint statues off their pedestals. Then, departing from the Roman Rite of the liturgy to come, he opened the ceremony with a small speech full of compassion about my father's mental illness, saying that Dad had come to confession and communion a day or two before his death.

Did Dad know the end was nigh? Suicide by cop?

The two altar boys, released from their classes to serve the mass, were about twelve or thirteen years old. The boys wore their formal mini-priest black cassocks and starched white surplice coverings. I admired their solemnity for their age. They gripped ornate, golden holders containing thick, flickering, white candles that towered over their heads as they stood alongside the priest. The three figures moved near the open window on the left side of the altar. The white gauze curtains lightly fluttered behind them. The soothing breeze reached our section and touched my cheek.

That peacemaking sensation shattered as suddenly one boy wiggled, and a candle caught the curtains. The flame ran up the fabric, unbeknownst to the priest and the boys. They kept praying with their backs to the scene.

At that moment, I looked up through my tears. I took in the ignited scene and signaled to the priest across the church with my hand. He turned, saw the fire, and quickly slapped out the flames.

Dad had made his presence known.

Waves of despair and strength alternatingly washed over me, crashing into the sands of my faltering shoreline. Mass ended, and we reentered the limo. The funeral parlor men planted little black flags of death on the car hoods. Our motorcade drove the long distance to St. Joseph's cemetery. The cemetery rested just beyond the racetrack.

We parked in a familiar section of the graveyard, walked to the freshly dug hole in the moist June ground, and stood in a circle around the open grave with the casket suspended. Green Astroturf carpeted the ground around the hole. Mom sat on a fold-out chair. More prayers from the priest. More holy water.

As Dad had served in the military, a large American flag now draped the casket, replacing the white pall. The undertakers ceremoniously folded it. In a respectful and mournful pass, one man bowed, knelt on one knee, and handed the flag to my mother.

Many from both sides of our family were buried there in proximity for eternity. We went around and visited their graves after the ceremony. It was a mortality picnic.

We departed the cemetery individually, without our regimented parade of cars. I assumed by making it through this far, I was beginning my descent from the thunderous clouds of total immobilizing pain to some fraction of initial recovery and hoped for relief from my pantyhose.

I was dead wrong.

We went to our Wynndy Knoll family home for the wake. Up the hill, we trudged. Inside the kitchen, dishes of food covered the table. People had begun to adjust their thinking and face our tragedy. At times like this, there are angels among us crushing the potato chips for the various casseroles.

Steve and I were changing from funeral clothes in a bedroom, and I said to him, "I can never go through anything like this again. I mean it. It would kill me." He appeared unnerved by this statement; he had been as calm as a still summer lake at sunrise throughout this hell on earth. He paused a moment and reflected. Then he told me that, as part of life, we need to face loss and death.

We went to the living room, and Mom said the priest had called and was coming over, which was not unusual. Father Yoris entered with a grave mien and settled his long body in a velvety fabric swivel chair by the front door.

Father dwarfed the seat as he leaned his elbows forward onto the knees of his pants, so often pressed that they appeared shiny as coal. He had a lot of charcoal-colored tousled hair. His face looked weary. We offered food and drink. Father said, first, he wanted to talk to all of us. We surrounded him as if he were going to tell us a camp ghost story around the fire. Someone nabbed Dad's primo seat/throne/recliner/ATM (where we had dug in the goldmine seat cushion for the lost change from his pockets after he napped there).

Father took a breath then gently told us Grandpa Wynn, Dad's dad, who had been housed at the nursing home for safekeeping during all the ceremonies, had just died.

The shock of having witnessed all that gunfire and bloodshed in his front yard caused even the strongest man I knew to falter. Upon receiving this dreadful news, Grandma Aggie cried, saying, "Poor Bob. Poor Bob."

I was dumbfounded and felt like I was in a Road Runner cartoon. Like Wile E. Coyote, I had run off the edge of a mountain with nothing to sustain me underneath. I would surely drop.

We were forced to put our grief-battered and sluggish brains to the task of processing how Dad's actions had hastened his own father's demise in the arena of collateral damage. They had been baptized Catholic the same day in 1921 when Dad was a newborn. Now, they entered the Great Beyond the same week in 1980.

We returned to our parish church for Grandpa's funeral just days later, but this time, there was an unanticipated cortege difference. Because my grandfather had been the Chief of Police in our city, there were surprise guests in addition to the usual motorcycle guide police. About seventeen police cruisers lined up in the church parking lot at the funeral. The uniformed officers planted themselves next to their cars, standing stock still and rigid in military stance as we parked and entered the church again.

The irony of this was not lost on us.

All our nerve endings were already burnt to a crisp like the church curtains at Dad's funeral Mass, with no more fuel left to fire us up. We began to verge on giddy, the next frontier after the devastation.

At the previous night's viewing for Grandpa Wynn, at the same funeral home as Dad, during the customary prayers, I resorted to an old trick of mine. I gave my sister, Kathleen, a look that I knew would make her laugh while I quickly rearranged my face to appear pious. It is an old routine of ours. It worked. She covered her face and had to pretend she was weeping. It had come to this.

This is how Grandpa's funeral went. The police could not have been more professional, dignified, respectful, and kind. They gave a military salute to Grandpa's coffin. They gazed forward, not at us, as we again processed down the center aisle of the same church in our encore display of a crushed family. It was a replay for Father Yoris, too, who officiated. Not as many people came; it had been a mere handful of days since Dad's service.

By this time, I was in the *I could not believe this was happening* zone, so I hovered on a comfy cloud of "Just carry on, everyone, while I take a breather," suspended above the action, flying like Peter Pan, being a good "little boy."

After Mass, the line-up of police in their cruisers joined the procession back out to the cemetery and to the new grave only a stone's throw from Dad's freshly dug forever home. Here this warring father and son could now find peace.

We laid Grandpa to rest.

Two days later, I returned to my classroom, wanting to get back into the swing of things and not dwell too long on the stranger-than-fiction events that befell us. I wrongly assumed I could file my agony under "F" for Forget Feeling This.

I went to lunch in the teacher's lounge at school. The funny complaint chatter, dark classroom humor jokes, and innocent ribbing of each other's quirks were absent. With the windows open, the warming spring alerted us that the school days were dwindling until glorious summer break. Usually, that would have us teachers in rapturous harmony of anticipation. But that day, there was a low hum of innocuous and gently polite chit-chat crisscrossing the round table, meaning to respect my fragile return.

Suddenly, our very self-possessed and proper librarian, a favorite of mine for her sly humor and smarts, stopped eating her sandwich and put it on the wrapper wax paper at her place. She burst into tears, expressing her emotions about my family's double whammy. She said, "It's just so sad, so tragic. I'm sorry. It is awful what has happened to all of you."

She knows a Dickensian tale of crushing plot lines when she sees one.

I knew people were uncomfortable that they might say the wrong thing, so they just acted like it was a typical day in the Normal World. Jean, the librarian, could not suppress her sympathy.

Although I didn't know it at the time, I had a bit of Gwydir's Lion and Eagle in me to help me avoid the pain. In a decade or so, those noble animals of strength and courage to face all would desert me and scram across the golden fields of the Welsh castle grounds.

As I returned to my classroom, one of my students stopped me in the hallway. Shelina lived in the inner city. She spoke in intelligible, yet characteristic, speech sounds of students who are deaf, and she also used sign language: "Mrs. Brown, I'm sorry your father [the sign for father is an open hand, thumb to the forehead] died. I understand. My dad was stabbed in a fight and died."

This child had suffered too.

Christmas that year of my dad's death, 1980, had our whole immediate family attending Midnight Mass together and returning to the same church where the two funerals took place. Everyone in the congregation knew what had happened in the Wynn family the previous May.

The carols sung stung like blistering hail. Here were joyful families in variations of red celebratory clothing and little children playing with their distracting toys while some nestled asleep in their mothers' laps. The mothers and fathers smilingly prayed together. All these sights bruised my soul. I was on the outside looking in again.

The liturgy felt more like pleading than praying,

"Forgive us our trespasses as we forgive those who trespass against us."

"Lord have mercy."

"Christ, have mercy."

But there are Christmas miracles. Mercy is sometimes granted.

The father of my former classmate Carolyn, Mr. McGrail, approached me after Mass and expressed his sadness for our family's loss. He then wanted to tell me a story.

I listened.

Families filed out of the church to go to bed and wake up in their pajamas to the enchantment of Christmas morning. Mr. McGrail became Santa. He told me about being in elementary school with Dad at St. Aloysius.

Mr. McGrail explained that he remembered Dad as the most beautiful solo singer as a little boy, and that is how he wanted to remember him. He said the women at Mass would weep from the glorious sound of Dad's sweet voice.

I told him that I had often heard the story of someone wanting to take Dad to London when he was a child to train his voice, but my grandparents would not hear of it.

Mr. McGrail said with a smile that there was one memory he would never forget, which explained a lot about Dad. He told me about when they were kids at St. Al's and Sunday Mass started. Dad was scheduled to sing.

Dad whipped into the church late, quickly dressed into the surplus and cassock in the sacristy, and then made it up to his place at the altar for his hymn. Mr. McGrail tilted his head, reviewing the episode, and grinned.

My little boy-dad had a big black eye, apparently having just been in a schoolyard fight. Dad went on to sing with a voice that made nonbelievers believe, and the congregation shook their heads in wonder. Mr. McGrail said it was like watching a poignant and comical scene from a movie.

The story also brought me a smile and a sense of joy. Dad, constantly fighting his way through, had been a shining star. That was the night Mr. McGrail saved Christmas.

Stories are my salvation.

I don't believe in magic, but I do believe in the power of stories.
—GREGORY PECK

Aunt Pat, Dad, Grandma Cavanaugh, and little me. Dad's look shows pride in me. I hope he feels the same toward me now as I write this memoir and tell the truth I learned about him.

Twilight and the darkness begin to seep under doors like liquid.
—Judy Corbett. Gwydir Castle.

Chapter 25

After All: What Happened to Dad

DAD, AT twenty-one, wrote a witty, boastful, and persuasive letter home, circa 1942, to his parents when he was in the Navy stationed in San Francisco, asking for money to buy a motorcycle. He wrote:

> [B]ut even with my cold, my ego, energy and stamina is something to be marveled at perhaps due to the scarcity of rum and women . . . Well, I've beat around the bush long enough, evading the point of this letter . . . I want to borrow $600.00 (gulp) from you to buy a motorcycle . . . This territory is just itching for someone to explore it on a popcycle [sic] and I'm just the dude to do it one way or the other . . .

They sent the money.

Dad loved motorcycles.

The letter requesting
money for a motorcycle.

> Well I've beat around the bush long
> enough, evading the point of this letter
> so I might as well tell you whats on
> my mind to start off with as I've told
> you before my chances of getting
> flight school are at the best and
> action twords going there should
> start at any time now so I sorta
> figured seeing as how I'm getting
> along with the navy and my work
> so well I want to ask a favor of you
> prepare for the blow. I want to
> borrow $600⁰⁰ from you to buy a
> motorcycle. I know those are pretty
> harsh figures and words seeing as
> how you've already done so much for
> me and I won't have any hard feelings
> at all if you don't send it, but I have
> decided to get a motor and my mind
> is made up I was going to buy it
> on the credit plan but I figured if you
> had a surplus 600 you wouldn't be need-
> ing for several months it would save me.
> Richard Leowyny Am't
> VP-91 Co. F.m. SanFrancisco Calif.

On his naval base assignment in 1943, a crucial, violent event would
take the "energy and stamina" he wrote home about with such bravado
and enjoyment and turn this easy rider into an angry, jumpy, psychotic,
depressed man for the rest of his life, eventually leading to his terrible and frightening death. The swift gusts of a maritime base tragedy
became a headwind that Dad could not counter.

As the chatelaine of this saga's truths, I employed a simple key on
my utility chain that unlocked eighty years of hidden circumstances.
While writing this memoir, I requested Dad's VA medical records, citing
the Freedom of Information Act. When I asked for them, I thought it
was as fruitless an endeavor as sending a fan letter to Beatle Paul in
1964 with no stamp. Much to my surprise, they sent me a CD with two
hundred pages of medical notes, some in the doctors' handwriting,
dating from 1943 to the day of Dad's death in 1980.

The reasons for Dad's crash and fall from sanity then became known
to me. The knowledge therein shocked me; it made me feel like a baf-

fling trick puzzle box had finally been opened. The secret compartment spilled forth revelations of examinations, hospital stays, treatments, and analyses resulting from the initial crisis itself, answering the one-word question about Dad's mental illness and the fate of our family that I have asked myself my entire life . . . why?

The answers follow.

1943. The Monticello Hotel in Norfolk, Virginia. Built in 1898 by businessman David Lowenberg, it was billed as "The South's Grandest Hostelry." The lauded hotel hosted stars and notables like Buffalo Bill Cody, Will Rogers, Gary Cooper, Jane Wyman, and General Douglas MacArthur.

At Christmas this year, the venerable hotel also housed one very short but stately, first-generation Irish American woman full of pluck: Agnes Anna Mitchell Wynn, my paternal grandmother. The Navy brass and doctors had summoned her because Dad had a dramatic and psyche-incendiary breakdown. Aggie was the woman for the job. Aggie would set herself steady with arms crossed under her ample bosom when encountering potential antagonistic forces.

A wild and crime-filled motorcycle joy ride and complete mental breakdown landed Dad in the hands of the Navy authorities and medical staff. They contacted Dad's parents back in Ohio. Grandma Aggie arrived at the Naval Station Norfolk while Grandpa Wynn remained on duty on the police force.

On Christmas night in 1943, Dad was arrested for speeding on a motorcycle. He was out of uniform. He had kicked in a plate glass storefront window to get "his beer." He accused the store clerk of stealing it from him when he was apprehended by civilian policemen.

The VA report says about his arrest that Dad thought a mob was after him, and that he engaged in a fight with a professional boxer.

The police hauled in Dad. Aggie is contacted somehow. They did not have a home phone. Aggie arrived. In Norfolk, Aggie reportedly listened to the list of Dad's troubling behavior, observed his personality disintegration, and with the authority of a former teacher of troubled boys, the wife of a police captain, the mother of four sons, three of whom were presently serving in this world-changing war, delivered her decree. Aggie told the authorities to, against his will, hospitalize Dad.

Pugnacious Dad entered the hospital with a "maximum amount of supervision." He was transferred to an advanced locked ward.

Reading these VA medical reports, I was excavating a hidden treasure almost too dark to reveal—the *known unknown*. I had known (we all had known) there was something wrong somewhere in Dad's history, but no one who knew about it said anything except: "There was some explosion." However, Grandma Aggie knew it all and said nothing. The VA reports finally broke the silence.

Now under psychiatric care after his *varoom* dash away Christmas night, in the VA reports, my dad told the examining psychiatrist that he put his mother up at the historic and beautiful Monticello Hotel because he desired her to be ensconced in "Officer's Country."

There, in the hotel with the dramatically rounded front, in one of the one hundred and ninety-eight rooms of this corner hotel, Grandma Aggie might have overlooked the Elizabeth River. Dad could ill afford this luxury stay.

Before he was locked away for months of psychiatric care, my father feted his mother in the elegant fifth-floor café-dining room, according to the medical interviews. They would have eaten from white dishes with a green and red trim. A shield at the top center of the plate featured a square with three faces inside, and the Latin words ABEO LIBERTAS A QUO SPIRITUS surrounded the insignia. This was the same coat of arms as Thomas Jefferson's Monticello, and the translation is: "He who gives life, gives liberty."

This extravagance was a rare and unknown gem to Grandma Aggie, who rarely traveled, let alone indulged in fine dining. The luxury starkly contrasted with the issues she was facing at the base and the decisions she had to make. Dad was booked into the world of mental illness from which he never emerged.

The doctor's initial intake report states: "He feels he has some special power to overcome the evils of the world and his alleged enemies." He thought his food had been poisoned. He was paranoid. He displayed

Monticello Hotel, Norfolk, Virginia, was built in 1898 by David Lowenber.

incoherent speech. He hallucinated. He heard voices. He tried to drown himself during the hydrotherapy session and had to be "forcibly withdrawn" from the tub. The report shook me.

Once stabilized, Dad was "sarcastic, boastful, struts around the ward in high boots telling all what a man he is. Full of obscenities toward authority figures. Sulky." And this: "Patient believes he has the abilities of a detective."

One VA medical evaluation report stated Dad worried about his future Navy assignments when the Japanese attacked Pearl Harbor, concerned about what peril he would face. Dad added he experienced profound anxiety about his older brother Bob being on the USS West Virginia at Pearl Harbor in the attack. But he also spoke of some long-ago deep-seated resentments for this brother who was strong, tall, handsome, and successful in all his endeavors and, on top of all that, was now a war hero. He had some reason to feel that way.

A Columbus newspaper story clipping from 1941, just after the bombing of Pearl Harbor, tells of my grandparents sitting by the radio throughout that Pearl Harbor Sunday of infamy when they had yet to receive word about their eldest son, Bob. Another article read: "Captain Wynn [of the police], worried and sleepless, reported for duty this morning at Central Police Station, having not heard of his son's whereabouts . . . Robert has not been home for four years."

Bob survived Pearl Harbor and eventually returned to his grateful

Oscar Says . . .

POLICE LIEUTENANT BOB WYNN, WHO SERVED THREE "HITCHES" IN THE NINTH INFANTRY, NOW HAS TWO SONS IN THE NAVY.

.SM.

Above: Drawn before Pearl Harbor by famed cartoonist and artist Leland McClelland.

Right: Uncle Bob in the news.

'Pretty Exciting' Says Robt. Wynn Of Pearl Harbor

"THINGS were pretty exciting at Pearl Harbor but at Midway we got in a few licks of our own."

Thus did Second Class Petty Officer Robert Charles Wynn, 24-year-old son of Police Capt. and Mrs. Robert E. Wynn, 148 North Warren avenue, laconically summarize two of the greatest naval battles of World war II when he came to Columbus last week.

Young Wynn is en route to Washington, D. C., where he will attend a school in fire control at the navy yard.

Wynn

In relating his experiences at Pearl Harbor, Dec. 7, Wynn said he was aboard ship when the Jap bombers struck and was near some of the vessels hit. While he was actually at the battle scene his parents were "listening in" over the radio.

Another son, Richard, age 22, is also in the navy being stationed with a bomber squadron while John, age 20, this week received his second papers for the army.

parents on leave. Cool cucumber Uncle Bob assessed the war doings this way in the piece: "'Things were pretty exciting at Pearl Harbor but at Midway we got in a few licks of our own'. . . Thus, did Second Class Petty Officer Robert Charles Wynn . . . laconically summarize two of the greatest naval battles of World War II when he came to Columbus last week."

A page from Grandma Aggie's scrapbook. Dad with a Japanese weapon.

Another newspaper article focuses on Dad before his 1943 breakdown; he is holding a souvenir Japanese sword in the picture. Sensationally, he is quoted as saying the Japanese soldiers are "hop-heads" who do heroin before missions to get them ready for battle. Dad added, "Personally I prefer a letter from home or some good jitterbug music when my morale needs jacking up."

After over a year in the hospital, Dad was given an honorable medical discharge from the Navy at the age of twenty-four. Yet, the VA visits and hospitalization reports, and Dad's war, will go on for thirty-six more years.

The initial 1944 intake pages catapulted me back to Dad in high school. The doctors were explorers charting his history, looking for emotional trapdoors. The VA cartography tells of a boy who wasn't

Naval Station Norfolk

living up to his, or his Dad's, expectations and who wanted to prove himself, but he struggled to do so.

I learned things I had never known before: Dad had dropped out of school at age seventeen and enlisted in the Navy, never to graduate high school. He had been expelled from classes twice for "insolence toward teachers." One psychiatrist surmised he was small in stature, very slim, and compensated by developing a tough guy attitude. Dad was quick to fight.

Dad entered the service in 1937. It was peacetime. He had great hopes of becoming a Navy pilot. The report lists his Navy assignments during his seven years of service without any reprimands: mess cook, boatman, seaman 1st class, work on the high-speed rescue crash boats, aviation metalsmith 3rd class, training in the South Pacific. The September incident that forever changed his life occurred during his final assignment at a naval base in Virginia.

The property on which the Naval Station Norfolk rests was purchased immediately after the United States entered the First World War. Construction on the site increased wildly in the late 1930s and early 1940s as another world war approached. The base was home to the Atlantic Fleet in WWII. It is the largest naval complex in the world.

Dad's service assignments included Suva, New Caledonia, Hebrides, Van Cora, Honolulu, and two months of pre-flight training. He quit when his math studies became too challenging, severely affecting his aspirations. Dad landed at the station in Norfolk for shore duty.

Dad in the Navy.

Seven months in, an incident, barely a blip on the WWII highlights screen at the time due to security concerns and more significant war news, formed the arc of his life and suffering.

America entered WWII. Demands on the enlisted escalated. Combat exercises increased to new levels. More powerful British-invented bombs were being delivered to Norfolk. Their arrival marked Dad's detonation. The VA reports led this story chatelaine to another key to put on my chains. I discovered this:

In 2012, journalist Joanne Kimberlin scribed for the first time a full-disclosure account of the tragedy on September 17, 1943, in the *Virginian-Pilot* newspaper. Kimberlin wrote:

Almost 70 years ago, a 300-pound depth charge detonated at the Norfolk naval base, bringing World War II home in the deadliest way. The first bomb set off 23 more. In the space of a single gap, bodies and buildings were blown to bits. Windows shattered as far as 8 miles away. All across Tidewater, eyes swiveled toward the base, where a column of red flames licked the clouds from the very sky.

A man-operated trolley carried these depth charges, which were more potent than previous bombs. Kimberlin writes, "The silver canisters, the size of garbage cans, were loaded with Torpex, the Allies' latest secret weapon . . . It had a hang time, an element that extended the pulse of its shock wave and its power to crack a submarine's shell."

These bomb canisters required vastly different care than they were being given at the time of the explosion. First, they were stacked too high and second, they were not strapped down. One slipped off, started sparking, and caused the explosions of all twenty-four canisters. This "punched a five feet deep crater through the concrete. A wall of fire 500 to 600 feet shot up. The booms could be heard in Suffolk, 20 miles away."

The death toll was twenty-five, with two hundred and fifty injured. The devastation included thirty-three aircraft and fifteen buildings. The trauma toll on those who survived was not measured.

On September 17, 1943, Dad left his night shift, which was doing quality control inspecting planes. He had been asleep for about two hours when, without warning, the twenty-four canisters exploded only about three hundred feet away from him. His barracks windows shattered, then blew in. I believe *this moment* inspired Dad's Hit the Deck game with us kids. The VA physician reports:

> He [Dad] ran out to help the wounded, working all day cleaning debris, and in the following two months developed 'a lot of weird ideas about things' [quoting Dad]. He developed a terrific fear of 'being bombed' and got quite 'radical' in his behavior, which was soon noticed by his colleagues and superiors.

One doctor wrote, "After seven months here [on the base], the sudden explosion of the twenty-four depth charges touched off his generally keyed-up condition and contributed to a rather sudden deterioration."

The newspaper article interviewed a female civilian working at the base. She and her husband, who also worked there, were injured in the blast. The woman, named Helen, said, "People were running like ants trying to get the heck out of there." Some assumed it to be an enemy attack. The reporter continues,

Tales would be told of people at the base scaling fences that were considered impossible to climb, and others who found themselves waiting

Naval Station Norfolk,
September 1943.
Photos: Hampton Roads
Naval Museum

Naval Station Norfolk,
September 1943.
Photos: Hampton Roads
Naval Museum

at streetcar stops with their shoes in their hands and no recollection of why. There was little time to mourn, less to dwell. In a matter of days, the Norfolk explosion vanished from even local headlines—a tiny footnote in a war whose victims would be measured in the tens of millions.

National security during the war also played a role in downplaying this major military failure.

When pressed for more details by the reporter, eyewitness Helen repeatedly said throughout the interview that she could not remember those facts. Helen surmised, "Maybe that's a blessing."

After the explosion, Dad started acting combatively while at work on the base, in "constant altercations with civilian employees." He complained that these civilian workers did not pull their weight. In his state of delusion, he decided to protect the women on base in the days after the explosions. VA accounts say, "he believed he was in the intelligence section" of the Navy.

"He entered the WAVE [Women Accepted for Voluntary Emergency Service] barracks and frantically tried to organize a rescue party and first aid team as he believed the place had been bombed." The WAVES immediately reported Dad to the authorities.

The doctor notes that Dad would "snoop around to find anything that would cause an explosion."

Upon returning stateside as a civilian, Dad's employment history is another source of his feelings of inadequacy and defeat throughout the VA pages.

1944. Columbus. Dad is home, living with his parents.

This happened: At Sunday Mass, just one month into his new police job in civilian life, Dad had another major breakdown. Dad said, as recorded in the report,

> I finally blew my stack in church. I had the feeling the church was going to blow up. I tried to get out. I started screaming like an idiot. My father grabbed me and held me down, and they took me to Ft. Hayes [a military facility in Columbus], where they put me in a cell [he had to be restrained], then down to Chillicothe [VA hospital].

August 26, 1947

The report goes on, "He lost contact with reality and thought someone was trying to shoot him through the window."

1947. Mom and Dad married three years after he was released from his long-term hospitalization.

Dad worked as a draftsman at General Motors for a few years. His symptoms continued, putting him on repeated disability leaves. The pages inform me that he had done a lot of union work and "distrusted management."

1951. I was born and listed in the report by name. Dad is shown in the records to be on complete disability and given a slight increase in payments for a dependent. A couple of the doctors over the decades of hospitalizations laid Dad out in their notes:

> One who thinks he has more ability than he has . . . hyperactive, restless, talkative, fault-finding, demanding, litigious, paranoid, showing defects in reasoning and judgment . . . demands to contact the FBI. Has gone AWOL while in the service . . . patient exhibits rather primitive, magical, almost delusional cognitive

processes . . . capable of any number of imaginative perceptions but few of them of the type useful in realistic adjustment to society.

The next hospitalization:

The patient's expressions of attitudes and opinions have the negativism and antisocial qualities one would expect from a juvenile delinquent, dislike of authority, disparagement of middle-class values, the tendency to act out of impulse. He possesses many of the techniques of the manipulator and the con man and shows some skill in perceiving the appropriate behavior for dealing with different kinds of people.

1950s. Defeated Dad: "I am good for nothing." "There is no fight left in me."

One doctor wrote, "Nothing counts or appears worthwhile anymore . . . He is afraid he will lose his home . . . He has a low opinion of himself." In the same evaluation, Dad responded to the interviewer, "I feel like I'm going to blow up."

This: "Significantly, he says that his father warned him that he would be lined up coming back here and appears to take great confidence in believing what his father says." Grandpa Wynn, always regimental in his thinking, sees straight lines of men doing what must be done.

Dad exhibited "a terrible fear of being bombed."

When I asked one of my uncles on my mother's side, who served at a desk job in Hawaii during the war, about "the explosion" causing Dad's issues, he scoffed at the idea that it could be significant enough to warrant all that mental illness. Yet, in my research for this memoir, there is newfound confirmation that non-combat PTSD due to accidents, viewing horrific events, or seeing dead bodies causes identical effects to combat-related PTSD. In addition, it is now known that loud explosions can cause brain injuries that can affect emotions and behavior.

1959. As I absorb Dad's years of torment, the report reads that Mom is pregnant for the fourth time, and Dad feels the pressure of more mouths to feed. He told the doctor his "wife is worn out." He says that "he himself is reluctant to strike the children or punish them physically and puts out a great deal of effort to persuade them to behave in the fashion he sees as correct." (Please reference all evidence I have presented to the contrary.) Dad also says he is too nervous to socialize. (I would amend the report to "unless at a bar.")

1962. Dad's ever-present pacing is noted as he returns to the VA for hospitalization. On this stay at the hospital, Dad self-reports: "I was a screaming idiot with voices and all."

On and on, it repeats until it ends.

1980: Hospital doctors described his last day before the shoot-out and recorded that Dad reported neck and eye pain. The attending physician observed twitching arms, and the doctor stated Dad was having "flashbacks to WWII." The next day, he would be dead, and two police officers shot.

A chapel doorway. Photo: Judy Corbett

The following is the final report from 1980 included on the VA disc sent to me in September 2021:

<u>The Columbus Division of Vital Statistics: Certificate of Death</u>

DATE OF DEATH: May 28, 1980
DEATH WAS CAUSED BY: Intra-thoracic and intra-abdominal hemorrhage
DUE TO OR CONSEQUENCE OF: Trauma Severe
DUE TO OR AS A CONSEQUENCE OF: Gunshot wound of trunk. Multiple. Three
APPROXIMATE INTERVAL BETWEEN ONSET AND DEATH: Three minutes
HOW INJURY OCCURED: In arrest by deputy and sheriff in struggle over gun. Was shot several times.
PLACE OF INJURY: along roadside
HOUR OF DEATH: 8:53 am

We Were The Wynns

Patricia, Robert, Kathleen, Dad (Richard), Mom (Dorothy), Richard Wynn.

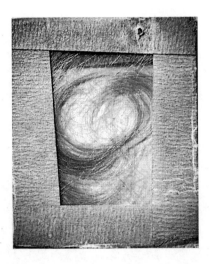

Dad's scant possessions were returned to us after he was killed. They fit into a shoe box. Among them was a lock of my baby hair preserved in his homemade cardboard frame with a plastic casing.

Judy Corbett writes: "A deeply mysterious morning here at Gwydir. As the mist descends, an otherworldliness takes hold."

As the Fog Lifts

It was my dream incarnate.
—JUDY CORBETT on discovering Gwydir Castle in 1994

Be true to the dreams of your youth.
—FRIEDRICH SCHILLER

OTHER WORLDS have held me up. Yes, I dabble in dreamscape and delusion as part of my *modus operandi*, which works for me. As I shift perspective, I navigate beyond life's bitter truths and transcend harsh realities, effectively rewriting my story to my advantage.

Upon seeing their daily Facebook posts, I often daydream about Gwydir Castle, as I dreamt when I was little about the Mouseketeers, the TV cowboys, Lucy, Atticus Finch as Super Dad, and later, the alluring Beatles. Taking flight in my imagination grounded me into my *becoming*. That helpful leap from one world to another led me to take significant steps toward furthering my education, falling in love, and marrying.

A thought occurred to me for the first time: Dad and I once spoke about how we both dreamed of flying like birds. In my dreams, I would soar from the top of Wynndy Knoll, feel the wind beneath my winged arms, and glide down the hill to the creek. Dad would say he ascended from the roof.

Dad wanted to fly, too, to be a Navy pilot. He once had career aspirations, just like me. He served in the Navy successfully for seven years but had one failure: at flight school because of poor math skills. Following that was the Naval Station Norfolk disaster and his breakdown. He was then medically discharged and cut off suddenly with no more hope of advancement after all his previous service. Once home, he saw himself as failing in his father's eyes in comparison to big brother, the hero. His mind suffered recurring supernova explosions that emotionally tortured him, and his dreams took the form of psychosis. This became his personal war, this battle with himself, and it was his ultimate downfall. He was ejected from this world.

Before I received the VA psych reports, I blamed Dad for it all. Atop the tower of knowledge, my perspective has changed.

Somehow, Dad learned to fly planes after the war. As a kid, I would look at the flight logbook he kept in the bottom drawer of the gun case, which held all his rifles, pistols, and ammunition. Just the flight log interested me.

Where Dad's mind was frequently untethered from actuality, *my* reimagining brought me closer to the reality of who I am and my capabilities. The severe trauma made him delusional and paranoid. He often felt the sinister, defeating sense of being hunted and on the verge of destruction.

My innocuous Walter Mitty-style delusions, with my love of storytelling and humor, and later my escapes into the ethereal world of dance, suspended me above the fray and helped me face another day. All of this became a helpmate in shedding the black shroud of shame laid on by society's disdainful attitude toward mental illness in those times.

The psychoanalyst, critique, and feminist writer Jacqueline Rose said in an interview, "I would like to live in a world where you didn't have to be ashamed of shame."

Discovering Gwydir Castle well into adulthood also helped. I enjoyed seeing the Wynn name associated with nobility instead of crazy. The royal part of Gwydir that resonates most with me is that of power over one's existence, and I love that the Gwydir Wynns focused on the arts and education. I decided early on—I believe as young as five years old—that I would reign over my life and not be a victim, despite my circumstances, trepidations, and self-doubts. I would battle on through the fears. The arts and education also became part of my life and remain so. I have wondered since 2011 if there is a part of those Wynns in me.

After writing the manuscript of this memoir, a woman named Angi Brasil from Texas messaged me. She is from a different branch of the

Wynn family. She saw some of my posts on the Gwydir Facebook page and noticed a resemblance between us. Angi does genealogy. She had already traced her line back to the Wynns of Gwydir. We began some correspondence.

Angi became one of my *Early Royal Readers* of this memoir. My stories touched her heart, and out of kindness, she went to work on my Wynn lineage.

Diligently, Angi read birth, death, military service, ship manifests, and marriage records. She sorted the begats, combed through histories, and exhausted reams of paper printing out family trees.

This is what she discovered.

My three siblings and I are sixteen generations from the Wynns of Gwydir. She sent the supporting paperwork in a notebook.

How does this change what has happened in our family? In the scope of Dad's suffering and our grief, it does not resolve anything. Concerning how I see myself and my life, it changes everything by widening the scope of possible horizons within me and my DNA.

The Wynns have many sides to our story, not just shame. We each weathered the disorder and heartache of dealing with Dad. It was a noble effort.

In concluding this memoir, I made a tough decision. It was one I battled over because it might cause me pain. Even worse, my Navy tour guide might brush aside my dad's war experience as ancient history to be filed and forgotten. Then, I rallied and made a personal pledge. I would go to Norfolk and visit the naval base where Dad's mind plunged to the lower depths.

I have just returned, and this is what transpired.

Steve and I had a conversation about the explosion in Norfolk with friends Annette and Sal Dominguez. Sal is a retired Navy man, and he knew people at the Norfolk base. He put me in touch with the Naval Station Norfolk Public Affairs Officer, Kelly Wirfel, who set up a tour for Steve and me. The base was not giving tours at the time, but I explained my mission and manuscript, and Kelly went full speed ahead with the planning. I had no idea what to expect. The 1943 base explosion was unknown to Kelly as it was so long ago and was downplayed during the strict security era of WWII. I sent Kelly some research I had done.

But would the tour be a cursory and rote exercise of goodwill? Would it bring up raw emotions that would unsettle my feelings? Would current world events that had sent the US Navy to patrol outside active war zones cause the tour to be canceled as soon as we made it to Norfolk?

Steve and I arrived at the base welcome center, and Public Affairs Officer Kelly, a retired Naval officer, met us with a smile as big as the Chesapeake Bay that borders the base's 4,300 acres. I knew we were in good hands. Kelly and I had an instant connection.

We hopped into her car. She held a map of the base in one hand and steered with the other. We proceeded at a slow speed as Kelly pointed out the sights. She had researched the location of the explosion. But before encountering the site of the historic tragic scene, we drove past some of the 55,000 sailors and 22,000 civilians at their tasks. We cruised by ships being repaired and cargo transported from docks, including Pier 2, where the twenty-four Torpex bombs had been unloaded and wrongly stacked on that fateful day.

We got out of the car and gazed at the massive ships along the vast harbor. Then we inched along Admiral's Row, passing beautiful houses with springtime front yards and walkways lined with snapdragons and azaleas in hearty bloom. The beauty and calm of that eased my tension.

At the end of the tour, Kelly found building V88, the place she had identified in her preparation for the tour. We arrived at the site.

I stood there and reimagined the horror of the series of twenty-four explosions rocking the base and leaving so many dead, dying, and some like Dad, forever reliving the din, danger, and destruction. I thought about the heroes, including Assistant Fire Chief Gurney E. Edwards, who rushed to the scene when the first canister started smoking. He attempted to extinguish it, but he failed and was killed instantly in the initial explosion.

My dad's barracks would have been, Kelly surmised, just across the road from where we stood. I looked where she pointed. I imagined him waking to his windows raining glass all over him. He must have thought they were under enemy attack. This was less than two years after his brother Bob survived the bombing of Pearl Harbor. That cataclysmic

Top left: With Public Affairs Officer Kelly Wirfel at Naval Station Norfolk.

Top right: Pier 2.

Middle: Touring the base with Steve, my steadying force.

Left: At the explosion site, building V88 is in the background. The previous buildings and Dad's barracks had been destroyed or severely damaged.

My "Navy" duds. Dad in the real thing.

event, which brought the US into the war and endangered his brother, is documented in Dad's medical records as having burdened him with dread and apprehension as the war heated up and his military duties intensified. Explosions figured into many of Dad's delusional episodes and conversations with his doctors.

Steve and Kelly anchored me, and I sensed them keeping their emotions "telescope up" to protect me. It may seem strange to some, but I planned this: I dressed like my dad's service wear that day. I not only wanted to witness the history but to be clothed in it, to stand at the place of the horror as an actor, to tune in to and justify Dad's psychic distress. I wanted the research to become real life.

It felt like raising a fist in the air, not in anger or protest of the Navy but to honor the fallen and maimed and to redeem Dad while fully recognizing what happened in the Wynn family. These two mindsets can coexist, and they came together for me like a solar eclipse, in sunshine and in shadow.

The night before the visit, I worried about becoming emotional. What I became was a sailor battling for the truth long lost. Doing so made me happy. I had the advantage of two moral support wingmen,

Steve and Kelly, whose understanding of the impact that the Norfolk catastrophe had on our lives helped remove my fear and anxiety. My dad's medical treatment at that time did not even directly address and treat his "shell shock" (now called PTSD). After all, he had not been in combat with the enemy. He had "just" been in an accident stateside; he suffered no physical injuries. He was to just get over it and move on. He did not.

Additional delving into what happened that led to this: the dead included Seaman 2nd Class Elizabeth Korensky, who was the first WAVE to die in the line of duty. I remembered that it was the WAVE barracks Dad was so worried about the day after the explosion.

Being there on the base was eerie, and, at the same time, it appeased my lifetime of hyperalert spirits. I felt in control of our family history; armed with the power of knowledge and truth, I freed myself from the Dark Ages. I thought about the cover of this book: that little girl looking tough with her dad's holster slung over her small hips and with his (real) pistol at the ready of her cocked hand.

The previous day, I had walked to the site of the former Monticello hotel, now only a historical marker, where Grandma Aggie Mitchell Wynn had stayed. I stood at this picture for some time and felt my grandmother's presence. My grandmothers are never far from my thoughts, but this brought a new light to Grandma Aggie's fortitude. What must she have been turning over and over in her mind, heart, and soul, so far from home and alone, as she met with Navy officers and

Last remnants of the Monticello Hotel.

USS Wisconsin was commissioned in April 1944. Dad was in psychiatric care on the base. The ship served in the Philippines, Iwo Jima, and Okinawa, was reactivated for the Korean War, and then went to "mothballs." She was recommissioned in 1988 for the Persian Gulf War. In 1991, she was decommissioned.

medical staff? Encountering her second son of four (three serving in the war), who was so badly deranged, must have been frightening for her.

I thought about all of this as Kelly drove us back to the entrance through the winding streets of this megalopolis. She also kept asking me specific and astute questions about the memoir she would be reading: Dad's history and all about policeman Grandpa Wynn and his overshadowing effects on our family. She was exceptionally sympathetic to all Mom needed to do to handle Dad and us, and she expressed this sentiment sincerely and often, "Your poor mom!" As we talked, she became even more passionate about the book's intent and engaged in conversation about what it could mean for Navy families. Kelly was on board.

When we left Kelly that day, I inadvertently left my notebook with my tour notes in her car. She texted to say we could meet the next day in front of the decommissioned USS Wisconsin, now a museum, where she was attending a special commemorative event on board with the base commander. There, she would return my notebook.

We discovered later that she had told Captain Janet H. Days, the first woman and first Black Commander of Naval Station Norfolk in its 106-year history, about Dad's base experience, our tour, and my book.

That next bright, blue-skied morning, we went to the USS Wisconsin. I stood by the ship, awaiting Kelly.

When Captain Days awarded me the Commander Coin.

Steve went ahead to another area near the Wisconsin in case Kelly was there. Then, whom should he meet but the commander, Captain Days! I meandered over to Steve and saw he was chatting with her. I could not believe my eyes. I had seen the commander's terrific interview on the *TODAY* show Kelly had sent me, and here she was in the flesh. She strikes a formidable figure, and that day, she was dressed in a black jacket over a white dress or skirt with white uniform heels, which she navigated like a runway model. Her white captain's hat extended her already impressive height nearly to the clouds.

I introduced myself with a look of sheer amazement and a few spontaneous bows that just popped out of me in the excitement. She said, "Oh, I know who you are. Kelly told me all about you and your dad. I have something special for you."

Then, she slipped her two strong hands over my hands and left a big coin in them. It felt like when I would play the child's game *Button-button, who's got the button* with Grandma Cavanaugh! I looked down and knew immediately what she had passed to me: a "challenge coin," a.k.a. a Commander Coin. This is awarded for special recognition for a military job well done. It is a true honor to receive one. I started to cry. The captain also wiped an eye.

She told me she is particularly interested in helping military families and grew up in one herself. Her dad was in the Army. To my astonishment, right then and there, Captain Days said the military did not have the most effective treatments for PTSD when my dad was hospitalized. This very truth I had come to understand about Dad, the truth that had bolstered my strength to come to the base. She told me she comprehended what my family endured and wanted me to know that the Navy appreciated our service, also. She emphasized the need for much more support for service members and their families, particularly the children, in terms of mental health. These were the words I needed to hear my entire life.

It was time for Kelly and the captain to board the USS Wisconsin for the private ceremony. However, the captain also wanted us to attend. She cleared it with the organizers, and on board the Wisconsin, we trooped together. There was VIP seating for Kelly and the captain, but Kelly said she would sit with us. The captain stood for a while, greeting admirals and politicians. It is part of her job, and she is good at it. I watched her. She has the charisma of Jack Kennedy. When she came over to where we sat, Kelly pointed out the VIP seat for the captain, but Captain Days said, "No, I want to sit with you guys."

The color guard marched to the front of the gathering, and we rose. They looked so young that I thought they must be high school students, but no, they were sailors from the base. An admiral spoke, bowing his head and taking a breath when he asked us to imagine such young people manning this vast ship and heading to war and an uncertain future. I had to pause with emotion for a moment, just as the admiral had. Dad was seventeen when he enlisted.

I put my hand on my heart as our flag passed by, and the captain stood stock still, saluting at attention. Nautical flags hung across the top of the ship, dancing jubilantly in the breeze, each displaying its own unique design, message, and vibrant colors. Captain Days held her salute firmly, with an air of pure pride as the Navy base band quartet began playing "The Star-Spangled Banner." We stood beneath the ship's cannons, once terrifyingly powerful, now forever stilled.

On the USS Wisconsin, just like when I went to Gwydir Castle, I felt an overpowering surge of pride sweeping the last of my rusty and barnacled feelings of shame out to sea. I'd been "seen" and my family

On board the 883-foot-long battleship USS Wisconsin, which is commemorating its eighty years. Some of its veteran sailors placed items in a time capsule, including an original 1944 mess hall menu.

The Latin "AD REM GLASSEN PARATUS" translates to: "To Prepare the Fleet." It is the motto of the Naval Station Norfolk, the largest naval base in the world. Left: front. Right: back.

"knighted" by Kelly and Captain Days. We came into possession of the Navy coin of the realm, the Commander Coin. The Wynn family received extraordinary twenty-one-gun-level honors that day.

The stories we tell ourselves about ourselves form our worldview. For so long, my narrative revolved around the story of Dad's insanity, which limited my independence from his identity. As a young child, I escaped that story by attaching my reveries to a fantasy world to see things differently than my everyday life allowed. In many ways, by visualizing these fantasies, they became my reality through writing, performing, and dancing.

For too long, my perception of my life had me self-doubting, anxious, hyperalert, and mistrustful. The positives in my life growing up, which I have recounted in these pages, were my armor. The revelations uncovered while writing the memoir are the bounty I have been searching for.

The fog has cleared. I have reimagined my life. Stories are my salvation.

The future belongs to those who believe in the beauty of their dreams.

—ELEANOR ROOSEVELT

There are things known, and there are things unknown, and in between are the doors of perception.

—ALDOUS HUXLEY

There is no truth. There is only perception.

—GUSTAVE FLAUBERT

Acknowledgments

WHO WOULDN'T WANT a fairy godmother to conjure up our hidden inner royalty? I've always desired one since I saw Disney's version of *Cinderella*. Now, I see that I have had many to get me to this point in life.

With a swish of the fairy godmother's wand in the movie, mice turn into prize horses, and a pumpkin becomes a festooned riding coach. The old horse transforms into a proper coachman, and Bruno, the bloodhound, is now a serving footman. A ball gown suitable for a princess appears with couture adjustments by bluebirds. Glass slippers are made to fit and become the jigsaw puzzle piece that helps Cinderella escape her life of drudgery.

Others help us reach beyond our limitations. We can never do it alone, especially when there are clues to be uncovered.

With my telling of this memoir, Liz Hopkin, a developmental editor, a.k.a. narrative specialist, was a prima donna fairy godmother, taking my tale from its ever-evolving rough forms and bringing the telling alive with her potion of insights, knowledge, compassion, and skilled understanding of where the story resided. Liz's inspired suggestions and red pencil wand corrections polished the prose to a higher shine. But there is more to it than story wrangling. Liz has helped me become brave enough to offer the truth of what I experienced and seek the truth of what happened to Dad in the Navy. And those revelations led me to a more peaceful reconciliation with my experience of our family life.

Sara T. Sauers cannot be thanked enough for the cover and book design. Her words in an email, "We will make a brilliant book," had me over the moon. Sara is a typographic designer and letterpress printer in Iowa City. She is also a freelance book designer for the University of Iowa Press. Sara and I met and became friends when I went onto the board at the (James) Thurber House Literary Center. She happens to be James Thurber's granddaughter. Gratitude is just the beginning of my deep feelings.

Gwydir Castle in Wales became a turning point in my life when we visited. As the ancient Wynn ancestral home, it contained magic all its own. Proprietors Judy Corbett and Peter Welford made us feel welcome. Judy's book *Castles in the Air* and her history of "the Illustrious Wynns" knocked me and my sense of shame for the mental illness in our family sideways and sent it scurrying off. Judy permitted words from her book and her beautiful photos on their Facebook page to be used in my memoir. Thank you, Judy.

Judy's social media posts about Gwydir summoned a new-to-me, distant Wynn cousin, Angi Brasil, who kindly contacted me and took on the genealogy work connecting us to the Wynns of Gwydir. What a gift, Angi.

At the earliest stages of this memoir, I posted on social media asking people if they wanted to read drafts of the book. I called them the *Early Royal Readers,* and over one hundred and sixty people accepted the raw pages. I received encouraging notes and critiques that supported my work and built up my confidence. Special thank you to readers and fervent cheerleaders, friends John Behmke and Jane Mulderig. Marian Hutson's email to me after reading the book is taped on my office window for a rallying cry. Hooyah! They convinced me I had a story that people needed to hear.

Inspiration in the window.

There is no better place on earth to write than Key West, and I had that privilege. Much of this memoir work happened at the beautiful home of Linda and Bill Webb (he is a retired Navy officer). The Hemingways lived just up the street. We have easy walks to the former homes of writers Tennessee Williams, Elizabeth Bishop, and Shel Silverstein and can stop at Judy Blume's bookstore. The Key West Literary Seminar has also been a boon to my writing for decades.

One of the first people to encourage me to share my funny, quirky, and sometimes sad life stories with others was my friend Lori Giuliani more than forty years ago. She nudged me into submitting some of them, and editor Bill Estep green-lit their publication in the alternative paper, *The View After Dark*. Thurber House in Columbus became the first stage for my writing with the warmest of audiences and the kindest of encouragement from then-director Donn Vickers.

Then, I was off to the races with columns in other newspapers, performances, and two books.

The people in my audience for my *Hair Theater Beauty School* shows deserve so much credit for confirming what I said resonated with them and lifted their spirits. *Mercis* to production assistants, the show's darling "Hairnettes," for helping me raise money for the wig fund for women in financial need experiencing hair loss from cancer. The same affirmation kudos go to my *Ladies of Success* classes at the Ohio Reformatory for Women. In their class notes to me at the prison, it is not uncommon for them to say that until our sessions, they had not laughed since they entered the prison and that I made them feel human again. This sense of purpose fuels me.

An extraordinary proclamation must ring out across the land to the Erma Bombeck Writers' Workshop creator, director, and loyal friend (M'lady) Teri Rizvi and the entire Bombeck family. After much begging from the podium as the workshop emcee, Bill Bombeck, Erma's husband, finally "adopted" me. Workshop attendee Louise Lucas led that playful petition effort.

James Thurber and Erma Bombeck are guiding literary lights for me, as is my friend and decades-long pen pal, writer Christopher Buckley. Their humor heals me. Confirming the Humor = Comedy + Tragedy equation foremost is Frank McCourt and his memoir *Angela's Ashes*, which influenced my writing tone here.

BiblioPublishing (Columbus, Ohio) has been helpful in meetings and emails, answering all my questions promptly.

The quality of many pictures in the book has been magically enhanced by the technological sorcery of Kim Kiehl, a photo manager and executive director of the Ohioana Library. Kim's work organizing people's picture collections, videos, and stories supported my efforts here. She is fascinated with the stories behind a family's picture images and taught me that this is sacred work.

I had an excellent education at each of my learning institutions. Still, I was thinking about this the other day when my friend Gina Barreca, also a keeper of magic wands of encouragement, asked on social media about which class we most benefited from in school. I answered, "Typing." Huge thanks to you, Mr. Morillo, typing teacher at Bishop Ready High School. I use what you taught me hours at a time every single day of my life.

While I was in high school, the Beach Boys' song "God Only Knows" was popular. I often think of that song when I wonder what my life would have been like had I not met Steve Brown. I would not say I was Cinderella waiting for a prince to save me; I think of us more as co-conspirators pursuing our shared hopes and dreams. I am grateful daily, Steve, for our life together and your encouragement in all my endeavors. You so often believe in me more than I do. This book is dedicated to you.

I thank our entire family and our friends for not only hanging in there with us through life's ups and downs but also for providing a source of great fun and togetherness. I especially had you in mind while writing, grandson John Lucas Rea (called Lucas), because it is important for you to know this family story. A special tip of the cap to maternal cousin Debbie Williams, whose work in L.A. as a stage manager taught me so much about show business and introduced me to *Ultimate Dad*, Gregory Peck. We are "identical cousins."

My fervent desire is that veterans and their families, and all families dealing with severe mental illness and struggles, will benefit from my stories. Thank you, US Navy's Kelly Wirfel, Public Relations Officer, and Captain Janet H. Days, commander of the Naval Station Norfolk, for the base tour and Commander Coin. You showed great compassion for my dad's seven-year Navy hitch, its tragic ending, and its war-like aftermath in our house. The Greater Columbus Arts Council awarded me a grant to help defray some of the cost of this trip to Norfolk. I am grateful.

I encourage you to tell your own tales through the arts or to a trusted friend or professional therapist. Telling our stories makes us the protagonist of our sagas, granting us three wishes: 1. Power over our existence, 2. Understanding the seemingly indecipherable, and 3. Freedom to become who we are meant to be.

Oh, Eternal Lord God, who alone rulest the raging of the sea; who has compassed the waters with bounds until day and night come to an end; be pleased to receive into Thy almighty and most gracious protection the persons of us Thy servants, and the fleet in which we serve.

—The Navy Prayer